Rarotonga

& the Cook Islands

a travel s

Tony
Nancy Keller

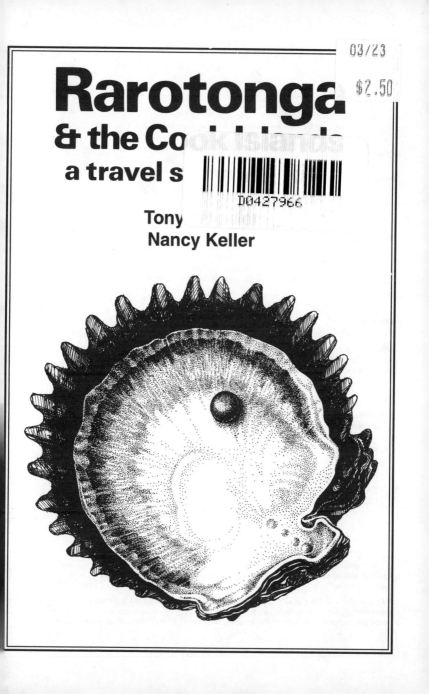

Rarotonga & the Cook Islands – a travel survival kit

3rd edition

Published by

Lonely Planet Publications
Head Office: PO Box 617, Hawthorn, Vic 3122, Australia
Branches: PO Box 2001A, Berkeley, CA 94702, USA
10 Barley Mow Passage, Chiswick, London W4 4PH, UK
71 bis rue du Cardinal Lemoine, 75005 Paris, France

Printed by

Colorcraft Ltd, Hong Kong

Photographs by

Tony Wheeler (TW), Nancy Keller (NK) and Trudi Canavan (TC)

Front cover: Sailing coral lagoon, Aitutaki, Cook Islands – Dallas & John Heaton, Scoopix

Illustrations

Historical: William Wyatt Gill from *Cannibals & Converts*, *From Darkness to Light in Polynesia* and *Cook Islands Customs*, all published by the Institute of Pacific Studies, University of the South Pacific.
Other: Judith Künzle (JK), Jillian Sobieska and Rick Welland.
Title page: Parau (Black-Lip Pearl-Oyster) *Pinctada margaritifera* (JK).

First Published

December 1986

This Edition

August 1994

National Library of Australia Cataloguing in Publication Data

Keller, Nancy J.
Rarotonga & the Cook Islands – a travel survival kit.

3rd ed.
Includes index.
ISBN 0 86442 232 6.

1. Cook Islands – Description and travel – Guide-books.
I. Wheeler, Tony, 1946- II. Title. III. Title: Rarotonga and the Cook Islands.
(Series: Lonely Planet travel survival kit).

919.62304

Tony Wheeler

Born in England, Tony spent his school years in Pakistan, the West Indies and the USA, returning to England to do a university degree in engineering. After a short spell as an automotive design engineer he returned to university to do an MBA, then dropped out on the Asia overland trail with his wife Maureen. They set up Lonely Planet in the mid-70s and have been travelling, writing and publishing guidebooks ever since. Travel for Tony and Maureen is now considerably enlivened by their children Tashi and Kieran, both of whom came to the Cook Islands during the research of the 1st edition of this book.

Nancy Keller

Born and raised in northern California, Nancy earned BA degrees in history and social science, later working in the alternative press doing every aspect of newspaper work from reporting and editorial to delivering the papers. She returned to university to earn a master's degree in journalism, graduating in 1986 after many breaks for extended stays on the west coast of Mexico. Since then she's been travelling and writing in Mexico, Central America, Israel, Egypt, Europe, New Zealand and various South Pacific islands. Nancy has also authored or co-authored Lonely Planet's *Mexico – a travel survival kit, New Zealand – a travel survival kit* and *Central America on a Shoestring*. Last we heard she was heading off to Mexico to work on her 10th book.

From Nancy

Thanks are due to many people throughout the Cook Islands for their help while researching and writing this edition. On Rarotonga, thanks to Chris Wong of the Cook Islands Tourist Authority, to Janice Siulepa, Dorice Reid and Diane Scott of the Cook Islands Chamber of Commerce, and to Ewan Smith and 'Bubs' of Air Rarotonga. Thanks to Gerald McCormack and Judith Künzle of the Cook Islands Natural Heritage Project for help with the Flora & Fauna and Rarotonga Walking & Climbing sections, and to Judith for the superb artwork she contributed for this book. Thanks also to artists Jillian Sobieska and Rick Welland, who also contributed art for the book, and to Nancy Griffith and Emil Cowan of the *Avatapu*, to Colin Hall, to Pa, to David Brettell and to Cindy Kay of Air New Zealand in Auckland for assorted helpfulness. Thanks to Kauraka Kauraka, Jon Jonassen, Rena Jonassen and Michael Taveoni for interesting conversation and/or good suggestions.

On the outer islands, greatest thanks and a big hello on Atiu to Andrea & Juergen Manske-Eimke, to Roger & Kura Malcolm and to Papa & Mama Puruto and family, wishing Papa Puruto a happy 80th birthday in June 1995; on Mauke, love and thanks (again!) to my dear friend Nan Greenwood; on Mangaia, the same to Dr Colleen Lal, and thanks to Mark & Tracy Drew for help with the map and a ride up the mountain.

Thanks also to many people on Aitutaki - to Mimau & Tom, Nelly & Ta, Josie & her husband, to Robert Imagire and Mr & Mrs Taefi, to Mr & Mrs Tunui Tereu for an interesting visit to several historic marae, to Greg Paynter for archaeological information, to Mareko Teao, and to Papa Tangaroa for many things, including a most enjoyable visit to Maungapu.

Greatest thanks of all to Papa Tangaroa Kainuku of Muri, oral historian, taunga, family genealogist, elder and generally royal person.

Dedication

Nancy dedicates this book to Papa Tangaroa Kainuku. Happy 70th birthday Uncle. My greatest thanks are to you.

This Book

Tony Wheeler researched and wrote the 1st edition of this book; the 2nd and 3rd editions were researched and written by Nancy Keller.

From the Publisher

This book was edited by Samantha Carew. Proofing was done by Kristin Odijk. The mapping was done by Margaret Jung. Design and layout by Rachel Black. Cover design by Jane Hart. Thanks to Diana Saad for editing supervision.

Thanks

Thanks must also go to the travellers who have written to us with suggestions, corrections and improvements. Thanks to:

Don Alchin, Dr Bob Baker (NZ), Emma Jane Beasant (UK), H J Best, J D Boatwood, Christian Braun (D), Jerry Brown (USA), Julie Caing (UK), Chris Couvee (Nl), Ian Diddams (UK), Rob & Heather Erickson (C), Chris Fox (UK), John Fuscoe (USA), Philip Game (Aus), Kim Grattudge (C), Ben Grummels (Cook), Larry Hardebeck (USA), David Huntzinger (USA), Iona Kargel (USA), Jochen Klaschka (D), Gary Koethner (UK), Myrta Koller (CH), Miranda Leare (Aus), Betsy Lipps (USA), Gabriele Losch (USA), Robyn Marshall (Aus), Neil McLeish (Aus), Frederico Medici (I), Charles Moncreiffe (UK), Garth Nicholson (UK), Jane Nielsen (Dk), Thys Nobels (Nl), Ann-Marie Parker (USA), Kathleen Pratt (C), Keith Rowe (C), Doug Schaffer (USA), Glen Shaw, Ed & Patricia Sibbald, A Strickland, Stephen Swabey (UK), John Talent (Aus), Betsy Tipps (USA), Richard Tyler (Aus), Armin Uhlig (B), C Van Der Huist (NZ), Jim Walker (Aus), Barbara Zodrow (USA)

Aus – Australia, B – Belgium, C – Canada, CH – Switzerland, Cook – Cook Islands, D – Germany, Dk – Denmark, I – Italy, Nl – Netherlands, NZ – New Zealand, UK – United Kingdom, USA – United States of America

Warning & Request

Things change – prices go up, schedules change, good places go bad and bad places go bankrupt – nothing stays the same. So if you find things better or worse, recently opened or long since closed, please write and tell us and help make the next edition better.

Your letters will be used to help update future editions and, where possible, important changes will also be included in a Stop Press section in reprints.

We greatly appreciate all information that is sent to us by travellers. Back at Lonely Planet we employ a hard-working readers' letters team to sort through the many letters we receive. The best ones will be rewarded with a free copy of the next edition or another Lonely Planet guide if you prefer. We give away lots of books, but, unfortunately, not every letter/postcard receives one.

Contents

MAP LEGEND

BOUNDARIES

- International Boundaries
- Internal Boundaries
- National Parks, Reserves
- The Equator
- The Tropics

SYMBOLS

- NEW DELHI .... National Capital
- BOMBAY .... Provincial or State Capital
- Pune .... Major Town
- Barsi .... Minor Town
- Post Office
- Airport
- Tourist Information
- Bus Station, Terminal
- 66 .... Highway Route Number
- Mosque, Church, Cathedral
- Temple, Ruin or Archaeological Site
- Lighthouse, Shipwreck
- Hospital
- Lookout
- Camping Areas
- Picnic Areas
- Hut or Chalet
- Mountain
- Railway Station
- Road Bridge
- Road Rail Bridge
- Road Tunnel
- Railway Tunnel
- Escarpment or Cliff
- Pass
- Ancient or Historic Wall

ROUTES

- Major Roads and Highways
- Unsealed Major Roads
- Sealed Roads
- Unsealed Roads, Tracks
- City Streets
- Railways
- Subways
- Walking Tracks
- Ferry Routes
- Cable Car or Chair Lift

HYDROGRAPHIC FEATURES

- Rivers, Creeks
- Intermittent Streams
- Lakes, Intermittent Lake
- Coast Line
- Spring
- Waterfall
- Swamps
- Salt Lakes, Reefs
- Glacier

OTHER FEATURES

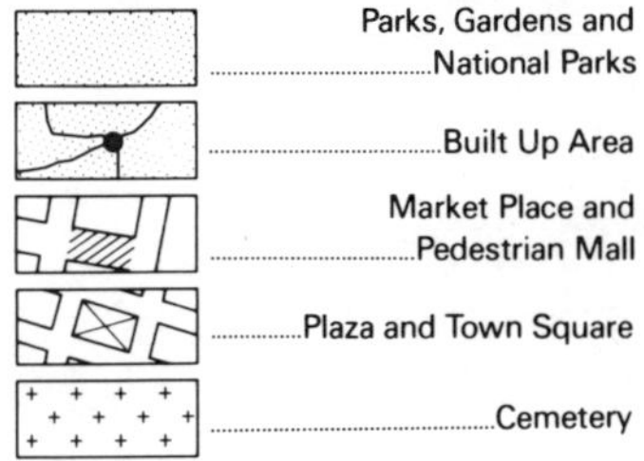

- Parks, Gardens and National Parks
- Built Up Area
- Market Place and Pedestrian Mall
- Plaza and Town Square
- Cemetery

Note: Not all the symbols displayed above will necessarily appear in this book

Introduction

The tiny and remote Cook Islands are Polynesia in a conveniently handy, though widely scattered, package. They offer something for nearly everyone. Rarotonga, the main island, is a spectacularly beautiful island – mountainous like Tahiti and cloaked in dense jungle. Surrounded by a protective coral reef, it has idyllic soft white-sand beaches fringed by rustling coconut palms and clear turquoise waters full of colourful tropical fish. It also has everything from modern resort facilities to backpackers' hostels, excellent restaurants and great entertainment, all on an island just 32 km around. 'Raro' is the entry point for 99% of visitors to the Cooks as it is the location for the international airport.

Rarotonga is only the starting point for exploring the Cook Islands. From Raro you can fly or, if you're feeling hardy and adventurous, ship by passenger freighter to the other islands of the southern group. Aitutaki is by far the best known with its huge turquoise lagoon fringed with tiny, picture-postcard islets. Aitutaki is a combination of high island and atoll and is a frequent nominee for any 'most beautiful island in the Pacific' award. If Raro is the Tahiti of the Cooks then Aitutaki is the Bora Bora.

Few visitors go farther than these two principal islands but that's a great shame because some of the others are equally interesting. Atiu, Mitiaro, Mauke and Mangaia are geological curiosities with a fringing, raised fossil reef known as a *makatea*, a weirdly beautiful area of razor-sharp coral formations riddled with limestone caves. Stalactites and stalagmites may seem a strange thing to find on a tropical island but the caves are full of them. There's also a cave on Atiu inhabited by a tiny, unique swallow known as the *kopeka* and the island has countless burial caves.

Finally there are the remote islands of the northern group. These are the classic low atolls of the Pacific and you need persistence to explore them. Though airstrips were built

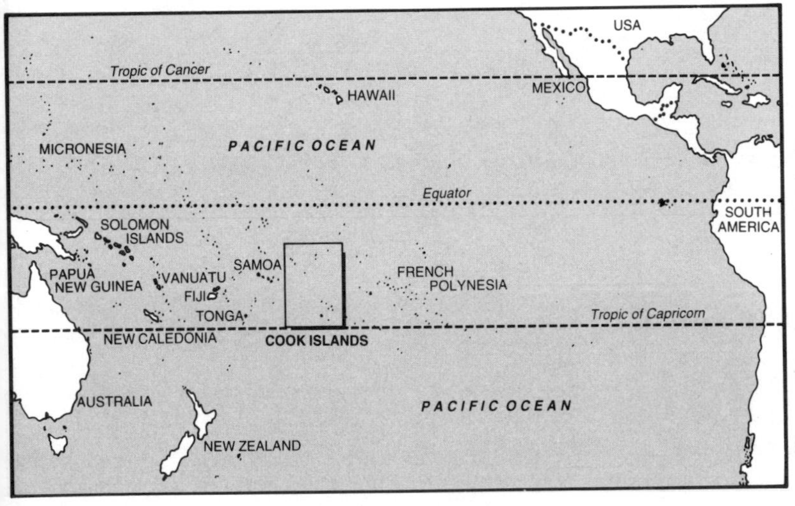

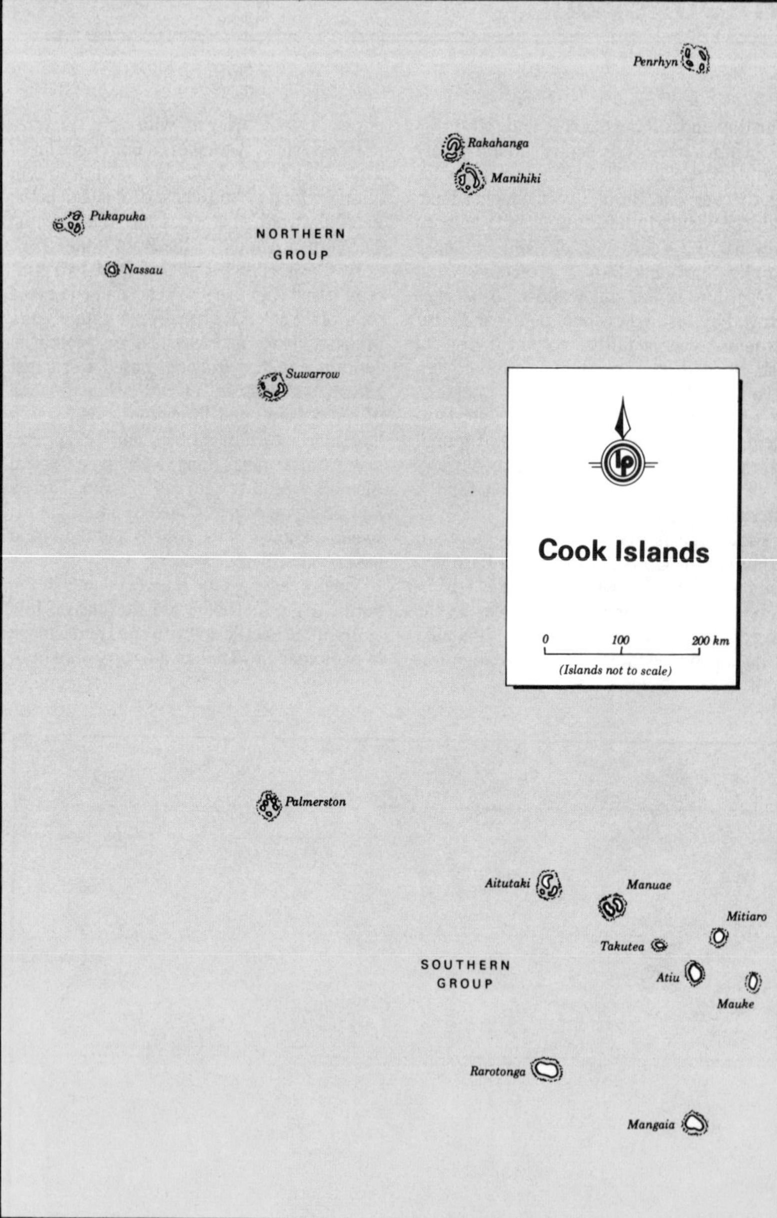
Penrhyn
Rakahanga
Manihiki
Pukapuka
NORTHERN GROUP
Nassau
Suwarrow
Cook Islands
0
100
200 km
(Islands not to scale)
Palmerston
Aitutaki
Manuae
Mitiaro
Takutea
SOUTHERN GROUP
Atiu
Mauke
Rarotonga
Mangaia

on a couple of them during WW II, they subsequently went without air connections for many decades due to their isolation and it's only within the past few years that three of them – Manihiki, Penrhyn and Pukapuka – have been reached by regular air services. It takes quite a while and costs quite a bit to get there, though, so most of the travel to the northern islands is still done on slow old freighters; these remote coral atolls are still seldom visited.

Of course islands aren't all there is to the Cooks – there are also the Cook Islanders themselves. Some say these handsome, easy-going people are the friendliest folk in the Pacific. They certainly have some of the most spectacular dancers and an evening at an 'island night' is an experience to remember.

There are plenty of activities to keep you busy if you're so inclined – swimming, snorkelling, scuba diving, deep-sea fishing, canoeing, sailing, windsurfing, bicycling, motorcycling, walking, hiking and climbing, and even tandem skydiving are all possibilities. Somehow, though, time seems to go slower in the Cooks than in other places and you may soon find that the most enjoyable thing to do is to slow down, take it easy and relax into the peaceful way of life and the voluptuous tropical beauty all around you. 'The Cooks are like Tahiti as it was 20 years ago,' say the promoters. It's a great place.

Facts about the Country

HISTORY

Although the Cook Islands only have a written history from the time of the arrival of Europeans, they have a rich oral history that has been passed on for many generations. Archaeologists have discovered many early religious ceremonial grounds, or *marae*, and traces of early settlements many centuries old on several of the islands. On Rarotonga the ancient road known as the Ara Metua, still encircling most of Rarotonga today, is about 1000 years old. Modern historians believe that the Polynesian migrations through the Cook Islands began around the 5th century AD.

Polynesian Settlement

The Cook Islanders are Polynesians, people of the 'many' *(poly)* islands of the South Pacific. They are Maoris, distantly related to the New Zealand Maoris, and their language is Cook Islands Maori, closely related to New Zealand Maori and also to the Polynesian languages of Tahiti and Hawaii.

It is thought that 40,000 years ago the Pacific region was totally uninhabited. Around that time people started to move down from Asia and settled Australia and Melanesia – the 'black islands' which include modern Papua New Guinea. The Australian Aboriginals and the tribes of New Guinea are the descendants of this first wave of Pacific settlers. The islands of Micronesia ('tiny islands') and Polynesia ('many islands') remained uninhabited until around 5000 to 6000 years ago. At this time the Austronesian people of South-East Asia started to move beyond New Guinea to the islands which now comprise the Solomons, Vanuatu and Fiji.

The Austronesian language group includes the languages of South-East Asia (from Indonesian to Vietnamese) and the languages of the Pacific which developed as a sub-group as people moved into the Pacific. Around 1500 BC people moved on from Fiji to Tonga and this group is assumed to have included the ancestors of all the Polynesian people. Their language gradually diverged to become Polynesian as settlers moved to Samoa around 300 BC and to the Society Islands and Marquesas (now both part of French Polynesia) in the early years AD. The final great waves of Polynesian migration are thought to have taken place around 400 AD to Easter Island and between 500 and 800 AD to the other islands of modern French Polynesia, the Cook Islands and to New Zealand. Pukapuka in the Cooks, however, is thought to have been settled directly from Samoa or even earlier from Tonga.

The 'Great Migration'

One of Rarotonga's most notable historical moments occurred around 1350 AD, when Avana Harbour in Ngatangiia was the starting point for the fleet of canoes now often referred to in New Zealand as the 'Great Migration'. It was in this year that the Maori canoes voyaged to Aotearoa ('the land of the long white cloud'), bringing the settlers that became the great ancestors of the present-day New Zealand Maori tribes.

These New Zealand Maori tribes, named after the canoes on which their ancestors came, all trace their genealogies to an ancestor that arrived on one of the 'Great Canoes'. You can go to Avana Harbour and see the spot from where the canoes departed. Opposite the big white Ngatangiia CICC church at Avana Harbour is a circle of seven stones, commemorating seven canoes that completed the voyage: *Takitumu, Tokomaru, Kurahaupo, Aotea, Tainui, Te Arawa* and *Mataatua*. ■

It's uncertain exactly when the first settlers did reach the Cook Islands. Oral history traces Rarotongan ancestry back about 1400 years.

In common with other Polynesian peoples, Cook Islands legends say that the ancestors of ancient times originated from the legendary homeland of Avaiki (spelt Hawai'i, Hawai'iki etc in other parts of Polynesia). The exact location of Avaiki has been lost in history; it isn't modern-day Hawaii, but the similarity of names suggests that modern Hawaii was probably named after the ancestral homeland.

Early Cook Islands Society

Rarotonga has always been the most important island of the Cooks and it's assumed the culture of its early inhabitants was largely duplicated on the other islands.

Pre-European Rarotonga was divided into six districts, each of which was governed by a hierarchy of chiefs, the most important of whom was the *ariki*, or paramount high chief. The districts were subdivided into *tapere* populated by a related group known as *ngati* and headed by a sub-chief ranking directly below the ariki, known as a *mataiapo*. Next in rank, just below and answerable to the mataiapo, were the *rangatira*. Tapere were typically around 150 hectares in area and had a population of around 100 to 200. Each tapere had its own marae. The *koutu* was a similar centre, used for meetings and political functions. Larger marae and koutu served entire districts.

Although in some respects this pattern of relationship and land ownership was firmly established, in other ways it was quite flexible. The line of chieftainship, for example, was not totally based on the male line and early European visitors gravely misunderstood the Rarotongan system by trying to translate what they observed into purely European terms. Hereditary titles could also be created and an ariki who became particularly powerful might have had to create rangatira titles as a reward for his faithful supporters.

A chief's control over his people was related to his *mana*, a sort of supernatural power which he was felt to possess. A person's mana came not only from his birth but also from his achievements and status. Mana could not only be gained; it could also be lost. An ariki who became unpopular (for example, by interfering excessively in the distribution of crops) might suddenly find that his followers perceived a dramatic decline in his mana, which could even lead to his losing control.

Control of *tapu* was a powerful weapon for an ariki. Certain activities were tapu, or forbidden, for supernatural reasons and since a chief could often decide what was or was not tapu this gave him considerable power. It was the people's strong belief in an ariki's combination of inherent mana and control of tapu which made the ariki so powerful and allowed them to exert control over their people without necessarily having the physical means to enforce their will. Unfortunately the early missionaries failed to fully understand the structure of the Rarotongan society and virtually ignored the operations of the pre-European religion.

Within the ariki system was another class of people with tremendous power – the *taungas*. Taungas were experts, and there were taungas in many fields; there could be a taunga for woodcarving, another for agriculture, another for navigation etc. Most powerful of all, even more powerful than the ariki in certain ways, was the taunga in charge of spiritual matters. The principal connection between the people and the powerful spirits of gods and ancestors, these taungas could have even more mana than the ariki they served under – for while an ariki could gain or lose mana through his actions in relation to the people, a powerful taunga had the much greater powers of the spirit world on his side and only a more powerful taunga would dare to challenge him. Another very important taunga was the one charged with memorising the tribal history and genealogy. These taunga were like living libraries in a society where there was no written word. Taungas were trained rigorously from childhood in their particular skills.

The islands were not as extensively cultivated as the first missionaries' reports may have indicated and many crops were disastrously susceptible to the occasional severe hurricanes. A bad storm could completely destroy an island's crops and lead to terrible famines until replanting could be completed.

European Explorers

The Spanish explorers Alvaro de Mendana and Pedro Fernandez de Quiros were the first Europeans to sight islands in the group. Pukapuka in the north was the first, sighted by Alvaro de Mendana on 20 August 1595. Eleven years later, on 2 March 1606, Spanish captain Pedro Fernandez de Quiros stopped at Rakahanga, also in the northern group, to take on provisions.

There is no record of further European contacts for over 150 years, until in his expeditions of 1773 and 1777 Captain James Cook explored much of the group, although the only island that he personally set foot on was the tiny atoll of Palmerston, which was uninhabited at the time.

Remarkably, Captain Cook never sighted the largest island, Rarotonga. That honour was left to the mutineers on HMS *Bounty* who touched upon Rarotonga in 1789. The mutiny actually took place after the *Bounty* sailed from Aitutaki. Those modern historians who place the blame for the famous event on the seductive qualities of Polynesian women, as opposed to Captain Bligh's cruelty, possibly had the Cook Islanders in mind! From Rarotonga the mutineers sailed on to Pitcairn Island in their search for a refuge where they would not be reached by the long arm of the British navy.

Cook, following what was virtually an English tradition of attaching truly terrible names to truly exotic places, dubbed the southern group islands the Hervey Islands in honour of a British Lord of the Admiralty. Half a century later a Russian cartographer, Admiral John von Krusenstern, published an atlas, the *Atlas de l'Océan Pacifique*, in which he renamed the islands to honour Captain Cook, who had been killed in Hawaii in 1779, a couple of years after his final visit to the Herveys. The northern group islands were called variously the Penrhyn Islands, the Manihiki Islands and a few other names. It was not until the turn of the century when the islands were annexed by New Zealand that the whole southern and northern group became known by one name.

Missionaries

Missionaries followed the explorers. The London Missionary Society's Reverend John Williams made his first appearance in the Cooks at the island of Aitutaki in 1821, after sailing from French Polynesia. He left two Polynesian 'teachers' behind and when he returned two years later they had made remarkable progress. Indeed the conversion of the Cook Islanders, generally accomplished in its initial stages by Polynesian converts, went far faster and more easily than it had done in the Society Islands, from where the missionaries generally came.

Papeiha, the most successful of these original missionaries, was moved to Rarotonga in 1823 and he laboured there for the rest of his life. In that period the missionaries totally swept across the islands and established a religious control which has held strong to this day. They did their best to completely wipe out the original island religion, establishing what was virtually a religious police state. The height of their power was from 1835 to 1880 when their rigid and fiercely enforced laws were backed up by a system where fines on wrongdoers were split between the police and judges. Naturally this turned police work into an extremely lucrative profession and in parts of Rarotonga one person in every six was in the police force, ready and willing to turn in their neighbours for a cut in the proceeds. The missionary 'Blue Laws' included strict limitations on what you could do and where you could go on a Sunday. There was even a law requiring any man who walked with an arm around a woman after dark to carry a light in his other hand!

Although their influence was huge, the missionaries left the actual government of the islands to the tribal chiefs, or ariki. Therefore while Rarotonga, established as the Cook Islands' headquarters for the London Missionary Society, became an important administrative and religious centre for the islands, it was not a government centre. The individual Cook Islands remained as separate and independent political entities. Due to their relative isolation, small populations, lack of economic importance and their generally poor harbour facilities the islands were largely neglected and ignored by traders, whalers and the European powers. The missionaries also worked hard at keeping other Europeans at arm's length.

The fact that the ariki system of government, the traditional land inheritance system, the indigenous language and many other cultural attributes have remained intact shows that the missionaries did not completely obliterate the original island culture, despite the drastic changes they brought. Even the old religion, which had been abandoned by the entire population as far as the missionaries knew, continued to survive among a select few.

Mission ship *John Williams*

Cannibalism At one time the Cook Islanders certainly practised cannibalism. Although the early islanders rarely ate meat (their pigs were poor specimens and difficult to breed) there were plenty of fish and cannibalism was not, as it has been in some areas of the world, a protein supplement. It appears that in the Cooks it was an activity more closely associated with the supernatural acquisition of the mana, or power of one's adversaries. It was also a way of exacting revenge: to eat your defeated opponent was probably the most telling indignity you could subject him to. The pioneering missionary William Wyatt Gill reported the following cannibal recipe:

> The long spear, inserted at the fundament, ran through the body, appearing again with the neck. As on a spit, the body was slowly singed over a fire, in order that the entire cuticle and all the hair might be removed. The intestines were next taken out, washed in seawater, wrapped up in singed banana leaves (a singed banana-leaf, like oil-silk, retains liquid), cooked and eaten, this being the invariable perquisite of those who prepared the feast. The body was cooked, as pigs now are, in an oven specially set apart, red-hot basaltic stones, wrapped in leaves, being placed inside to insure its being equally done. The best joint was the thigh.

If you really want to learn something about the practice of cannibalism in the Cooks, read *Cannibals & Converts* by Maretu (see the Books section of the Facts for the Visitor Chapter), who is the only author who has written not only as a historian but also a participant.

Disease, Population Decline & Slavers

The missionaries intended to bring far more than just Christianity to the islands of Polynesia: they planned to bring peace, an end to cannibalism and infanticide, and a general improvement in living standards. Unfortunately they also brought previously unknown diseases and did many things to destroy the islanders' traditional culture. The consequences were a drastic and long-lasting population decline. The poor Cook Islanders took the onslaught of deadly new diseases as a message from above to abandon their old religion and fall in with the new.

Undoubtedly the diseases would have soon arrived – courtesy of traders and whalers – whether or not the missionaries had brought them, but the statistics are nevertheless horrifying. When the missionaries first arrived on Rarotonga in 1823 the population was probably around 6000 to 7000 (it's around 10,000 today). The first major assault on this population was the arrival of dysentery from Tahiti in 1830. It killed nearly 1000 people in a single year. A series of common European diseases, from whooping cough to measles, smallpox and influenza, followed. Each was previously unknown in the Cooks and each took a terrible toll.

Throughout the 19th century deaths exceeded births and by 1854, when an accurate census was finally taken, the population of Rarotonga was less than 2500 – about two-thirds of the population having died in just 31 years. By 1867 the population had dropped to 1856 and although migration from other islands began to create an artificial increase in the population of Rarotonga the decline in the group's total population did not start to level out until the late 19th century. It was not until early this century that a real increase in population began.

The trend of migrating from the outer islands to Rarotonga that commenced in the 19th century continued, so that although the population decline on Rarotonga slowed it was only at the expense of a greater decline on other islands. Many islanders left for work on other Pacific islands, particularly Tahiti, but also on various plantation islands established by European traders. This migration continues to the present day as islanders move first to Rarotonga and then on to New Zealand or Australia.

Disease was not the only cause of the drop in population. The new housing designs introduced by the missionaries were damp and poorly ventilated and probably contributed to the death rate. In addition, a brutal Peruvian slave trade took a terrible toll on the islands of the northern group, despite only lasting a mere seven months from late 1862 to 1863. At first the traders may have genuinely operated as labour recruiters but they quickly turned to subterfuge and outright kidnapping to round up their human cargoes. The Cook Islands were not the only ones visited by the traders but Tongareva (Penrhyn) was their very first port of call and it has been estimated that three-quarters of the population was taken. Rakahanga and Pukapuka were also victims of the slavers.

Few of the recruits, whether they went freely, as many did in the beginning, or through baser methods, ever returned to the islands. Over 90% either died in transit to Peru, died in Peru, or died while being repatriated. At the time of repatriation efforts Peru was suffering from a terrible smallpox epidemic and many Polynesians died from this while travelling back and, far worse, brought the disease back to their islands. One ship left Peru with 29 islanders and landed 15 smallpox-infected survivors on the island of Nuku Hiva in French Polynesia; the subsequent epidemic killed nearly 1000 people on Nuku Hiva and a further 500 on a neighbouring island.

The islanders' limited contact with Westerners and the fact that what little contact they had experienced had been relatively benign was a major factor in why they were easy prey for the South Americans. As the missionary William Wyatt Gill commented:

Their simplicity of character, their kindness to visitors, their utter ignorance of the depths of depravity and deceit in the hearts of wicked white men, render them the easy dupes of designing characters.

Protectorate & Annexation

Despite their considerable influence via the missionaries, the British did not formally take control of the Cook Islands until 1888. In that year the islands were declared a British protectorate by a Captain Bourke who arrived off Rarotonga in the warship HMS *Hyacinth*. To some extent this inevitable, although reluctant, extension of British control was due to fears that the French might decide to extend their power from neighbouring Tahiti in the Society Islands.

It's indicative of the hasty manner in which the British finally took over the islands that they failed to make a firm decision on just which islands would be included in the protectorate. The unfortunate Captain Bourke also managed to get the ceremony wrong and technically *annexed* the islands rather than simply bringing them under British protection! This caused some embarrassment and the process later had to be reversed in the southern islands where he had hoisted the flag, although for some reason Aitutaki remained annexed. One by one the others islands in the southern and northern groups were brought under British control.

The first British Resident, F J Moss, arrived in 1891 but his period in the islands was not a great success. In part this was due to his basic failure to understand the complexities of the ariki system, and the inappropriate application of European economic assumptions to a wholly different system. Moss was given the shove with some lack of ceremony in 1898 and the new Resident, W E Gudgeon, adopted a totally different method of running the islands. He ruled with an iron hand but his methods were also far from universally successful.

In the late 1890s the question of whether the islands should be associated with Britain or New Zealand was batted back and forth. Finally in 1900 Rarotonga and the other main southern islands were annexed to New Zealand and in 1901 the net was widened to encompass all the southern and northern islands.

Population & Economics

A major problem facing the islands during the early years of British power was the steadily declining population. The combination of disease, slavery and migration meant that the population of the islands had fallen to less than half the pre-contact level. Gudgeon, whose opinion of the islanders under his charge was far from complimentary, was convinced they were a dying race. Finally in the early part of this century the population started to slowly increase, although there were continuing migration losses, first to Tahiti and later to New Zealand.

Economics was another major problem and an answer to the islands' economic difficulties is still far away. Prior to their takeover, the New Zealand Government was convinced that the Cooks could easily be made self-sufficient but this turned out to be a frequently repeated fallacy. The easy-going Polynesian nature, combined with shipping difficulties which continue to this day, defeated all attempts to tap the obvious agricultural richness of the islands, particularly the volcanic islands of the south.

The difficulty of improving the economic situation in the islands was felt by some officials to be related to the ariki system and land-ownership patterns. Since land was traditionally controlled by the ariki, commoners did not have land to grow produce and the ariki often preferred to leave land unused rather than set a precedent for use by outsiders. The power of the ariki has gradually been weakened but they wield a lot of influence even today and the land-ownership system is still a major disincentive to improving the use of agricultural land.

Independence

During WW II the USA built airstrips on Penrhyn and Aitutaki, but the Cooks remained a quietly forgotten New Zealand dependency. In the 1960s it was belatedly realised that colonies were becoming an aberration and the path to independence was plotted with considerable haste. In 1965 the Cook Islands became internally self-governing but foreign policy and defence were left to New Zealand. The continuing problem of the population drain accelerated after independence.

The close links with New Zealand have precluded the Cook Islands from taking a seat in the United Nations, and it has to be admitted that a country with a population of less than 20,000 is bound to face considerable difficulties in achieving real self-sufficiency in the modern world. The Cook Islanders derive a number of benefits from their relation to New Zealand, including New Zealand citizenship and the right to come and go at will from both New Zealand and Australia. Not only is the population of Cook Islanders in New Zealand actually greater than in the Cook Islands themselves but it's also a very important source of income for the nation.

Modern Politics

Elections in 1968 brought Albert Henry, leader of the Cook Islands Party and a prime mover in the push for independence, to power. In 1972 he was once again elected Prime Minister and in January 1974 he was knighted by Her Majesty the Queen. Sir Albert was an Aitutakian and it's said that the people of this island are such keen arguers and debaters that they'll get themselves into trouble simply for the joy of talking their way out of it. In the 1978 elections Sir Albert got himself into deep trouble.

The problem revolved around the great number of Cook Islanders living overseas, principally in New Zealand. Sir Albert feared that the forthcoming election was going to be a close one and dreamt up the ingenious plan of organising a series of charter flights from Auckland, New Zealand, to Rarotonga, bringing back hordes of Cook Islanders for a short vacation and a quick visit to the polling booths – where they would gratefully vote for the provider of their free tickets. It worked a treat: 445 Cook Islanders were flown back by the Australian airline Ansett at a cost of A$290,000 and Sir Albert was duly re-elected.

Then came the protests of electoral fraud. A High Court case followed and eventually Sir Albert was kicked out of office by the Chief Justice for misappropriation of public funds. In 1980 he was stripped of his knighthood and in early 1981 he died, some say broken-hearted. (Go by and see his unusual grave in the Avarua CICC church graveyard, complete with a bronze bust peering down at you wearing Sir Albert's own black spectacles.)

A truly multi-dimensional man, Dr Tom Davis, leader of the Democratic Party, became the new Prime Minister. Before returning to the Cook Islands to enter politics he'd qualified as a doctor in New Zealand, become Chief Medical Officer to the islands, written a book titled *Doctor to the Islands*, studied in Australia, sailed a yacht to the USA and studied at Harvard, and become an expert on space medicine with NASA.

In the next election in 1983, however, the Democratic Party was bundled out and another Henry took over as Prime Minister. Dr Davis had become Sir Thomas Davis during his period in power but in the 1983 election he even lost his seat in Parliament. Unfortunately for the new leader, Geoffrey Henry, a cousin of Albert Henry, politics in the Cook Islands is a family affair and his family quickly turned against him. When another important Henry withdrew his support Geoffrey Henry soon found he'd lost his parliamentary majority. Parliament was dissolved, a new election was called and this time around the Democratic Party squeezed back in with Sir Thomas Davis once more Prime Minister. In his own electorate Sir Thomas' majority was just five votes in this second 1983 election.

In 1984, a split occurred in the governing Democratic Party. As a result, they lost their majority, and the loyal Democrats started lobbying with the opposing Cook Islands Party (CIP). This led to the first coalition, with the Democrat and CIP members facing off against the rebel Democrats. Also in

1984, Geoffrey Henry came in again, this time as Deputy Prime Minister under Sir Thomas.

It was not to last for long. In 1985, just a couple of days before the South Pacific Forum convened on Rarotonga, Sir Thomas sacked Geoffrey Henry, and Terepaii Maoate, the former deputy leader of the opposition under Geoffrey, took over as the Deputy Prime Minister. This caused another split, resulting in another coalition, this time with loyalist Democrat and CIP members in alliance against a mixture of rebels from both parties.

In 1987, yet another split occurred. The entire Cabinet was sacked by Parliament and Sir Thomas was booted out as Prime Minister. Then the Democrat/CIP coalition elected all the same cabinet ministers back in again, with Dr Pupuke Robati, the former minister from the northern group island of Rakahanga, as Prime Minister. The Deputy Prime Minister, Terepaii Maoate, retained his seat.

In 1989 Geoffrey Henry was again returned to power as Prime Minister after five years in opposition. However, the CIP only managed to secure 12 out of the 24 contested seats.

Geoffrey, who became Sir Geoffrey during his five-year term of office, presided over the construction of the Sir Geoffrey Henry National Cultural Centre in Avarua and the Maire Nui cultural festival in October 1992. Though his administration enjoyed many successes, as the March 1994 election approached there was widespread public discontent with his government for various reasons, including his February '94 revelation that the government had run up a massive NZ$247.5 million national debt. Other issues included his refusal to make public the government's 1993 national financial report, saying something to the effect that it was none of the public's business. Also, a scandal was exposed a few weeks before the election revealing that during his term, in which he served as both Prime Minister and Minister of Finance, the Cook Islands Government had apparently been involved in a massive tax fraud scam against other governments involving hundreds of millions of dollars, in connection with the offshore banking industry in the Cooks. Then there was also the matter of around NZ$30 million connected with the Sheraton boondoggle that somehow got 'lost' around the time his government took power.

Nevertheless, despite all of this, Sir Geoffrey's party, the CIP, won a landslide victory in the March '94 election, winning 20 of the 25 parliamentary seats. The Democratic Party secured three seats and the Alliance, a new coalition party formed by a mixture of rebel former Demos and CIPs, won two. Norman George, leader of the Democratic Party, kept his seat as MP from Atiu, but former Prime Minister Sir Tom Davis, who had returned from the USA to lead the Alliance Party, did not win even the MP position he sought. Now in his mid-80s, author of several books and with a long and varied career behind him, Papa Tom said he thought he'd give the political fray a rest for a while.

A referendum to measure public opinion on a number of issues, held at the same time as the general election, revealed that the majority of voters were happy to maintain the status quo on all the referendum issues. They voted to retain the name 'Cook Islands' for the country rather than change it to a Maori name, to retain the national anthem and national flag as they are, to retain the five-year parliamentary term of office, and to retain the Overseas Constituency MP seat, allowing many thousands of Cook Islanders living overseas to have representation in parliament.

Politics may be colourful but the Cook Islands are generally quite stable, despite all the ins and outs of the various individual characters. The government's biggest problem is managing the economy and trying to keep some sort of balance between the meagre exports and the avalanche of imports.

GEOGRAPHY

The Cook Islands have a total land area of just 241 sq km – that's about a quarter of the area of the Australian Capital Territory or of Rhode Island (the smallest US state). This inconspicuous land mass is scattered over about two million sq km of sea, an area as large as Western Europe. The islands are south of the equator, slightly east of the International Date Line and about midway between American Samoa and Tahiti. Rarotonga, directly south of Hawaii and about the same distance south of the equator as Hawaii is north, is 1260 km from Tahiti and 3447 km from Auckland, New Zealand.

The 15 islands are conveniently divided into northern and southern groups, separated by as much as 1000 km of empty sea. The islands are:

Southern Group

Island	*Land Area (in sq km)*	*Type*
Rarotonga	67.2	high volcanic
Mangaia	51.8	raised atoll
Atiu	26.9	raised atoll
Mitiaro	22.3	raised atoll
Mauke	18.4	raised atoll
Aitutaki	18.1	high volcanic & lagoon atoll
Manuae*	6.2	coral lagoon atoll
Palmerston	2.0	coral lagoon atoll
Takutea*	1.2	low coral atoll

Northern Group

Penrhyn	9.8	coral lagoon atoll
Manihiki	9.8	coral lagoon atoll
Pukapuka	5.1	coral lagoon atoll
Rakahanga	4.1	coral lagoon atoll
Nassau	1.2	low coral atoll
Suwarrow	0.4	coral lagoon atoll

* unpopulated

There are some clear differences between the two groups quite apart from their geographical separation. The southern islands are generally larger, more heavily populated, economically better off and more closely connected with the outside world. They're actually a continuation of the Austral Islands in the south of French Polynesia. They lie along the same north-west to south-east fracture in the earth's crust. The southern islands are volcanic islands, while the northern islands are coral atolls. The southern islands make up about 90% of the total land area of the whole Cook Islands.

That simplistic definition of volcanic islands in the south versus atolls in the north can be further refined. Only Rarotonga, which is the youngest island in the group, is a straightforward volcanic, mountainous island like Tahiti in French Polynesia. Aitutaki has one small mountain, actually more of a large hill, but also a surrounding atoll reef like Bora Bora in French Polynesia.

Four of the southern group islands – Atiu, Mauke, Mitiaro and Mangaia – are raised atolls. They have been raised up from the ocean floor in the past and their fringing reef has become a rocky coastal area known as a makatea, surrounding a central region of volcanic soil. In Atiu and Mangaia the makatea surrounds a hilly central plateau while Mauke and Mitiaro are virtually flat with a swampy central region. Two of the southern group islands, Manuae and Takutea, are uninhabited and very small, while Palmerston is a coral atoll like the northern group, and indeed is often included with those islands.

All the northern group islands are coral atolls and most take the classic Pacific form with an outer reef encircling a lagoon and small islands dotting this reef. An atoll of this type is basically a submerged volcano – only the outer rim of the volcano breaks the surface of the sea and this is where the reef and islands are. The lagoon in the centre is the volcano crater. All the northern islands except Penrhyn rise from the Manihiki Plateau, an area of the ocean bottom 3000 metres deep. Penrhyn rises from west of this platform where the ocean is 5000 metres deep. The Penrhyn volcano is thus much 'higher' than those of the other northern group islands. Nassau is unique in the northern group because it is simply a single island with an encircling reef – not a group of islands around a lagoon. All the northern group atolls are very low – waves can wash right over them in hurricanes and you have to be very close to see them from a ship.

FLORA & FAUNA

Flora

The island flora varies widely from island to island. The two most noticeable features are probably the coconut palm and the great variety of flowers which seem to grow with wild abandon almost everywhere.

Rarotonga has a wide variety of vegetation in a number of distinct vegetation zones. Gerald McCormack of the Cook Islands Natural Heritage Project has identified several types of 'plant communities', varying according to elevation and the types of terrain where they live. Communities include valley forest, native fernland, native slope forest, native ridge forest, native rockface and highest of all, a native cloud forest community; the damp, mountainous central part of the island is densely covered in a luxuriant jungle with ferns, creepers and towering trees. Look for the book *Rarotonga's Mountain Tracks and Plants* by Gerald McCormack & Judith Künzle (Cook Islands Natural Heritage Project, 1994, paperback) for more about Rarotonga's plant life and a number of interesting walks on the island.

The raised atoll islands of the southern group such as Mangaia or Atiu are particularly interesting for the sharp dividing line between the fertile central area with volcanic soil, the swampy transition zone between the fossil coral makatea and the central region and the wild vegetation on the makatea itself. Although the makatea is rocky, it's covered with lush growth and a considerable variety of plants supported by pockets of volcanic soils. Pandanus trees, whose leaves are so important in traditional handicrafts of the islands (mats, baskets etc) grow on the makatea; they used to grow on all the southern group islands but are now rare on Rarotonga and Atiu. On the atolls of the northern group the soil is usually limited and infertile and there is little vegetation apart from the coconut palms.

Fauna

In common with most other Pacific islands the fauna is limited.

Mammals The only mammals considered native are Pacific fruit bats (formerly known as flying foxes), which are found only on Mangaia and Rarotonga. The bats were introduced from Mangaia onto Rarotonga around the 1870s; recent archaeological evidence indicates that these mammals were already present on Mangaia when the ancient Polynesians arrived, though it's not known if they originated on Mangaia or arrived there at some more remote time in the distant past and if so, how they would have gotten there.

Rats and pigs were introduced to the islands at some early stage. Today there are many domestic pigs which are usually kept by the simple method of tying one leg to a coconut tree. There are also a great many dogs on Rarotonga, a number of cats and goats, and a few horses and cattle. The island of Aitutaki has the distinction of having no dogs at all.

Birds Birds are more plentiful, both land and sea varieties. The number of native land birds is very limited, and on Rarotonga you have to get up into the hills to see them. They have been driven up there by a number of human-related factors, including changes in the natural vegetation, cats, guns and the ubiquitous mynah bird.

A native of India, the mynah was introduced to Rarotonga from Tahiti in 1906 to control coconut stick insects. These green insects, about 10 to 15 cm long, were once a great destroyer of the coconut trees on the island. The mynah bird was so successful in drastically reducing the number of coconut stick insects that you rarely see one of these insects today, and they never reach plague proportions now as they used to. Other islands also wanted the mynah to control their coconut stick insect problems, and today the mynah is found in great numbers on all the inhabited southern group islands except Mitiaro. Although the coconut stick insect is no longer a problem, the sometimes obnoxious mynah birds have proliferated abundantly, becoming quite a nuisance and contributing to the lack of native birds in the lowlands.

Despite the limited number of birds there are some of great interest to bird-watchers including a surprising number of endemic birds – birds found only in the one localised area. Birds of particular interest include the cave-dwelling Atiu swiftlet (kopeka) on the island of Atiu, the chattering kingfisher of

Atiu and Mauke and the Mangaia kingfisher of Mangaia. The most colourful endemic bird is the Cook Islands fruit dove, found in the inland areas of Rarotonga and on Atiu. The Rarotonga flycatcher, or *kakerori*, which is found only on a limited area of Rarotonga and is on the endangered species list, is slowly making a comeback.

The *Guide to Cook Islands Birds* by D T Holyoak (Cook Islands Library & Museum, Rarotonga, 1980, paperback) is an illustrated field guide to the birds of the islands. The Cook Islands Natural Heritage Project has published some interesting poster/pamphlets about various birds.

Fish & Marine Dwellers Of course there are many fish in the waters around the islands. Snorkellers in the lagoons inside the reefs and divers outside the reefs will find plenty of colourful tropical fish to keep them enthralled. Fortunately for swimmers, sharks are not a problem – the islands of the southern group generally have such shallow lagoons that sharks and other large fish are usually found only outside the reef. Outside the reef, sharks are present but there are none which pose a danger to humans; the coral structures support a variety of fish and other reef life and the high visibility makes wonderful opportunities for scuba divers. *Cook Islands Reef Life*, a colourful poster printed in 1992 by the Cook Islands Natural Heritage Project, is helpful for identification of species.

Unga Putua (Chocolate Hermit) (JK)

There are some other sea creatures you're likely to come across in the Cooks. Around Rarotonga, on the sandy lagoon bottom of Aitutaki and on other islands there are great numbers of sea cucumbers, also known as *bêche de mer* or, in Maori, as *rori*. There are about 15 species of rori in the Cooks, about six of which are common; certain varieties of these strange slug-like creatures are a noted delicacy. Large bright-blue starfish are also a common sight. On land as well as in the water the Cooks have a great number of crabs, ranging from tiny, amusing hermit crabs to large coconut crabs.

U'u (Parrot Fish) *Scarus spp* (JK)

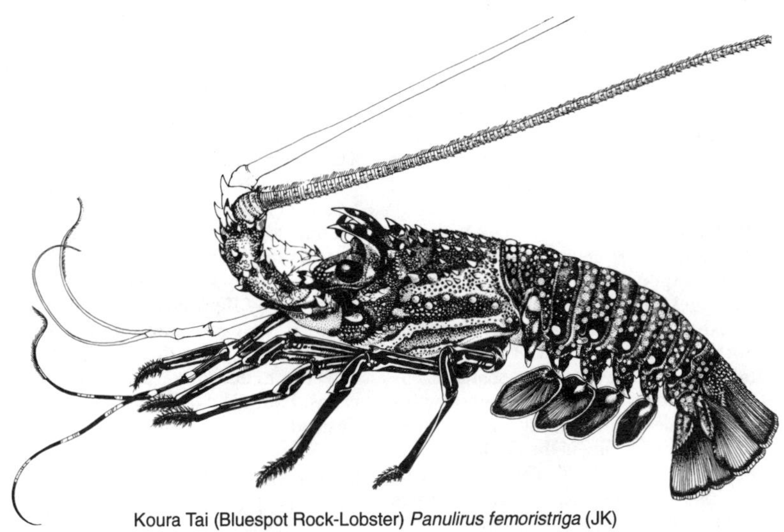

Koura Tai (Bluespot Rock-Lobster) *Panulirus femoristriga* (JK)

Humpback whales visit Rarotonga and other Cook Islands every year in August and September. Humpbacks, which can reach up to 11 metres in length, are the 'singing whales' – various recordings have been made of the males 'singing' to the females to attract them during the mating season. Not many humpbacks come to the Cook Islands – only around 12 to 20 each year – but they come up from the Antarctic every year to mate and to calf. With an 11-month gestation period, the whales mate one year, bear young the next, rear their young in Antarctica during that year and mate again the following year. Oddly enough the whales don't eat much while they're here; during most of the year, they live in Antarctica where their food is very plentiful, build up a lot of blubber, and mostly survive off their blubber during their time in the Cooks.

GOVERNMENT

The Cook Islands is a semi-independent nation, in free association with New Zealand. It has its own government responsible for all internal affairs, while its international relations and defence matters are handled by New Zealand.

The Cook Islands has a Westminster parliamentary system of government like that of England, Australia and New Zealand. Of course with a population of 20,000 it's on a small scale. The Cook Islands Parliament inhabits an inconspicuous building beside the Rarotonga airport. It was originally built as a hostel for airport workers during the airport's construction in 1974 and later converted for use as the Parliament building. The Prime Minister has an office here and another one in Avarua.

The Parliament has two houses. The lower house or Legislative Assembly has 25 elected members, with 24 from the various districts of the Cook Islands and one 'overseas constituency' seat representing the thousands of Cook Islanders living in New Zealand. The upper house or House of Ariki represents the island chiefs but they have only advisory powers. Her Majesty the Queen of England is represented by a Queen's Representative (QR), whose residence on the south side of Rarotonga is a stately affair overlooking the lagoon.

Away from Rarotonga each island has at least one elected Member of Parliament

(MP), plus a resident appointed Chief Administrative Officer (CAO). This is a direct carryover from the Resident Agent of colonial times and indeed the CAO's house on each island is still known as The Residency. The CAO generally has more power than the elected Island Council.

ECONOMY

The Cook Islands' economy is far from balanced – exports are far lower than imports. The biggest factor in making up the shortfall is good old foreign aid, particularly from 'big brother' New Zealand. Considerable amounts of money are also sent back by Cook Islanders living abroad – remember there are more Cook Islanders living overseas than are actually in the Cooks.

Exports are almost totally dependent on New Zealand so if the Kiwis sneeze the Cook Islanders catch a cold. New Zealand is a small market and for the Cooks it has sometimes been a fickle one. The biggest export category is clothing and footwear which enjoys privileged entry into New Zealand. Next up comes fresh fruit and vegetables. Citrus fruit is the major agricultural export, although other tropical fruits such as bananas and papaya (pawpaw) and vegetables such as beans, tomatoes, capsicums (bell peppers) and zucchini (courgettes) are also exported. Much of this produce is air-freighted out; an important plus for tourism is that agriculture creates an additional demand for aircraft. The inevitable copra (dried coconut), produced throughout the Pacific, is another important export and there is also a continuing supply of pearl shell.

The most important money earner for the Cooks, however, is tourism. It's number one and growing faster than anything else; it's estimated that 50,000 tourists visited Rarotonga in 1993, with 55,000 expected for '94 – a significant number for a small island with a population of only around 10,000. Other important money earners include the Cook Islands' beautiful and cleverly marketed postage stamps, offshore banking and the status of the islands as a tax haven.

For the casual visitor it's very hard to get any sort of handle on the economy of the Cooks, or more particularly of Rarotonga. On one hand the balance of trade is undoubtedly pretty horrific and the Cook Islanders live far beyond their means. On the other hand everybody is undeniably well fed. There's definitely a lot of food around, even a surplus, with exotic fruits growing in profusion all around the island. Avocadoes and coconuts grow in such abundance that they're often used as pig food. It's a popular joke that when *Merry Christmas Mr Lawrence* (a WW II prison camp drama starring David Bowie) was filmed on Rarotonga it proved impossible to find 500 people who looked thin enough to appear as prison camp extras. Extras had to be flown in from New Zealand.

POPULATION & PEOPLE

In the 1991 census the population of the Cook Islands was 18,617. The figure for Cook Islanders living outside the Cook Islands is even greater; most of the expatriate Cook Islanders live in New Zealand and Australia, where Cook Islanders have residence rights. The story of the Cook Islands' population is a story of continuing movement from the outer islands to Rarotonga and from there to New Zealand, and to a lesser extent to Australia. This draining trend has slowed somewhat recently, though, as the economic problems and high unemployment figures in New Zealand and Australia are making it more difficult to just go over and pick up a job. A number of Cook Islanders who went to New Zealand to make their 'fortune' are now back in the Cooks, trying to work it out one way or another.

Over 90% of the population lives on the southern group islands. None of the lightly populated atolls of the northern group have a four-figure population. Population estimates are:

Island	*Group*	*Population in 1986*	*Population in 1991*
Rarotonga	southern	9678	10,886
Aitutaki	southern	2391	2357
Mangaia	southern	1235	1214

Atiu	southern	955	1006
Mauke	southern	687	639
Mitiaro	southern	272	247
Pukapuka	northern	760	670
Manihiki	northern	508	663
Penrhyn	northern	496	503
Rakahanga	northern	283	262
Nassau	northern	118	102
Palmerston	northern	50	49
Suwarrow	northern	6	6

There are a number of unpopulated islands in both the northern and southern groups. These unpopulated islands are not normally visited by anyone – locals or tourists. And the only way they are accessible is by private yacht.

The population is over 90% Polynesian – closely related to the Maoris of New Zealand. New Zealand Maoris and Cook Islanders speak a similar language and the oral history of the Cook Islands relates how the ancestors of the New Zealand Maoris set out from Rarotonga to settle New Zealand. There's also a small minority of people of European descent, principally New Zealanders, and a couple of families of Fijians, Indians and Chinese.

There are often subtle differences between the islands, in some cases due to their isolation. The people of Pukapuka in the north, for example, are in some ways more closely related to Samoa than to the other islands of the group; geographically the northern Cook Islands are closer to Samoa than they are to the southern Cook Islands.

EDUCATION

Education is free and compulsory for children from ages six to 15. There are 28 primary schools throughout the islands and seven secondary schools, with secondary school education available on all the inhabited islands of the southern group. The New Zealand Government offers Cook Islanders scholarships for secondary and tertiary education and career training programmes in New Zealand, resulting in many Cook Islanders leaving the islands to be educated. The University of the South Pacific (USP), based in Suva, Fiji, has a small extension centre in Avarua.

ARTS

A number of distinctive arts are practiced on the Cook Islands:

Dance

Dancing in the Cook Islands is colourful, spectacular and popular. The Cook Islanders are reputed to be the best dancers in Polynesia, even better than the Tahitians, say the connoisseurs. You'll get plenty of opportunity to see dancing as there are dance performances all the time, particularly at the ubiquitous 'island nights'. Entry charges to see the performances are usually only about NZ$5 if you arrive at an island night around 9 pm, after the buffet. Some of the nightclubs also host dance performances.

The dancing is often wonderfully suggestive and, not surprisingly, this caused some upset to the Victorian European visitors. You can almost sense William Wyatt Gill, the observant early missionary, raising his eyebrows as he reported that:

> Respecting the *morality* of their dances, the less said the better; but the 'upaupa' dance, introduced from Tahiti, is obscene indeed.

Things haven't changed much!

The sensual nature of Cook Islands dance is rooted in its history when dances were performed in honour of Tangaroa, god of fertility and of the sea. This also explains the similarity in the dances of the Cook Islanders, Tahitians and Hawaiians, all of whom shared the same religion, taking their god Tangaroa with them as they migrated from one island group to another.

If you go to the annual dance championships on Rarotonga the points which judges watch for will probably be outlined. They include the difficulty of the dance, the movements of the hands which must express the music, the facial expressions and the grace with which the dance is done. Male dances tend to be aggressive and energetic, female dances are often all languid suggestiveness and gyrating hips. It's a lot of fun. Don't concentrate solely on the dancers – the musicians are wonderful to watch and the

The Maire Nui

In October 1992, representatives from 24 nations around the Pacific gathered in Rarotonga for the sixth Festival of Pacific Arts, a 10-day festival showcasing the traditional and modern arts of the Polynesian, Micronesian and Melanesian countries. It was the first time the festival had been held in such a small country – previous festivals had been held in Australia, New Zealand, Fiji, Western Samoa and Tahiti – but Rarotonga rose to the challenge admirably, making a name for itself throughout the Pacific. In the local Cook Islands parlance, the festival was called simply the *Maire Nui* or Grand Festival.

And grand it was. Demonstrations and performances were given of many diverse arts from around the Pacific with dance, music and song, painting, woodcarving, weaving, tapa cloth making, traditional tattooing, culinary arts, clothing and textile arts and a wide variety of other arts & crafts all represented.

Perhaps most spectacular of all was the 'canoe festival'. Large double-hulled canoes were carved by traditional methods in a variety of places around the Pacific, with preparations beginning long before the festival, and sailed to Rarotonga from places as distant as New Zealand, Hawaii and Tahiti, as well as from the outer islands of the Cooks. A deep respect and admiring thrill was felt by everyone when all the canoes sailed in unison into Avana Harbour, Rarotonga's ancient harbour on the south-east side of the island. The arrival of the canoe from New Zealand was an especially emotional event, as Avana Harbour was the spot from which the great Polynesian migrations set sail for New Zealand (Aotearoa) around 1350 AD, resulting in the Maori settlement of New Zealand. This was the first time in many centuries that a double-hulled canoe had made the journey home, back to Rarotonga.

Festival participants and observers streamed into Rarotonga from around the Pacific and around the world. Overseas participants, giving performances and demonstrations of their arts, numbered about 1900. Cook Islands participants were difficult to count, since so many people participated in so many ways, but it was estimated that around 1600 Cook Islanders participated in the opening ceremony alone. An additional 7000 or so observers arrived from around the Cook Islands, the Pacific and around the world. People were housed in every conceivable place around the island – in hotels, hostels, schools, clubhouses, meeting houses and in private homes.

A lot of construction was done in preparation for the festival. Some of the more notable constructions of this time that can still be seen today include the Sir Geoffrey Henry Cultural Centre complex, the Punanga Nui open-air market, Vaka Village and the Ara Maire Nui coast road in Avarua.

The Maire Nui left many other lasting changes in Rarotonga, besides the physical ones. The festival mobilised a sort of cultural renaissance throughout the Cook Islands. There's a palpable feeling of what might be called 'Polynesian Pride' here in the islands now. There seems to be a greater knowledge of and respect for Polynesian culture in general – and Cook Islands culture in particular. Hosting and experiencing the sharing of cultures from all around the Pacific showed the Cook Islanders a lot about their traditional culture and about its standing in relation to other Pacific cultures. The festival showed everyone that the Pacific has a lot to be proud of. ■

audience often gets involved in a big way. Some of the fat mamas are simply superb and, despite their weight, can shake a hip as well as any young *vaine*. Take note of how it's done though; a feature of almost every island night is dragging some unsuspecting *papa'as,* or foreigners, up on stage to perform!

Of course Western ideals of beauty have gained considerable ascendancy these days and it's only as they get older that some Polynesian women start to widen so dramatically. In the missionary period William Wyatt Gill wrote:

> The greatest requisite of a Polynesian beauty is to be fat and as fair as their dusky skin will permit. To insure this, favourite children in good families, whether boys or girls, were regularly fattened and imprisoned till nightfall, when a little gentle exercise was permitted. If refractory, the guardian would even whip the culprit for not eating more, calling out 'Shall I not be put to shame to see you so slim in the dance?'

Another interesting thing to see is how much the traditional dance movements permeate even the modern 'Western-style' dancing. Go to any nightclub and you'll see disco, pop, rock-n-roll and even sometimes ballroom dancing spiced with hip-swaying, knee-knocking and other classic island movements. Don't be afraid to join in and try it yourself, after you've seen how it's done – the locals will love it and you'll have a great time too!

Traditional Arts & Crafts

Although the arts and crafts of the Cook Islands today are only a shadow of their former importance, they were once widespread and of high quality. The early missionaries, in their passion to obliterate all traces of 'heathenism', did a comprehensive job of destroying much of the old art forms but, fortunately, they also saved some of the best pieces, many of which can now be found in European museums.

There was no real connection between the southern volcanic islands and the northern atolls in the pre-European period and the art of the small islands to the north was much more limited. Domestic equipment and tools, matting, and inlaid pearl shell on canoes and canoe paddles were about the extent of their work. In the south, however, a variety of crafts developed with strong variations between the individual islands.

A number of fine books have been published about the arts and crafts of the Cook Islands; see the Books section in the Facts for the Visitor chapter.

In this section we'll speak only about the ancient, traditional arts and crafts of the islands, but many arts and crafts are still practiced in the islands today. See the Things to Buy section in the Facts for the Visitor chapter, and in each individual island chapter, for an idea of the types of arts and crafts that are found in the islands today.

Woodcarving Figures of gods carved from wood were amongst the most widespread art forms and were particularly common on Rarotonga. These squat figures, variously described as fisherman's gods or as images of specifically named gods such as Tangaroa, were similar to the Tangaroa image which has become symbolic of the Cook Islands today. Staff gods with repetitive figures carved down a pole; war clubs and spears were other typical Rarotongan artefacts. The incredibly intricately carved mace gods, often from Mangaia, and the slab gods from Aitutaki, were other examples of woodcarving which are no longer found today.

Ceremonial Adzes Mangaian ceremonial adzes were an important craft. At first, these axe-like hand tools probably had an everyday use but with time they became purely ceremonial objects and more and more stylised in their design. Each element of these adzes was beautifully made – from the stone blade to the carefully carved wooden handle and the intricate sennit binding that lashed the blade to the handle. Some of the best examples of Mangaian ceremonial adzes are on exhibit in some of the world's great museums. Some people believe that the art of ceremonial adze making has died out. Not so – when we went to Mangaia we met a couple of woodcarvers who still make the traditional adzes in the traditional way.

Canoes Canoes, or *vakas,* were carved with great seriousness and ceremony in pre-European times. Not only did the canoes have to be large and strong enough for long-distance ocean voyages, they also had to be made in accordance with strict rules of tapu. Taunga, or experts, not only in the matter of canoes and woodcarving but also in spiritual matters, had to guide every step of the process. A suitable tree had to be found, chosen and cut, with proper supplication to the god of the forest. Once cut, the carving had to proceed in a certain way, all the way to the launching of the canoe, which once again had to be done in accordance with all the proper spiritual as well as physical laws and requisites. None of the ancient, huge pre-European canoes survive in the Cook Islands today.

Buildings Houses and other buildings were made of natural materials which decayed rapidly so no ancient buildings survive to the present day and very few buildings of traditional construction remain on any of the southern islands. Woodcarving was only rarely used in houses, although some important buildings, including some of the first locally built mission churches, had carved and decorated wooden posts. Artistically impressive sennit lashing was, however, found on many buildings. Since nails were not available the wooden framework of a building was tied together with carefully bound sennit rope. Each island or area had its own distinctive style for the binding of the sennit and this is still followed today. If you are on the island of Mangaia you can see fine sennit lashing on the roof beams of the CICC churches. The Rarotongan Resort Hotel on Rarotonga commissioned craftspeople to bind the beams of verandahs and walkways with sennit.

Other Crafts Woven fans, feathered headdresses bound with sennit, woven belts and baskets, and wooden seats from Atiu were other artistic crafts of the pre-European period. Some of these crafts have survived but others are found only in museums.

CULTURE

Visitors to the Cooks often get only a superficial impression of the place and are disappointed, upon seeing the close-cut lawns, the Western-style clothing, the electricity and the New Zealand-type houses, that there is so little sign of Polynesian culture. Yet right underneath this thin Western veneer, layer upon layer of the old Cook Islands culture survives. It's in the land system – how it's inherited, how it's managed, how it's leased but never sold. It's in the way people transact business. It's in the concept of time. Tradition survives intact in hospitality, in how to dance and make music and celebrate, in the wearing of flowers and in many other day-to-day ways of doing things.

Every native Cook Islander is part of some family clan, and each family clan is connected in some distinct way to the ancient system of chiefs (ariki), sub-chiefs (mataiapo) and landed gentry (rangatira) which has survived for centuries in an unbroken line. Rarotonga's six ariki clans are still based on the original land divisions from when the Maoris first arrived on the island many centuries ago.

Even today, when an ariki is installed, the ceremony takes place on an ancient family marae. The new ariki and all the attendants are dressed in the traditional ceremonial leaves, and the ancient symbols of office – a spear, woven shoes, a feather-shell-tapa cloth headdress, a woven fan, a huge mother-of-pearl shell necklace and other emblems – are presented. You'll see these things in

Land Ownership

The Cook Islands' land ownership policy has a great influence on the islands' economy and its social patterns. A law prohibiting anybody from selling or buying land makes it impossible for outsiders to own land in the Cooks. Land ownership is purely hereditary and land can only be leased, not sold, to an outside party. The maximum term of a lease is 60 years.

Because land is passed from generation to generation, people start to own curiously divided chunks of property. Many families seem to have a house by the coast, a citrus plantation somewhere else, a taro patch somewhere else again and the odd group of papaya trees dotted here and there. It can be a full time job commuting from one farmlet to another. ■

Island Houses

Today the houses you see around the islands are almost all cheaply made imitation-European-style with fibro walls and tin roofs. Very few of the old *kikau* houses with their pandanus-thatched roofs remain. In the southern group islands, only Aitutaki has a traditional-style village, New Jerusalem; it was built by a religious group called the Free Church in the early 1990s on the south end of the island, well away from the other villages. In Rarotonga it's illegal to build and live in the traditional type of house that today's generation of elders grew up in. ■

museums, but for Cook Islanders, they are not just museum pieces.

You'll see many graves of the ancestors beside modern houses. For many Cook Islanders, the spirits of the ancestors are an ever-present reality. The spirits are not feared as 'ghosts' are in some other cultures. It is simply a fact of life that they live here along with everyone else.

RELIGION

Only a few people today know much about the pre-European religion of the Cook Islands, with its sophisticated system of 71 gods, each ruling a particular facet of reality, and its 12 heavens – seven below the sun, five above it, plus another dominion below the earth – each the dwelling place of particular gods and spirits. The early missionaries held 'pagan beliefs' in such utter contempt that they made virtually no effort to study, record or understand the traditional religion. They did, however, make great efforts to wipe it out and destroy any 'heathen images' they came across. Fortunately some fine pieces of religious art were whisked away from the islands and are now prized pieces in European museums.

The Cook Islands today are overwhelmingly Christian – in fact people from Christian cultures who haven't been to church for years (weddings and funerals apart) suddenly find themselves going back to church for fun! The major local sect is the Cook Islands Christian Church or CICC. Founded by those first London Missionary Society missionaries who came to the islands in the early 1820s, it's a blend of Church of England, Baptist, Methodist and whatever else was going on at the time – Roman Catholicism definitely excepted. Today the CICC still attracts about 70% of the faithful, on Rarotonga at least, and probably even a higher percentage on the outer islands. The remaining 30% is squabbled over by the Roman Catholics, the Seventh Day Adventists, the Church of the Latter Day Saints (Mormons, looking as out of place in their white shirts and ties as ever), Assembly of God, Apostolic Revival Fellowship and various other sects, plus a small but avid following of Baha'is .

The CICC still has an overwhelming influence on local living habits and in many cases the pattern is exactly that established by those original British missionaries in the 19th century. Rarotongan villages are still divided into four sections which take turns in looking after the village church and its minister. Each family in the congregation contributes a monthly sum into the church fund which goes towards church costs. The church minister is appointed for a five-year period after which he moves to another church. He gets a small weekly stipend but in addition the village group responsible for that week also collects to provide him with a more reasonable weekly salary. The weekly contribution is read out during the Sunday service to the shame or pride of that week's responsible group!

This village responsibility has two sides for the church minister. He is responsible for far more than just his church: if the village teenagers are playing up or hanging around the local bars the blame is likely to be laid at the CICC minister's door! And if he doesn't do something about it then a pitifully low weekly contribution can be interpreted as a strong hint to get on with the job. In fact islanders say that they prefer to have a minister with no local connections – someone from an outer island, say. That way if they decide to kick him out by cutting the money supply he's not going to find it so easy to fall back on the food from his local gardens!

Visitors are more than welcome to attend a Sunday church service and it's a delightful event. You're looked upon as a useful way of augmenting the collection and anyway, there's nothing much else happening on a Sunday morning. The service is held mostly in Maori, although there will be a token welcome in English and parts of the service may be translated into English as well. The islanders all dress in their Sunday best and the women all wear strikingly similar wide-brimmed white hats. When you go, show respect by observing a few simple rules of dress: no shorts for men or women and no bare shoulders. CICC services all over the island are held at 10 am Sunday, with other services held on Sunday evenings and other evenings throughout the week.

The major attraction of a CICC service is the inspired hymn singing – the harmonies are superb and the volume lifts the roof! This wonderful singing has a pre-European origin. When the missionaries arrived they found the people were already singing praise to their gods, so they simply put Christian words to the existing songs. Thus the harmony, rhythm and basic structure of the music you hear has its roots in a time long before the arrival of Christianity. Of course you will also hear a familiar tune or two, but sung in a distinctively Cook Islands style.

Early Missionaries

Important figures in the early spread of Christianity through the islands included:

Aaron Buzacott Following in John Williams' footsteps, Buzacott not only did most of the work in translating the Bible into Maori, he also composed most of the hymns in the CICC Maori hymn book. Buzacott also supervised the construction of the church in Avarua, Rarotonga, and died in 1864 after 30 years' work in the Cook Islands. The story of his life and labours is told in *Mission Life in the Islands of the Pacific*.

William Gill Author of *Gems from the Coral Island*, William Gill built the present CICC church at Arorangi, Rarotonga, and also its predecessor, destroyed by a hurricane in 1846. He worked at Arorangi from 1839 to 1852 when he returned to England. His brother George was the first resident missionary on Mangaia.

William Wyatt Gill Author of *From Darkness to Light in Polynesia*, William Wyatt Gill was no relation to William Gill. He spent 20 years on Mangaia – see the Books section of the Facts for the Visitor chapter for more details.

Maretu Maretu's accounts of the spread of Christianity are particularly interesting because they are by a Cook Islander rather than a European (see the Books section of the Facts for the Visitor chapter). A native of Rarotonga, Maretu later worked as a missionary on the islands of Mangaia, Manihiki and Rakahanga.

Papeiha Probably the most successful of the local mission workers, Papeiha was brought to the Cook Islands from Raiatea in the Society Islands, now part of French Polynesia, in 1821 by John Williams. Papeiha introduced Christianity to the Cook Islands – to Aitutaki in 1821 and to Rarotonga in 1823. He died on Rarotonga in 1867, having spent 46 years in the Cook Islands.

John Williams A pioneer mission worker in the Pacific, he was instrumental in the spread of Christianity to the Cook Islands. He was killed (and eaten) on the Vanuatu island of Eromanga in 1839.

LANGUAGE

The language of the Cook Islands is Cook Islands Maori, but English is spoken as a second language by virtually everyone and you will have no trouble at all getting by with English.

Among themselves, however, the people speak their own language. If you'd like to learn a little of it yourself, pick up a copy of *Say it in Rarotongan* by Mana Strickland (Pacific Publications, Sydney, 1979, paperback) which is widely available in the Cook Islands. It will get you started. If you'll be here for some time and are serious about learning the language, the Cook Islands Library & Museum Society in Avarua has a number of books for studying the language, and the University of the South Pacific (USP) centre in Avarua offers classes.

English can present its own special difficulties for Cook Islanders. In their language there is no differentiation between male and female; 'he' and 'she', 'him' and 'her' are all expressed by the one word *aia*. You'll fre-

Names

To our ears the Cook Islanders have some pretty strange given names. There's no differentiation between male or female names and they're often given to commemorate some event that happened around the time the name's recipient was born. Big brother just left your island to go off to school on another island? Well you might end up as 'Schooltrip'. The school was far away in Whangarei, New Zealand? You could be named 'Whangarei'. Big brother won a medal in the Commonwealth Games? You're 'Silver Medal'! But why would somebody be named 'Tipunu' or 'Teaspoon'? ■

quently hear Cook Islanders mix up all the different English words to express what they have only one word for, calling men 'she' and women 'he'!

Although each island has its own distinctive speech, people from all the Cook Islands can understand one another. Cook Islands Maori is also closely related to the Maori language of New Zealand and to the other eastern Polynesian languages including Hawaiian, Marquesan and Tahitian. A Cook Islander would have little trouble understanding someone speaking those languages.

Cook Islands Maori was traditionally a spoken language, not a written one. The language, in its Rarotongan form, was first written down by the missionaries in the 1830s. Later they produced a Rarotongan version of the Bible.

Pronunciation

The Cook Islands alphabet has only 13 letters: *a, e, i, k, m, n, ng, o, p, r, t, u, v*. The *ng* sound is pronounced the same as in English (eg, running, sitting etc) but in Cook Islands Maori it's often at the beginning of a word (eg, Nga, Ngatangiia). Practise by pronouncing the sound in an English word and see how it feels in the throat; then say it alone by itself; then use it to begin a word, and you'll have it. All the other consonants are pronounced as they are in English.

Vowels The pronunciation of vowels is very important. Each vowel has both a long and a short sound. Using the one other than the right one results in a completely different word (eg, *pūpū* = class, group or team; *pupu* = a type of small shell). Sometimes the long vowels carry a macron over them when written (ā, ē, ī, ō, ū), but not always; the language can correctly be written either with or without the macrons. The long and short pronunciation of the vowels is like this:

Short		**Long**	
a	as in about	ā	as in all
e	as in pet	ē	as in hen
i	as in sit	ī	as in bee
o	as in cot	ō	as in worn
u	as in put	ū	as in tune

Another symbol used in the written language is an apostrophe before or between vowels (eg, *ta'i)*, indicating a stop in the enunciation (eg, *tai*, pronounced with one syllable, as the English 'tie', vs *ta'i*, pronounced with two syllables, as 'TA-i').

The classic joke about the pronunciation of Cook Islands Maori vowels – a true joke – is that if you pronounce the word *ika* in one way it means 'fish', while pronounced in another way it means the 'female genitalia'! If you want to say 'fish', pronounce it as if it had an 'e' sound in front – *e ika*.

Greetings & Civilities

Hello; all purpose greeting ('may you live!').
Kia orana!

How are you? (said to one person).
Pe'ea koe?

How are you? (said to two people).
Pe'ea korua?

How are you? (said to three or more people).
Pe'ea kotou?

Good; also, thank you.
Meitaki.

Very good; also, thank you very much.
Meitaki ma'ata.

Goodbye (said by the person staying to the person leaving; literally, 'go along').
Aere ra.

Goodbye (said by the person leaving to the person staying; literally, 'remain').
E no'o ake ra.
Goodbye (said by both people, when each is leaving to go).
Aere atu ra.
Welcome!
Turou!
Good luck (a toast)!
Kia manuia!

Please (used at the end of the statement).
Ine.
Please come here.
Aere mai, ine.
Thank you.
Meitaki.
Thank you very much.
Meitaki ma'ata.

Small Talk

What's your name?
Ko'ai to'ou ingoa?
My name is Nancy.
Ko Nancy toku ingoa.
Where are you from?
No'ea mai koe?
I'm from Rarotonga.
No Rarotonga mai au.
Where are you going?
Ka aere koe ki'ea?
I'm going to the shop.
Te aere nei ki te toa.
I'm going to Aitutaki.
Te aere nei ki Aitutaki.

Yes	*Ae*
No	*Kare*
Maybe	*Penei ake*
Who knows?	*E a'a nei?*
person; people	*tangata*
man	*tane*
woman	*vaine*
child	*tamariki*
boy	*tamaroa*
girl	*tama'ine*
baby	*pepe*
father	*papa*
mother	*mama*
brother	*tungane*
sister	*tua'ine*
friend	*oa, taeake*
husband	*tane*
wife	*vaine*
me/I	*au*
you (one person)	*koe*
you (two people)	*korua*
you (three or more)	*koutou*
him/her/he/she	*aia*
we (two)	*taua, maua*
we (three or more)	*tatou, matou*
they (two)	*raua*
they (three or more)	*ratou*
beautiful	*manea*
ugly	*vi'ivi'i*
the mountain is beautiful	*manea te maunga*

Around Town

store; shop	*toa*
house	*are*
town	*taoni*
village	*tapere*
beach	*tapa ta'atai*
island; lagoon islet	*motu*
lagoon	*roto*
land	*enua*
mountain	*maunga*
ocean	*moana*
reef	*akau*
sky	*rangi*

Religion

Bible	*Bibilia Tapu*
church	*ekalesia; are pure*
God	*Atua*
holy; sacred	*tapu*
hymn	*himene*

Food & Drink

food	*kai*
underground oven	*umu*
food cooked in an underground oven	*umukai*
arrowroot	*maniota*
banana	*meika*

beef	*puaka toro*
beer	*pia*
breadfruit	*kuru*
chicken	*punuamoa*
coconut (for drinking)	*nu*
coconut (for meat)	*akari*
coffee	*kaope*
fish	*ika*
juice	*vai venevene*
mango	*vi*
orange	*anani*
passionfruit	*parapotini*
pawpaw (papaya)	*nita*
pineapple	*ara painapa*
pork	*puaka*
potato	*pitete*
rice	*raiti*
sweet potato	*kumara*
taro	*taro*
taro leaves	*rukau*
tea	*ti*
water	*vai*
watermelon	*mereni*

Fauna

bee	*rango meri*
bird	*manu*
butterfly	*pepe*
cat	*kiore, ngaio*
centipede	*veri*
dog	*puakaoa*
mosquito	*namu*
moth	*kikiona*
rat	*kioretoka*
pig	*puaka*
wasp	*rango patia*

Time

day	*ra*
night	*po*
hour	*ora*
one o'clock	*ora ta'i*
two o'clock	*ora rua*

Numbers

1	*ta'i*
2	*rua*
3	*toru*
4	*a*
5	*rima*
6	*ono*
7	*itu*
8	*varu*
9	*iva*
10	*ta'i-nga'uru*
11	*ta'i-nga'uru-ma-ta'i* (one ten plus one)
12	*ta'i-nga'uru-ma-rua* (one ten plus two) & etc, to
20	*rua-nga'uru* (two tens)
21	*rua-nga'uru-ma-ta'i* (two tens plus one) & etc, to
99	*iva-nga'uru-ma-iva*
100	*ta'i-anere*
101	*ta'i-anere-ma-ta'i* (one hundred plus one) & etc, to
110	*ta'i-anere e ta'i-nga'uru* (one hundred plus one ten) & etc, to
999	*iva-anere e iva-nga'uru-ma-iva*
1000	*ta'i-tauatini*
1001	*ta'i-tauatini-ma-ta'i* (one thousand plus one) & etc

Days of the Week

Monday	*Monite*
Tuesday	*Ru'irua*
Wednesday	*Ru'itoru*
Thursday	*Paraparau*
Friday	*Varaire*
Saturday	*Ma'anakai*
Sunday	*Tapati*

Months of the Year

January	*Tianuare*
February	*Peperuare*
March	*Mati*
April	*Aperira*
May	*Me*
June	*Tiunu*
July	*Tiurai*
August	*Aukute*
September	*Tepetema*
October	*Okotopa*
November	*Noema*
December	*Titema*

Facts for the Visitor

VISAS & EMBASSIES

No visa is required to visit the Cooks. A visitor's permit, good for 31 days, is granted on arrival for all nationalities. The only things you need do are present a valid passport, an onward or return airline ticket, and honour the loosely policed 'prior booking' arrangement (see Accommodation later in this chapter).

If you want to stay longer than the initial 31 days you should have no problems so long as you can show you've got adequate finances and still have your vital return ticket. Extensions are granted a month at a time and each one-month extension costs NZ$30. You're allowed five one-month extensions to take you to a total of six months. If you want to stay more than six months, apply in advance to the Principal Immigration Officer, Department of Immigration, PO Box 473, Rarotonga (☎ 29-363, fax 29-364).

Visitor's permits can be extended on Rarotonga at the Department of Immigration office on the main road, next door to the airport. If you are intending to visit the northern islands it's wise to extend your permit before heading up as there are often delays. One long-stay visitor wrote that extending his family's visas in Aitutaki took forever.

> The immigration officer was always waiting for information from Rarotonga and we finally got our visas in order three days before we left the Cooks and three months after they had officially expired!

Cook Islands Consulates

Cook Islands consulates in other countries include:

Australia
: Cook Islands Consulate, 1/177 Pacific Hwy, North Sydney, NSW 2060 (☎ (02) 955-0444, fax 955-0447)
: Cook Islands High Commission, Canberra (☎ (06) 281-5329, 281-5456, fax 281-5501)
: Cook Islands Consulate, c/o Roy Spratt & Associates, 17/12 Crips Ct, Bruce, ACT 2617 Canberra (☎ (06) 253-2977, fax 476-7106)

New Zealand
: Cook Islands High Commission, 11 Park St, Thorndon, PO Box 12-242, Wellington (☎ (04) 472-5126, 472-5127, fax 472-5121)
: Cook Islands Consulate, 330 Parnell Rd, PO Box 37-391, Auckland (☎ (09) 379-4140, fax 309-1876)

Norway
: Cook Islands Consulate, Bydgoy Alle 64, 0265 Oslo 2 (☎ (02) 430-910, fax (22) 444-611)

USA
: Cook Islands Consulate, Kamehameha Schools No 16, c/o 144 Ke Ala Ola Rd, Honolulu, Hawaii 96817 (☎ (808) 842-8216, fax 842-3520)

Foreign Consulates in the Cook Islands

Foreign consulates in the Cook Islands include:

France
: French Consul, Mrs Diane McKegg, upstairs in CITC Building, Avarua; Private Bag 1, Rarotonga (☎ 22-000, fax 20-857)

New Zealand
: New Zealand High Commission, upstairs over the Philatelic Bureau, beside the post office, Avarua; PO Box 21, Rarotonga (☎ 22-201, fax 21-241)

DOCUMENTS

The only document you'll need in the Cook Islands, aside from your valid passport and visitor's permit, is a Cook Islands driver's licence if you want to drive on Rarotonga. See under Rental Cars in the Getting Around section in the Rarotonga chapter for details.

CUSTOMS

The usual customs restrictions of two litres of spirits or two litres of wine or 4½ litres of beer, plus 200 cigarettes or 50 cigars or 250 grams of tobacco apply. The usual agricultural quarantines also apply: bringing in plants or plant products, animals or animal products etc is restricted or prohibited, and used camping or sporting equipment may have to be fumigated. There are also the usual restrictions about firearms, weapons, drugs etc.

MONEY

All prices in this book are quoted in New Zealand dollars (NZ$) since the Cook Islands dollar is tied to and valued the same as the New Zealand dollar.

Currency

New Zealand and Cook Islands paper money is used interchangeably in the Cooks, but New Zealand coins are not accepted. Cook Islands notes are in denominations of $3, $10, $20 and $50. The $3 note is a rarity, only one other country has such a note. There is also a complete set of Cook Islands coins – 5c, 10c, 20c, 50c, $1, $2 and $5. Most of the coins are the same size and shape as the New Zealand coins (and Australian ones for that matter) so you can use New Zealand coins for pay phones or other such uses quite easily. The old huge $1 Tangaroa coin is now a collectors' item – they're available at the Philatelic Bureau on Rarotonga – having been replaced by a smaller, wavy-edged $1 coin, still bearing Tangaroa's image. The $2 coin is also an oddity, it's triangular! The $5 coin is larger than the rest and made of brass.

Cook Islands money, whether coins or paper bills, cannot be changed anywhere else in the world, so be sure to either spend it or change it back into New Zealand or other currency before you leave the country.

Exchange Rates

The Cook Islands use both Cook Islands and New Zealand currency, which are equal in value. The exchange rates are:

US$1	=	NZ$1.60	NZ$1	=	US$0.62
A$1	=	NZ$1.18	NZ$1	=	A$0.84
UK£1	=	NZ$2.40	NZ$1	=	UK£0.41
C$1	=	NZ$1.22	NZ$1	=	C$0.81
DM1	=	NZ$0.89	NZ$1	=	DM1.11
Y100	=	NZ$1.43	NZ$1	=	Y69.54

You get about 4% more for travellers' cheques than for cash. There are not many places you can change money – the Westpac and ANZ Banks in Avarua, the Administration Centre in Aitutaki and at some hotels. You're better off changing all your money on Rarotonga rather than hoping to be able to change money on the outer islands. Westpac has a branch at the Rarotonga International Airport, open for all arriving and departing international flights.

Credit Cards

Bankcard, Visa and MasterCard are readily accepted at most places in Rarotonga, and the Westpac and ANZ banks in Avarua give cash advances on all three cards. American Express and Diners Club are accepted at the better hotels and restaurants.

Costs

Thumbing through the pages of this book will show you the costs for everything from accommodation and dining out to hiring a motorcycle, riding the bus or going diving.

The Cook Islands are more expensive than Fiji, but they're nowhere near the horrendous levels of Tahiti and French Polynesia.

The New Zealand connection is both a factor for and against the steep costs. The Cook Islands are heavily dependent upon New Zealand for their imports so there's a healthy slug on top of New Zealand prices to cover the shipping costs. Shipping is a major element in the high prices of most Pacific islands. Additionally, and again like many other Pacific islands, there's a sad lack of self-sufficiency. It's something of a shock to see the tins of mackerel and tuna in every trade store when the reef abounds with fish. Similarly, Rarotonga is extravagantly fertile but produce is still imported at a high cost.

The plus point about the Cook Islands' strong links to New Zealand is that for a number of years the New Zealand dollar has not been the world's strongest currency. So if the New Zealand dollar sinks, relative to your home market currency, then prices in the Cook Islands also translate into that much less.

Cheaper accommodation, though

camping out is not allowed, can also help to cut costs. Most importantly, nearly all accommodation offers opportunities for preparing your own food which is substantially cheaper than eating out. See the Accommodation and Food sections later in this chapter for details.

Many visitors to the Cooks come on all-inclusive package holidays. Check out the package holidays available from travel agents; sometimes you can get an accommodation-and-airfare package for about the same price as you'd pay for airfare only, or even less.

Tipping & Bargaining

Tipping and bargaining are not traditional customs in the Cook Islands. The price marked on items for sale, or on the bill in restaurants, is the price the merchant expects to receive. Haggling over prices is considered very rude.

Consumer Taxes

A 10% tax is figured into the quoted price of just about everything. If a price is quoted to you 'plus tax', you must add 10% to see what you'll actually pay.

CLIMATE & WHEN TO GO

Rarotonga, the largest and most visited of the Cook Islands, is virtually directly south of Hawaii and about the same distance south of the equator as Hawaii is north. The climate is therefore very similar to that of Hawaii, although the seasons are reversed: December is the middle of summer, August the middle of winter.

The Cooks have a pleasantly even climate year-round with no excesses of temperature, humidity or rainfall, although it can rain quite often. Rarotonga, with its high mountains, is very likely to be wet and although you'd have to be unlucky to suffer one of the rare week-long rainy periods, be sure to bring rain gear with you at any time of year. The wettest months are usually December to March when around 25 cm of rain can fall each month. These are also the hottest months, although the seasonal variation is very slight, ranging from high/low temperatures of 29/23°C in February, the hottest month, down to 25/18°C in the coldest months of June, July, August and September. The summer months can feel quite warm at times, though, due to the combination of temperature and humidity, and the winter nights can sometimes feel quite cool, even chilly.

Despite the relatively heavy annual rainfall some of the islands, particularly the

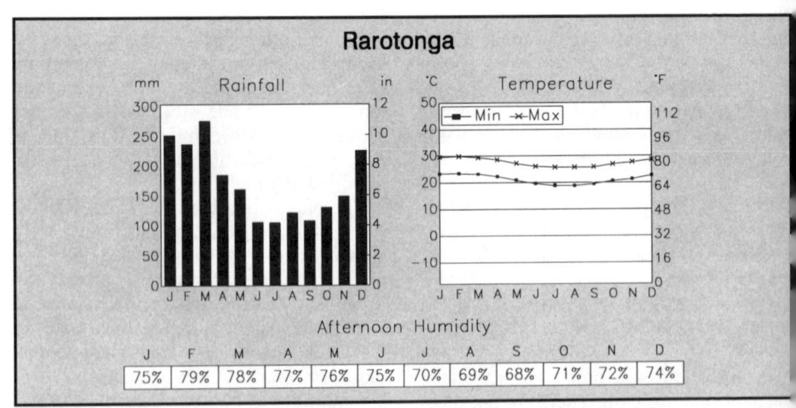

J	F	M	A	M	J	J	A	S	O	N	D
75%	79%	78%	77%	76%	75%	70%	69%	68%	71%	72%	74%

atolls of the northern group, suffer from severe water shortages and great care must be taken to conserve water supplies.

Hurricane season is from November to March. On average a mild hurricane will pass by two or three times a decade but extremely severe hurricanes are a much rarer occurrence, happening only about once every 20 years.

The last one was Hurricane Sally, which struck the northern group island of Suwarrow on 26 December 1986, moved southwards and made a loop or two before hitting Palmerston on 31 December, and then made a fair bee-line for Rarotonga, arriving with full force at Rarotonga on 1 January '87. Lots of material damage occurred, but no lives were lost, and international relief efforts helped to put the island back together before long.

So when is the best time to come to the Cooks? We've been there during all seasons and we'd say that any time is a good time!

WHAT TO BRING

The Cook Islands' balanced and moderate climate makes clothing choice a breeze. You rarely need anything warmer than a short-sleeve shirt or T-shirt, but bring along a jumper (sweater) just to be on the safe side, especially during the cooler months of June to September. An umbrella or other rain gear is worth packing for any time of year.

You'll need an old pair of running shoes or sneakers for walking on the reefs – there are some things you'd rather not step on, and coral cuts take a long time to heal. You'll also need those runners, or a pair of sturdy shoes or hiking boots, if you intend to go walking or climbing on Rarotonga, or walking across the razor-sharp makatea of Atiu, Mauke, Mitiaro or Mangaia.

A torch (flashlight) will come in handy, especially if you visit the outer islands, where the power goes off at midnight. There are also caves to explore, for which a torch is essential.

The Cook Islands are, of course, wonderful for snorkelling and scuba diving. You can bring your own equipment with you or rent or buy it on Rarotonga.

The Cook Islands are a major supplier of clothes to New Zealand so there's a pretty good choice of clothes locally, although prices tend to be high.

Most Western consumable commodities are readily available but, again, somewhat expensive. It may be more economical to bring a spare tube of toothpaste or another spool of film rather than buy it locally.

Don't forget sun screen or suntan lotion, although these are readily available. You may find you prefer the age-old local favourite, pure coconut oil, available everywhere. It does wonders for both skin and hair and smells good too, whether it's the plain variety or scented with local flowers. Mauke Miracle Oil, a little more expensive, contains herbs which act as a natural sun screen.

If you're planning to travel farther afield, particularly if you travel deck class on the inter-island ships to the islands of the northern atolls, come prepared. You'll probably want a sleeping bag and some sort of foam mat to lay out on the deck. Cooking equipment and, of course, food supplies can also be useful.

TOURIST OFFICES

Local Tourist Office

The local tourist office, called the Cook Islands Tourist Authority (☎ 29-435, fax 21-435, telex RG62054, PO Box 14, Avarua, Rarotonga) is on the main road in the centre of Avarua; look for the 'i' sign (it stands for 'information') out on the street and Visitors Centre written on the building. You can contact them for information about the Cook Islands before you arrive – they'll send you some printed information – and stop in for information, answers to questions, free maps etc while you're here. The office is open Monday to Friday from 8 am to 4 pm.

Overseas Tourist Offices

Overseas offices or representatives of the Cook Islands Tourist Authority include:

Australia
   Cook Islands Tourist Authority, 1/177 Pacific Hwy, North Sydney NSW 2060 (☎ (02) 955-0444, fax 955-0447)
Germany
   TCSP, Klugstrasse 114, D-8000 Munchen 19 (☎ (49) 89-155021, fax 89-1577593)
Hong Kong
   Pacific Leisure, Box 2382, Tung Ming Building, 40 Des Voeux Rd, Central (☎ 524-7065, cable MYPLEASURE, telex 73038 MY PLSHX)
New Zealand
   Cook Islands Tourist Authority, 330 Parnell Rd, PO Box 37-391, Auckland (☎ (09) 379-4140, fax 309-1876)
United Kingdom
   TCSP, Suite 433, High Holborn House, 52-54 High Holborn, London WC1V 6RB (☎ (71) 242-3131, fax 242-2838)
USA
   Cook Islands Tourist Authority, 6033 West Century Blvd, Suite 690, Los Angeles, CA 90045 (☎ (310) 216-2872, toll-free 1-800-624-6250, fax 216-2868)

BUSINESS HOURS & HOLIDAYS

Monday to Friday, 8 am to 4 pm is the usual business week, and shops are also open on Saturday morning until noon. Small local grocery stores keep longer hours, often from around 6 or 7 am till around 9 pm. The Westpac and ANZ Banks in Avarua are open Monday to Friday from 9 am to 3 pm.

Nearly everything is closed on Sunday – bars close at midnight on Saturday and even the local airline doesn't fly on Sunday. The only exceptions, again, are the small local groceries, some of which open for a couple of hours very early Sunday morning and for a couple of hours again in the evening. A couple of shops are operated by Seventh Day Adventists, who celebrate the Sabbath on Saturday rather than Sunday, so they're closed on Saturday and open on Sunday. Even most restaurants are closed on Sunday, except for hotel restaurants, which are open seven days a week. Several of the larger hotels serve up special Sunday meals – brunches in the late morning, barbecues in late afternoon.

Holidays

There are lots of public holidays in the Cook Islands and they're good opportunities to see dancing and other activities.

New Year's Day
   1 January
Good Friday & Easter Monday
   The two principal Easter days.
Anzac Day
   As in New Zealand and Australia, 25 April is an annual memorial day for the soldiers of the two world wars, with a special parade and services.
Queen's Birthday
   As in New Zealand and Australia, the Queen's 'official' birthday is celebrated on the first Monday in June.
Gospel Day
   Nuku religious plays are performed to commemorate the arrival of Christianity to Rarotonga, when British missionary John Williams and Raiatean missionary Papeiha arrived on 26 October 1823. Every major church participates with Biblical dramatisation involving music, processions, colourful costumes etc.
Flag Raising Day
   The raising of the British flag over Rarotonga on 27 October 1888 by Captain Bourke of the HMS *Hyacinth* is celebrated on 27 October, with traditional string band and drumming competitions.
Christmas Day
   Church services celebrate 25 December.
Boxing Day
   The day after Christmas; 26 December. Its name comes not from the sport, but from Olde England where traditionally the leftovers from Christmas dinner were 'boxed' and distributed to the poor the day after Christmas.

CULTURAL EVENTS

In addition to the annual holidays, many other island-wide events continually pop up. 'Any excuse for a good time' seems to be the motto, and the locals exuberantly turn out to support all manner of marches, runs, walks, sports competitions, music/dance/art/cultural events, youth rallies, religious revivals, raffle drawings, international mobilisations for one cause or another – you name it! Don't be shy about attending any function – visitors are always welcome.

The two major sports in the Cooks are rugby, which is played with all-out passion from May to August, and cricket, played over the summer months, particularly December to March.

The following are some of the more interesting and important festivals and events.

Cultural Festival Week In the second week of February, this week features *tivaevae* quilt competitions and arts and crafts displays.

Cook Islands Sevens Rugby Tournament International and local teams compete in this tournament held in mid-February.

Star Quest Stretching over two weeks in mid-April, singers, musicians and performers from all the Cook Islands come to Rarotonga to compete for stardom.

Island Dance Festival Week In the third week of April, dance displays and competitions include the important individual Dancers of the Year Competition.

Masters' Golf Tournament This mid-July golf tournament is for those age 40 years and over. Visitors are welcome to enter.

Lawn Bowling Tournament This tournament, with local and overseas participants, runs from mid-July to the first week in August.

Constitution Celebration This 10-day festival starts on the Friday before 4 August and celebrates the 1965 declaration of independence with sporting activities, dances, musical performances, historical and cultural displays, and many other events. This is the major festival of the year.

Aitutaki Open Golf Tournament This open golf tournament is held on Aitutaki in mid-September.

Rarotonga Open Golf Tournament Held in late September, just after the Aitutaki tournament.

Linmar's 15 km Road Race Taking place a couple of weeks before the Round Rarotonga Run, the Linmar's shop sponsors a 15-km foot race.

Round Rarotonga Road Race & Round the Rock Relay These popular fun runs held in early October, one for individual runners and a few days later for teams, circle the island on the coast road. The record for the 32-km distance is just over 98 minutes. Visitors are welcome to run with the locals.

Polynesian Music Festival Music groups from around Polynesia assemble on Rarotonga in the third week in October for this festival of traditional and contemporary Polynesian music.

Cook Islands Fashion Week Also held the third week in October, it features local fashion and accessories.

All Souls Day (Turama) The Catholic community decorates graves with flowers and candles on 1 November.

International Food Festival A festival of international foods is held on Rarotonga the second Saturday in November.

Tiare (Floral) Festival Week In the third week in November, floral float parades, and flower display and arrangement competitions are held. All the public businesses on Rarotonga decorate their premises with flowers.

New Year's Eve The new year is welcomed with dancing and other entertainment.

POST

Postage stamps are a major source of revenue for the government. They produce some beautiful stamps and by limiting the supply and availability they've managed to make many of them valuable collectors items. The Cook Islands Philatelic Bureau was set up by an American entrepreneur, Finbar Kenney. He was entangled in the late Sir Albert Henry's fly-in-the-voters programme in 1978 but despite NZ$80,000 in fines and court costs he continued to manage the lucrative stamp trade. You'll find the Philatelic Bureau office next to the post office in Avarua, offering a wide selection of stamps, coins and bills.

As an ideal souvenir, you can send some attractively stamped postcards home from the Cooks. Postage rates include:

To	*Postcards*	*Letters*
New Zealand & Australia	NZ$0.80	NZ$0.85
USA, Canada, Latin America & Asia	NZ$0.85	NZ$1.05
Europe & Africa	NZ$0.90	NZ$1.15

You can receive mail care of Poste Restante at the post office, where it is held for 30 days. To collect mail at the post office in Avarua it should be addressed 'Your Name, c/o Poste Restante, Avarua, Rarotonga, Cook Islands'. On the other islands it can be addressed 'Your Name, c/o Poste Restante, Island Name, Cook Islands'.

TELECOMMUNICATIONS

All the southern group islands, including Rarotonga, have modern telephone systems. The front pages of the telephone directory contain a section with details on international telephone calls. International collect calls can be made free from any telephone. Other international calls can be made from private phones, pay phones or from Telecom offices. Each island has a Telecom office. On Rarotonga, the Telecom office in Avarua is open 24 hours, seven days a week (limited hours on other islands). In addition to international and inter-island telephone services it also offers fax, telegram and telex services.

Of course telephone charges may change, but at the time of writing, the cost per minute was:

Destination	*Operator-Assisted*	*Direct-Dial*
all Cook Islands	NZ$1.20	NZ$1.00
New Zealand	NZ$2.53	NZ$2.31
Australia & the Pacific Islands	NZ$3.63	NZ$3.30
other Countries	NZ$6.16	NZ$5.83

International and inter-island calls are always charged at the same rate – there is no cheaper time to call.

The country code for the Cook Islands is 682. Country codes for some other countries include:

Australia	61
Canada	1
Fiji	679
France	33
French Polynesia	689
Germany	49
Great Britain	44
Japan	81
New Zealand	64
Niue	683
Samoa (American)	684
Samoa (Western)	685
Tonga	676
USA	1

To direct dial from the Cook Islands to another country, dial '00', then the country code, city code and number. No code is required for inter-island calls. Dial the international operator '015' for international and inter-island operator-assisted calls or for international information. The local information operator is '010'.

TIME

The Cook Islands are east of the International Date Line. This is effectively one of the last places in the world; tomorrow starts later here than almost anywhere else. More precisely, when it's noon in the Cooks the time in other places (making no allowances for daylight saving and other seasonal variations) is:

London, England	9 pm same day
New York & Toronto	5 pm same day
San Francisco & Los Angeles, USA	2 pm same day
Tahiti & Hawaii	noon (same time)
Samoa	11 am same day
Tonga	11 am next day
Auckland, New Zealand	11 am next day
Sydney & Melbourne, Australia	9 am next day

The International Date Line

The early LMS missionaries generally came to the Cook Islands from Sydney, Australia, and were unaware that they had crossed the International Date Line and should have turned the calendar back a day. This anomaly continued for 75 years until 1896 when Christmas was celebrated two days in a row and the Cooks came into line with the rest of the world. Or at least some of the Cooks came into line; it took a bit longer for the message to get to all the other islands and for it to be accepted. Accounts of visiting ships at that time indicate that considerable confusion existed for a while. ■

Remember, however, that in common with many other places in the Pacific the Cook Islands also have Cook Islands Time, which means 'sometime, never, no hurry, no worries'.

ELECTRICITY

Electricity is 240 volts, 50 cycle AC just like in Australia and New Zealand and the same three-pin plugs are used.

On Rarotonga and Aitutaki the power supply operates 24 hours a day; it's usually regular and quite dependable. On smaller islands it may be available more limited hours – the other southern group islands have power from 5 am to midnight.

LAUNDRY

Most accommodation places make some provision for their guests' laundry needs. On Rarotonga there's a laundry in Avarua with another branch in Arorangi.

WEIGHTS & MEASURES

The Cook Islands uses the metric system. See the conversion table at the back of this book.

BOOKS

There have been a surprising number of books written about the Cooks or in which the Cooks make an appearance. Unfortunately some of the most interesting are out of print and you will have to search libraries or second-hand bookshops if you want to find them. There are also, however, an increasing number of interesting books about the Cook Islands being written today, with many available in the Cook Islands.

All the bookshops in the Cook Islands are in Avarua. The University of the South Pacific (USP) centre probably has the largest selection of books about the Cook Islands, and they have the best prices on all the books USP publishes. Good selections of books about the Cook Islands are also on sale at the Cook Islands Library & Museum Society, opposite USP, and at the Cook Islands Trading Company (CITC) department store, which also has a good selection of other general interest paperbacks and children's books. Other shops in Avarua with books about the Cook Islands include the Bounty Bookshop, Island Crafts and Pacific Supplies.

You can borrow books from the Cook Islands Library & Museum Society – including their extensive Pacific Collection – and from the National Library, both in Avarua, by signing up for a Temporary Borrower's Card. See the Rarotonga chapter for details.

History

Alphons M J Kloosterman's *Discoverers of the Cook Islands & the Names they Gave* (Cook Islands Library & Museum, Rarotonga, Bulletin No 1, 1976, paperback) gives a brief history of each island, the early legends relating to that island and a record of its European contact. It makes interesting reading and there's an exhaustive listing of the early descriptions of the islands by European visitors.

History of Rarotonga, up to 1853 by Taira Rere (Rangitai Taira, Rarotonga, 1981, reprinted 1991, paperback) is a short locally-written history of Rarotonga. *The Gospel Comes to Rarotonga* by the same author (Rarotonga, 1980, paperback) is a concise account of the arrival of Christianity in the Cook Islands, particularly in Rarotonga, with interesting thumbnail sketches of the various important participants in this chapter of the islands' history.

The Cook Islands, 1820-1950 by Richard Gilson (Victoria University Press, Wellington, 1980, paperback) is a rather starchy and dry history of the Cooks. There is an introductory chapter on the pre-European history of the islands but basically it relates the story from soon after the first missionary contact up until just after WW II, concentrating heavily on boring descriptions of the economics and politics of the Cook Islands since annexation by New Zealand. It's almost exclusively a Rarotongan history; little mention is made of the other islands in the group.

Years of the Pooh-Bah: A Cook Islands History by Dick Scott (Cook Islands Trading Corporation, Rarotonga, and Hodder & Stoughton, Auckland, 1991, hardback) is a newer and more readable book. Illustrated with plenty of historical photos, it tells the history of the Cooks with an emphasis on how they have been administered by the British and New Zealand.

H E Maude's *Slavers in Paradise* (Australian National University Press, Canberra, and Stanford University Press, Stanford, 1981, paperback) provides a readable yet detailed analysis of the Peruvian slave trade which wreaked havoc in Polynesia from 1862 to 1864. Some of the northern atolls were particularly badly hit by this cruel and inhumane trade. This book is available in the Cook Islands as a paperback from the University of the South Pacific (Suva, 1986).

Missionaries' Accounts

The Reverend William Gill turned up on Rarotonga in 1839 and lived in the Cooks for the next 30 years. His book *Gems of the Coral Islands* (1858) is perceptive but heavily slanted towards the missionary view of life.

The Cooks had a second William Gill: William *Wyatt* Gill was no relation at all to the other William Gill (he was only 11 years old when the older Gill started his missionary career) but he lived on the island of Mangaia for 20 years from 1852 and wrote several important studies. *From Darkness to Light in Polynesia* was originally published in 1894 but has been reissued as a University of the South Pacific paperback (Suva, 1984). *Cook Islands Customs* (University of the South Pacific, Suva, 1979, paperback) is a direct reprint of a fascinating illustrated manuscript originally published in 1892, telling of the customs of the Cook Islanders as the missionaries found them when they arrived.

Mission Life in the Islands of the Pacific (University of the South Pacific, Suva, 1985, paperback) is another recently reissued missionary account. It traces the life and work of the Reverend Aaron Buzacott, who arrived on Rarotonga in 1828 and laboured as one of Rarotonga's foremost missionaries until his death in 1864. On Rarotonga his name is remembered in the Avarua CICC church which he constructed, the Maori Bible which he helped to translate and in the many hymns which bear his name in the CICC hymn book.

Amongst these reports on the Cook Islands by foreign-born missionaries there are also a couple of interesting books telling the story from an island point of view. One author, Maretu, was born in the Ngatangiia area of Rarotonga sometime around 1802. He was an older child when Europeans first visited Rarotonga in 1814 and a young man when the missionaries first arrived in 1823. Maretu later became a missionary himself and worked on several other islands in the Cooks. In 1871 he sat down to write, in Rarotongan Maori, an account of the extraordinary events he had witnessed during his lifetime. Translated into English and extensively annotated, his illuminating work has been published as *Cannibals & Converts* (University of the South Pacific, Suva, 1983, paperback).

Another Ngatangiia-born native son, Taunga, was about five years old when the missionaries arrived. He attended the mission school and became one of its star pupils, subsequently spending most of his long life as a missionary in the Pacific. *The Works of Taunga: Records of a Polynesian Traveller in the South Seas 1833-1896* by Ron & Marjorie Crocombe (Australian

National University Press, Canberra, 1968; reprinted by University of the South Pacific, Suva, 1984, paperback) presents Taunga's accounts of his adventures, with notes putting his writings into historical perspective. *If I Live: The Life of Taunga* by Marjorie Tuainekore Crocombe (Lotu Pasifika Productions, Suva, paperback) is a short, simple story of Taunga's life, based on the larger book.

Impressions of Tongareva (Penrhyn Island), 1816-1901, edited by Andrew Teariki Campbell (University of the South Pacific, 1984, paperback) reproduces 48 historical references and accounts of visits to Penrhyn by missionaries, seafarers and others.

Residents' Accounts

A number of Cook Islands residents have gone into print with their tales of life in the South Pacific. Unfortunately very few books are currently in print.

Robert Dean Frisbie's books *The Island of Desire* (1944) and *The Book of Puka-Puka* (1928) are classics of South Pacific life. Frisbie was born in the USA and ran a store on Pukapuka; his eldest daughter Johnny also wrote of the Cook Islands in *Miss Ulysses from Puka-Puka* (1948) and *The Frisbies of the South Seas* (1959). Frisbie's first book, *The Book of Puka-Puka*, subtitled 'A Lone Trader on a South Sea Atoll', is a collection of articles he wrote for *Atlantic Monthly* and is now available in paperback (Mutual Publishing, Honolulu). See the Pukapuka section of the Northern Group chapter for more information about the colourful Frisbies.

One of the best known resident writers would have to be Tom Neale, who wrote of his life as the hermit of Suwarrow in *An Island to Oneself* (Holt, Rinehart & Winston, New York, 1966; Fontana Silver Fern, Auckland, 1975; and Avon paperback). Tom Neale lived by himself on the beautiful but totally isolated northern atoll of Suwarrow for a total of six years in two, three-year spells, in the late '50s and early '60s; his book recounts these periods. He then returned to Suwarrow and lived there for most of the '70s until he was brought back to Rarotonga, shortly before his death in 1977. Many Rarotongan residents have anecdotes to relate about Tom Neale or opinions of him and it seems that his book, which was actually ghost written, makes him out to be a much more reasonable fellow than he actually was. One person's opinion was that he was so cantankerous that an uninhabited island was the only place for him. See the Suwarrow section of the Northern Islands chapter for more details.

Isles of the Frigate Bird (Michael Joseph, London, 1975, hardback) and *The Lagoon is Lonely Now* (Millwood Press, Wellington, 1978, hardback) were both written by the late Rarotongan resident Ronald Syme. The first book is mainly autobiographical and relates how the author came to the Cook Islands in the early '50s and eventually settled down. Before finally ending up on Rarotonga he spent some time travelling around the islands and also lived on Mangaia for a while. The second book is more anecdotal, relating legends, customs and incidents of island life. It becomes a little tiresome at times with its constant reiteration of how much better things were in the 'old days' and how much better things could be if progress wasn't forced down the islanders' throats. Nevertheless, both books make interesting reading and are a good introduction to life in the Cook Islands, particularly during the period of great changes in the years since WW II.

There are countless earlier accounts of life in the Cooks, few of them currently available. F J Moss, for example, wrote of the islands in 1888 in his book *Through Atolls & Islands*. Julian Dashwood (*Rakau*, or 'wood' in Maori) was a long running islands character who wrote two books about the Cooks. *I Know an Island* was published in the 1930s and he followed that with a second book in the '60s published as *Today is Forever* in the USA and as *Island Paradise* in England. *Sisters in the Sun* by A S Helm & W H Percival (Robert Hale, London, 1973) tells of Suwarrow and Palmerston.

Politics & Politicians

Cook Islands Politics: the Inside Story (Polynesian Press, Auckland, 1979, paperback) is an anthology of articles by 22 writers. Representing many points of view, it tells the story of the toppling of Prime Minister Sir Albert Henry from power: the historical background, the intrigues, the corruption and the bribery.

Tom Davis, KBE (known as 'Sir Tom' or 'Papa Tom' in the Cooks), Prime Minister of the Cook Islands from 1978 to 1987 and a candidate for office again in 1994, has written a number of books. *Island Boy – An Autobiography* (University of the South Pacific, Suva, 1992, paperback) tells the story of his life up to 1992. Another autobiographical book, *Doctor to the Islands* by Tom & Lydia Davis (Michael Joseph, London, 1955, hardback) is an earlier autobiographical work by Sir Tom and his wife, about his years as an island doctor. Sir Tom has also written another book, *Vaka* (see under Legends, Literature, Poetry & Song later in this section).

Nature, Plants & Birds

Rarotonga's Mountain Tracks and Plants by Gerald McCormack & Judith Künzle (Cook Islands Natural Heritage Project, 1994, paperback) is a guide to the mountain tracks of Rarotonga and the plants you'll see when you walk them, as well as a general guide to the plant life of the island.

Guide to Cook Islands Birds by D T Holyoak (1980, paperback) has colour photos and text for identification of a number of local birds. *Kakerori: Rarotonga's Endangered Flycatcher* by Gerald McCormack & Judith Künzle (Cook Islands Conservation Service, Rarotonga, 1990, paperback) is a small, illustrated book on the efforts to save one of Rarotonga's rare birds.

Academic Reports

Akatokamanava: Myth, History and Society in the Southern Cook Islands by Jukka Siikala (Polynesian Society, Anthropology Department, University of Auckland, 1991, paperback) is an anthropological study of the cosmology of the southern Cook Islanc with analyses of their myths, history and on, written by a Finnish anthropologist.

People of the Cook Islands: Past ar Present (Cook Islands Library & Museu Society Bulletin No 5, 1988, paperback) is report of the physical anthropological ar linguistic research conducted in the Coc Islands from 1985 to 1987 by a group Japanese scholars.

Richard Walter's *Prehistory of Mauke: A Ethnoarchaeological Report* (Cook Islanc Library & Museum Society, Museu Journal No 1, 1989, paperback) give archaeological reports about 39 sites o Mauke, together with traditional stories th are connected with each site and othe archaeological observations about th island. *An Archaeological Survey c Pukapuka Atoll, 1985 (Preliminary Repor* by Masashi Chikamori and Shunji Yoshid (Department of Archaeology & Ethnolog Keio University, Tokyo, 1988, paperback) i the Cook Islands Library & Museur Society's Bulletin No 6. All of their publications are on sale at the Cook Islands Librar & Museum Society in Avarua.

Agriculture in the Cook Islands: Nev Directions by Saifullah Syed & Ngatokoru Mataio (University of the South Pacific Suva, 1993, paperback) is a specialists report on the topic.

Legends, Literature, Poetry & Song

Once you're in the Cooks you'll see numerous paperback books about the traditiona legends of the various islands, many of them published by the University of the South Pacific's Institute of Pacific Studies. *Cook Islands Legends* (University of the South Pacific, Suva, 1981, paperback) and *The Ghost at Tokatarava and Other Stories from the Cook Islands* (Ministry of Cultural Development, Rarotonga, 1992, paperback) are both written by notable Cook Islands author Jon Jonassen. *Te Ata O Ikurangi – The Shadow of Ikurangi* by J J MacCauley (Cook Islands Library & Museum Society, Rarotonga, Bulletin No 2, paperback) is another book of old-time legends. *Atiu Nui*

Maruarua (University of the South Pacific, Suva, 1984, paperback) presents legends and stories from the island of Atiu in two languages, Atiuan Maori and English.

Vaka: Saga of a Polynesian Canoe by Tom Davis, KBE (University of the South Pacific, Suva, 1992, paperback), is a historical novel based on the story of the Takitumu canoe, one of the canoes of the 'great migration' to New Zealand around 1350 AD, over a span of 12 generations. It's a novel, not a history book, so it doesn't stand as solid history, but it makes fascinating reading.

Kauraka Kauraka, a Manihikian author and poet currently residing on Rarotonga, has published a number of books of legends, stories and poetry. *Oral Tradition in Manihiki* (University of the South Pacific, Suva, 1989, paperback) is a fascinating scholarly analysis of the Maui myth (Maui being an important figure in the legends of many parts of the Pacific), of Manihiki culture and the relation between the two.

Kauraka's books of Cook Islands legends, principally from his home island of Manihiki, include *Legends from the Atolls* (1983) and *Tales of Manihiki* (1991), both published in paperback by the University of the South Pacific, Suva. His books of poems include *Return to Havaiki/Fokihanga ki Havaiki* (University of the South Pacific, Suva, 1985, paperback), *Dreams of a Rainbow* (South Pacific Creative Arts Society, Rarotonga, 1987, paperback) and *Manakonako/Reflections* (University of the South Pacific, 1991, paperback). All of these books are bilingual, with the text published side by side in English and Manihikian Maori language.

Korero (Mana Publications, Suva, 1977, reprinted 1991, paperback) by Makiuti Tongia is another book of poetry, all in English this time, by a Cook Islands poet.

Te Rau Maire: Poems and Stories of the Pacific, edited by four prominent Cook Islands authors – Marjorie Tuainekore Crocombe, Ron Crocombe, Kauraka Kauraka and Makiuti Tongia – was published in paperback in 1992 for the Pacific Arts Festival, jointly by the Cook Islands Ministry of Cultural Development, the University of the South Pacific, the South Pacific Creative Arts Society, the University of Victoria (Wellington, New Zealand) and the University of Auckland. A sampling of stories and poetry from many Pacific nations, it contains several poems and one story from the Cook Islands.

E Au Imene Tamataora: Songs and Songwriters of the Cook Islands by John J Herrmann (University of the South Pacific, Suva, 1988, paperback) presents the lyrics (in Cook Islands Maori) to six songs by each of seven Cook Islands composers, with a brief story (in English) about each song, its composition and composer.

Arts & Crafts

Cook Islands Art by Dale Idiens (Shire Publications, Buckinghamshire, 1990, paperback) is illustrated with black & white photos of all kinds of arts and crafts from around the Cook Islands, explaining how they are or were used and their significance in Cook Islands culture. *The Art of Tahiti* by Terence Barrow (Thames & Hudson, London, 1979, hardback) is more accurately a guide to the art of Polynesia and includes an interesting chapter on the Cook Islands.

Tivaevae: Portraits of Cook Islands Quilting by Lynnsay Rongokea, with photos by John Daley (Daphne Brasell Associates Press, Wellington, 1992, paperback) introduces 18 Cook Islands women from five southern group islands, with colour photos of the women, the environment around them and the colourful tivaevaes they sew. It won New Zealand's highly prestigious Wattie Book Award for 1992.

Patterns of Polynesia: The Cook Islands by Ailsa Robertson (Heinemann Education, Auckland, 1989, paperback) is a collection of patterns for things you can make yourself, including tivaevaes and Mangaian masks.

Cook Islands Drums by Jon Jonassen (Cook Islands Ministry of Cultural Development, Rarotonga, 1991, paperback) tells about Cook Islands drums and drumming, including rhythms, cultural significance and diagrams of how to make the various kinds of drums.

Pareu and Its Many Ties (Te Pua Inano, Rarotonga, 1992, paperback) gives colour photos and instructions on how to tie the Cook Islands pareu (wrap around sarong-type garment) in a variety of ways for both men and women.

The culinary art of the Cook Islands is celebrated in the *Cook Islands Cook Book* by Taiora Matenga-Smith (University of the South Pacific, Suva, 1990, paperback), a collection of Cook Islands recipes side by side in English and Maori. If you ever wanted to learn how to make raw fish in coconut sauce *(ika mata)*, curried octopus in coconut sauce *(eke takare i roto ite akari)*, stuffed breadfruit *(anga kuru akaki ia)* or Cook Islands fruit pudding *(poke)*, here's your chance.

Travellers' Accounts & Guidebooks

Across the South Pacific by Iain Finlay & Trish Shepherd (Angus & Robertson, Sydney, 1981, paperback) is an account of a trans-Pacific jaunt by a family of four. The Cook Islands section is particularly interesting for its description of taking the old Silk & Boyd ship *Mataora* from Rarotonga through the northern group and across to Western Samoa. If you're considering island-hopping through the Cooks on a local freighter, read this first.

How to Get Lost & Found in the Cook Islands by John & Bobbye McDermott (Orafa, Honolulu, 2nd edition, 1986, paperback) is another in the Air New Zealand funded series by a Hawaiian ex-adman, with a concentration on the Cooks' many colourful characters. The Cook Islands (you soon realise after reading a few books on them) are a pretty small pool. The same big fish keep popping up in every account!

Exploring Tropical Isles & Seas by Frederic Martini (Prentice-Hall, Englewood Cliffs, New Jersey, 1984, paperback) makes interesting reading if you want to know more about what types of islands there are, how they are formed and what lives in the sea around them.

If you just want a souvenir of the Cooks *Rarotonga* by James Siers (Millwood Press, Wellington, 1977, hardback) has some pretty though dated photos. A newer book of Cook Islands photos is *The Cook Islands: Images of Polynesia* (Cook Islands Typographical Services, Rarotonga, 1988, paperback) by Rick Welland, Robin Brill and Russell Bishop, three expatriates who lived on Rarotonga for a number of years. Their collection of colour photos of Rarotonga and other islands in the southern group are some of the best you'll see, and the book also gives insight into the islands' culture.

The same publisher also produced *A Hurricane Warning is Now in Force for Rarotonga* by Russell Bishop (1987, paperback), documenting the impact of Hurricane Sally on Rarotonga in 1987. Looking at the island today, it's hard to imagine the devastation.

If you're travelling farther afield in the Pacific, check out the other Lonely Planet books on the Pacific nations. Titles include *Tahiti & French Polynesia, Samoa, Tonga, Fiji, Vanuatu, New Caledonia, The Solomon Islands, Papua New Guinea, Bushwalking in Papua New Guinea, Micronesia, New Zealand, Tramping in New Zealand, Australia, Bushwalking in Australia, Islands of Australia's Great Barrier Reef* and *Hawaii*. The *South Pacific Handbook* by David Stanley (Moon Publications, Chico, California, 1993, paperback) is an overall guide to the region.

If you can read German, *Die Südsee: Inselwelten im Südpazifik* by Sabine Ehrhart (Du Mont Buchverlag, Köln (Cologne), Germany, 1993, paperback) is an excellent overall guide to the South Pacific, with well-written history, natural history and culture sections and superb illustrations.

Language & Dictionaries

Say it in Rarotongan by Mana Strickland (Pacific Publications, Sydney, 1979, paperback) gives a good general introduction to the language of Rarotonga. A visit to the Cook Islands Library & Museum Society in

Avarua will turn up a number of other resources for tackling the language.

A Dictionary of the Maori Language of Rarotonga by Stephen Savage (University of the South Pacific, Suva, 1980, paperback) is a reprint of the dictionary first published in 1962, many years after the author's death in 1941. It was the most authoritative dictionary of Rarotongan language ever published up to that time and it's been in use ever since, though now it's rather dated.

A newer, more modern Maori-to-English dictionary, the *Cook Islands Maori Dictionary* by Jasper E Buse & Raututi Teringa (Australian National University Press, Canberra, 1994, hardback) is scheduled to appear sometime in 1994.

Other

Television and Video in the Pacific Islands edited by Michael R Ogden & Linda S Crowl (Pacific Islands Communication Journal, Vol 16, No 1, University of the South Pacific, Suva, 1993, paperback) features one chapter about the Cook Islands ('Introducing Television: Seven Lessons from the Cook Islands' by Duane Varan) and other references to the Cooks throughout the book, with other chapters about the new experience of TV and video in a number of other Pacific countries. TV began on Rarotonga on Christmas Day, 1989, and on Aitutaki one year later; within a five-year period around the same time, Fiji, Nauru, Niue, Papua New Guinea, Western Samoa and Vanuatu also introduced TV. It's a hot issue for the region and the book makes interesting reading.

Voluntary Service and Development in the Cook Islands by R G Crocombe University of the South Pacific, Suva, 1990, paperback) is a listing, with commentary, of the many voluntary organisations currently operating in the Cooks.

MAPS

The Cook Islands Survey Department publishes a fine series of colour topographical maps of each island, showing natural features as well as roads and other introduced features. Cost is around NZ$7 to NZ$12 per map. The maps are sold at many shops around Avarua, or you can buy them at the Survey Department office on Rarotonga (☎ 29-434, fax 27-433, PO Box 114).

What's On in the Cook Islands and *Jason's*, free tourist publications available at the Tourist Authority Office in Avarua and at hotels and shops around Rarotonga, contain maps of Rarotonga and Aitutaki with items of interest to visitors (hotels, restaurants, sights etc) clearly marked.

MEDIA

Newspapers & Magazines

Rarotonga's daily newspaper, the *Cook Islands News*, is published every day except Sunday and provides coverage of local events and a brief summary of international events. The Saturday edition has a pull-out entertainment section with dining and nightlife guides, plus the upcoming week's cinema and TV programming, and feature articles.

The *New Zealand Herald* is sold on Rarotonga the day after it's published. A small selection of foreign magazines is also available, principally at the Bounty Bookshop in Avarua.

Radio, TV & Video

The Cooks have two local radio stations, one AM frequency and the other FM frequency, the first FM station in the South Pacific. Apart from local programmes they also broadcast Radio New Zealand news and Radio Australia's overseas world news service.

TV arrived on Rarotonga on Christmas Day, 1989. On Rarotonga it broadcasts daily from 5 pm until around 11 pm, starting earlier on Sunday with a Sunday afternoon movie. On weekdays, the *Karioi* entertainment and cultural programme and the *Te Rongo Veka* local news programme (half in Maori, half in English) provide local coverage. Later in the evening there's a half-hour news programme from New Zealand's Channel One.

Each evening, the TV broadcast is taped and sent by airplane to Aitutaki, where it is shown the following evening. The other outer islands do not have TV.

Video was present on Rarotonga several years before TV. Perhaps this explains the large number of video shops around – TV sets were on the island years before there was any TV broadcasting, so videos became enormously popular. On Rarotonga you can hire a video machine and even the colour TV to go with it.

FILM & PHOTOGRAPHY

You can buy colour print and slide (transparency) film at the CITC Pharmacy in Avarua. Cliff's Photos, also in Avarua, also sells film but the selection is much more limited. Prices are a couple of dollars higher than what you'd probably pay back home, though, and if this one shop ran out of the type of film you're looking for there would be nowhere to get any more in all the Cook Islands. It's a good idea to bring your film with you to the Cooks.

The CITC Pharmacy has a good selection of Kodak, Fuji and Agfa films and it also sells cameras and does photo processing. Film costs around NZ$8/10 for a roll of 24/36 colour prints and NZ$15/19 for a roll of 24/36 colour slides. Both CITC and Cliff's offer one-hour colour print processing; cost is about NZ$18/25 for 24/36 prints. Cliff's is the only place you can get colour slide film processed; cost is NZ$16 per roll, but he only does the processing once in a while, when there are about eight rolls to be processed. If you have that many he may do it right away, but for only one roll you may have to wait until seven other people have brought rolls in!

Unfortunately, they'll tell you that their colour print processing is the same here as elsewhere and so the results should be the same, we took our colour prints to be processed at CITC and wished we hadn't – they came back cloudy and with very dim colours. Since then, several people have told us that this is about what you have to expect on Rarotonga. It's probably better to wait until you get to a more 'developed' country to get your film processed.

There is no film or film processing available on the outer islands – they have to send their film to Rarotonga to be done.

The Cook Islanders are generally quite happy to be photographed but the usual rule applies – it's polite to ask first. It's also worth bringing some high speed film with you. If you're photographing in the densely forested mountain country of Rarotonga or in the makatea of Atiu or Mauke it can be surprisingly dark. Bring a flash if you plan to take photos in the caves in any of the outer islands.

HEALTH

The Cook Islands is generally a healthy place for locals and visitors alike. Food and water are generally good, fresh, clean and readily available, there are few endemic diseases, and the most serious health problem most visitors will experience is sunburn from overdoing it at the beach. Nevertheless, it never hurts to know some basic travel health rules, anytime you travel.

Travel health depends on your pre-departure preparations, your day-to-day health care while travelling and how you handle any medical problem or emergency that develops.

Travel Health Guides

There are a number of books on travel health. *Staying Healthy in Asia, Africa & Latin America* by Volunteers in Asia (paperback) is probably the best all-round guide to carry, as it's compact but very detailed and well organised. *Travellers' Health* by Dr Richard Dawood (Oxford University Press, paperback) is comprehensive, easy to read, authoritative and also highly recommended, although it's rather large to lug around. *Where There is No Doctor* by David Werner (Hesperian Foundation, paperback) is a very detailed guide intended for someone, like a Peace Corps worker, going to work in an undeveloped country, rather than for the average traveller. *Travel with Children* by Maureen Wheeler (Lonely Planet Publications, paperback) includes basic advice on travel health for younger children.

Pre-Departure Preparations

Health Insurance A travel insurance policy to cover theft, loss and medical problems is a wise idea. There are a wide variety of policies and your travel agent will have recommendations. The international student travel policies handled by STA or other student travel organisations are usually good value. Some policies offer lower and higher medical expenses options but the higher one is chiefly for countries like the USA which have extremely high medical costs. Check the small print:

- Some policies specifically exclude 'dangerous activities' which can include scuba diving, motorcycling, even trekking. If such activities are on your agenda you don't want that sort of policy.
- You may prefer a policy which pays doctors or hospitals direct rather than you having to pay on the spot and claim later. If you have to claim later make sure you keep all documentation. Some policies ask you to call back (reverse charges) to a centre in your home country where an immediate assessment of your problem is made.
- Check if the policy covers ambulances or an emergency flight home. If you have to stretch out you will need two seats and somebody has to pay for them! Hospitals and medical care do exist in the Cook Islands, but they are not up to the standards of the major developed countries. Most Cook Islanders fly to New Zealand for medical care when there's a serious problem. Their national health insurance programme provides for them to do so, but you will have to either pay your own way or have your own insurance to cover it if the need arises.

Medical Kit A small, straightforward medical kit is a wise thing to carry and have on hand. It could include:

- Aspirin, Disprin or Panadol – for pain or fever. The generic drug Ibuprofen, sold under various trade names including Nurofen, Motrin, Advil etc, is especially useful for certain types of pain including menstrual cramps and arthritis.
- Antihistamine (such as Benadryl) – useful as a decongestant for colds, allergies, to ease the itch from insect bites and stings, and to help prevent motion sickness.
- Antibiotics – useful if you're travelling well off the beaten track, but they must be prescribed and you should carry the prescription with you.
- Kaolin preparation (Pepto-Bismol), Imodium or Lomotil – for stomach upsets.
- Rehydration mixture – for treatment of severe diarrhoea, this is particularly important if travelling with children.
- Antiseptic, mercurochrome and antibiotic powder or similar 'dry' spray – for cuts and grazes.
- Calamine lotion – to ease irritation from bites or stings.
- Bandages and Band-aids – for minor injuries.
- Scissors, tweezers and a thermometer (note that mercury thermometers are prohibited by airlines).
- Insect repellent, sunscreen or suntan lotion, chap stick and water purification tablets.

Ideally antibiotics should be administered only under medical supervision and should never be taken indiscriminately. Overuse of antibiotics can weaken your body's ability to deal with infections naturally and can reduce the drug's efficacy on a future occasion. Take only the recommended dose at the prescribed intervals and continue using the antibiotic for the prescribed period, even if the illness seems to be cured earlier. Antibiotics are quite specific to the infections they can treat. Stop taking them immediately if there are any serious reactions and don't use one at all if you are unsure if you have the correct one.

In many countries, if a medicine is available at all, it will generally be available over the counter and the price will be much cheaper than in the West. However, be careful of buying drugs in developing countries, particularly where the expiry date may have passed or correct storage conditions may not have been followed. It's possible that drugs which are no longer recommended, or have even been banned, in the West are still being dispensed in many Third World countries. This is probably not a big problem in the Cook Islands, but it pays to be aware.

Health Preparations Make sure you're healthy before you start travelling. If you are embarking on a long trip make sure your teeth are OK; there are lots of places where a visit to the dentist would be the last thing you'd want to do.

If you wear glasses take a spare pair and your prescription. Losing your glasses can be a real problem; there's nowhere in the Cooks you can get another pair made, and if you had to have another pair made and sent to you it could take quite a while for them to arrive.

If you require a particular medication take an adequate supply, as it may not be available locally. Take the prescription, with the generic rather than the brand name (which may not be locally available), as it will make getting replacements easier. It's a wise idea to have the prescription with you to show you legally use the medication – it's surprising how often over-the-counter drugs from one place are illegal without a prescription or even banned in another.

Immunisations No vaccinations are required for entry to the Cook Islands. It's always a good idea to keep your tetanus shot up to date, though, no matter where you are – a booster is required every 10 years.

Basic Health Rules

Care in what you eat and drink is the most important health rule; stomach upsets are the most likely travel health problem but the majority of these upsets will be relatively minor. Don't become paranoid, though – after all, trying the local food is part of the travel experience.

Water Tap water is usually safe to drink on Rarotonga and on most of the outer islands. Do ask about it, though. In Aitutaki, for example, there are some places where you should take your drinking water from a rainwater tank beside the house or hotel, rather than from the tap. Even on Rarotonga, the tap water is not chlorinated and while most visitors like the water and have no complaints, if you suffer any upsets (mild diarrhoea, for example) you might try boiling your water before drinking it.

On rare occasions when rainfall has been either unusually heavy or unusually light, tap water can become cloudy. On our last visit we experienced cloudy water from both causes – a drought on Atiu meant that water from rainwater tanks was the dirty water from the bottom of the tank, and exceptionally hard rain on Rarotonga caused mud and silt to enter the water supply. If you are suspicious of water for any reason, boil it for about five minutes before drinking. In heavy rain, remember you can always collect rainwater!

In hot climates always make sure you drink enough – don't rely on feeling thirsty to indicate when you should drink. Not needing to urinate or very dark yellow urine is a danger sign. Excessive sweating can lead to loss of salt and therefore muscle cramping. Salt tablets are not a good idea as a preventative, but in places where salt is not used much, adding salt to food can help.

Nutrition Good food is readily available in the Cook Islands so getting proper nutrition presents no special problems.

Whenever you travel, make sure your diet is well balanced. Fish, eggs and dairy products, pork, chicken, beef and mutton chops, as well as non-animal products, including tofu, beans, lentils and nuts, are all available in the Cook Islands and all are good ways to get protein. Fresh fruits and vegetables are a good source of vitamins. Try to eat plenty of grains and bread, preferably wholemeal bread. Remember that overcooked food loses much of its nutritional value. If your diet isn't well balanced or if your food intake is insufficient, it's a good idea to take vitamin and mineral supplements.

Everyday Health A normal body temperature is 98.6°F or 37°C; more than 2°C higher is a 'high' fever. A normal adult pulse rate is 60 to 80 beats per minute (children 80 to 100, babies 100 to 140). You should know how to take a temperature and a pulse rate. As a general rule the pulse increases about 20 beats per minute for each °C rise in fever.

Respiration (breathing) rate is also an indicator of illness. Count the number of breaths per minute: between 12 and 20 is normal for adults and older children (up to 30 for younger children, 40 for babies).

People with a high fever or serious respiratory illness (like pneumonia) breathe more quickly than normal. More than 40 shallow breaths a minute usually means pneumonia.

Many health problems can be avoided by taking care of yourself. Wash your hands frequently – it's quite easy to contaminate your own food. Avoid climatic extremes: keep out of the sun when it's hot, dress warmly when it's cold. Avoid potential diseases by dressing sensibly. You can get dangerous coral cuts by walking over coral without shoes. You can avoid insect bites by covering bare skin when insects are around, by screening windows or beds or by using insect repellents. Seek local advice: if you're told the water is unsafe due to currents, jellyfish or for any other reason, don't go in. In situations where there is no information, discretion is the better part of valour.

Medical Problems & Treatment

Potential medical problems can be broken down into several areas. First there are the climatic and geographical considerations – problems caused by extremes of temperature, altitude or motion. Then there are diseases and illnesses caused by insanitation, insect bites or stings, and animal or human contact. Simple cuts, bites or scratches can also cause problems.

Self-diagnosis and treatment can be risky, so whenever possible seek qualified help. Although we do give treatment dosages in this section, they are for emergency use only. Medical advice should be sought before administering any drugs.

In some places standards of medical attention are so low that for some ailments the best advice is to get on a plane and go somewhere else. Basic medical care is available in the Cook Islands – every island has a hospital. For serious conditions, however, many Cook Islanders go to New Zealand for treatment. See under the Health Insurance section earlier in this chapter.

Climatic & Geographical Considerations

The Cook Islands have a temperate tropical climate, neither extremely hot nor extremely cold. The northern islands are much closer to the equator and thus considerably hotter than the southern islands, where most visitors stay. During the summer rainy season, though, the high humidity decreases the ability of the body to cool itself by perspiring, and you'll feel hotter.

Sunburn You can get sunburnt surprisingly quickly in the tropics, even through cloud. Use a sunscreen if you're sensitive to the sun and take extra care to cover areas which don't normally see sun – eg, your feet. A hat provides added protection, and you can also use zinc cream or some other barrier cream for your nose and lips. Calamine lotion is good for mild sunburn.

Prickly Heat Prickly heat is an itchy rash caused by excessive perspiration trapped under the skin. It usually strikes people who have just arrived in a hot climate and whose pores have not yet opened sufficiently to cope with greater sweating. Keeping cool and bathing often, using a mild talcum powder or even resorting to air-conditioning may help until you acclimatise.

Heat Exhaustion Dehydration or salt deficiency can cause heat exhaustion. Take time to acclimatise to high temperatures and make sure you get sufficient liquids. Salt deficiency is characterised by fatigue, lethargy, headaches, giddiness and muscle cramps and in this case salt tablets may help. Vomiting or diarrhoea can deplete your liquid and salt levels. Anhydrotic heat exhaustion, caused by an inability to sweat, is quite rare. Unlike the other forms of heat exhaustion it is likely to strike people who have been in a hot climate for some time, rather than newcomers.

Heat Stroke This serious, sometimes fatal condition can occur if the body's heat-regulating mechanism breaks down and the body temperature rises to dangerous levels. Long, continuous periods of exposure to high temperatures can leave you vulnerable to heat stroke. You should avoid excessive alcohol or strenuous activity when you first arrive in a hot climate.

The symptoms are feeling unwell, not sweating very much or at all and a high body temperature (39°C to 41°C). Where sweating has ceased the skin becomes flushed and red. Severe, throbbing headaches and lack of coordination will also occur, and the sufferer may become confused or aggressive. Eventually the victim will become delirious or convulse. Hospitalisation is essential, but meanwhile get patients out of the sun, remove their clothing, cover them with a wet sheet or towel and then fan continuously.

Fungal Infections Hot weather fungal infections are most likely to occur on the scalp, between the toes or fingers (athlete's foot), in the groin (jock itch or crotch rot) and on the body (ringworm). You get ringworm (which is a fungal infection, not a worm) from infected people or animals or by walking on damp areas, like shower floors.

To prevent fungal infections wear loose, comfortable clothes, avoid artificial fibres, wash frequently and dry carefully. If you do get an infection, wash the infected area daily with a disinfectant or medicated soap and water, and rinse and dry well. Then apply an anti-fungal powder like the widely available Tinaderm. Try to expose the infected area to air or sunlight as much as possible, and wash all towels and underwear in hot water as well as frequently changing them.

Motion Sickness Eating lightly before and during a trip will reduce the chances of motion sickness. If you are prone to motion sickness try to find a place that minimises disturbance – near the wing on aircraft, close to midships on boats, near the centre on buses. Fresh air and looking off into the distance or at the horizon usually helps; stale air, cigarette smoke and reading make it worse. Commercial antimotion-sickness preparations, which can cause drowsiness, have to be taken before the trip commences; when you're feeling sick it's too late. Dramamine, sold over the counter at pharmacies, is the usual preferred medication. Sea Legs tablets or the Scopamine patch, worn behind the ear, are also good. Ginger is a natural preventative and is available in capsule form.

Diseases of Insanitation

Diarrhoea A change of water, food or climate can all cause the 'runs'; diarrhoea caused by contaminated food or water is more serious. Despite all your precautions you may still have a bout of mild travellers' diarrhoea but a few rushed toilet trips with no other symptoms is not indicative of a serious problem. Moderate diarrhoea, involving half-a-dozen loose movements in a day, is more of a nuisance. Dehydration is the main danger with any diarrhoea, particularly for children, so fluid replenishment is the number-one treatment. Weak black tea with a little sugar, soda water, or soft drinks allowed to go flat and diluted 50% with water are all good. With severe diarrhoea a rehydrating solution is necessary to replace minerals and salts. Eating pawpaw (papaya) seeds is a natural remedy if the diarrhoea is not too severe – eat nine seeds at once, followed by three more seeds every hour. You should stick to a bland diet as you recover.

Lomotil or Imodium can be used to bring relief from the symptoms, although they do not actually cure the problem. Only use these drugs if absolutely necessary – eg, if you *must* travel. For children, Imodium is preferable, but do not use these drugs if the patient has a high fever or is severely dehydrated.

Antibiotics can be very useful in treating severe diarrhoea especially if it is accompanied by nausea, vomiting, stomach cramps or mild fever. Ampicillin, a broad spectrum penicillin, is usually recommended. Two capsules of 250 mg each, taken four times a day, is the recommended dose for an adult. Children aged between eight and 12 years should have half the adult dose; younger children should have half a capsule four times a day. Note that if the patient is allergic to penicillin, ampicillin should not be administered. Three days of treatment should be sufficient and an improvement should occur within 24 hours.

Diseases Spread by People & Animals

Tetanus This potentially fatal disease is found in undeveloped tropical areas. It is difficult to treat but is preventable with immunisation. Tetanus is no more of a problem in the Cook Islands than in any other part of the world, but it's still a good idea to keep your tetanus booster shot up to date.

Tetanus occurs when a wound becomes infected by a germ which lives in the faeces of animals or people – so clean all cuts, punctures and animal bites. Tetanus is known as lockjaw, and the first symptom may be discomfort in swallowing, or stiffening of the jaw and neck; this is followed by painful convulsions of the jaw and whole body.

Sexually Transmitted Diseases Sexual contact with an infected sexual partner spreads these diseases. While abstinence is the only 100% preventative, using condoms is also effective. Gonorrhoea and syphilis are the most common of these diseases; sores, blisters or rashes around the genitals, discharges or pain when urinating are common symptoms. These may be less marked or not observed at all in women. Syphilis symptoms eventually disappear completely but the disease continues and can cause severe problems in later years. Gonorrhoea and syphilis are treated with antibiotics. There are many other sexually transmitted diseases, and while most can be treated effectively, there is no cure for herpes and there is also currently no cure for AIDS.

Although in early 1994 no cases of AIDS had yet been reported in the Cook Islands, practically no-one had ever been tested for the disease, either, so it can't be said with confidence that the HIV virus is not present.

AIDS can be spread through contact with the body fluids of another person, primarily blood and semen, and can be spread through infected blood transfusions as well as by sexual contact. It can also be spread by dirty needles – vaccinations, acupuncture and tattooing can potentially be as dangerous as intravenous drug use if the equipment is not clean.

Insect-Borne Diseases

Malaria Malaria is not present in the Cook Islands.

Dengue Fever Dengue Fever has been reported in the Cook Islands. There is no prophylactic available for this mosquito-spread disease; the main preventative measure is to avoid mosquito bites. A sudden onset of fever, headaches and severe joint and muscle pains are the first signs before a rash starts on the trunk of the body and spreads to the limbs and face. After a further few days, the fever will subside and recovery will begin. Serious complications are not common.

Cuts, Bites & Stings

Cuts & Scratches Any puncture of the skin can easily become infected in the tropics, and may be difficult to heal. Treat any cut with an antiseptic solution and mercurochrome or other protective antiseptic cream. Where possible avoid bandages and Band-aids, which can keep wounds wet; if you have to keep a bandage on during the day to protect the wound from dirt or flies, take it off at night while you sleep to let it get air.

Coral cuts are notoriously problematic – they seem to be particularly susceptible to infection, they can take a long time to heal and they can be quite painful. If you do get cut on coral, be sure to clean the wound thoroughly, get all the coral out, and keep it clean and disinfected until it heals. You can treat the wound with mercurochrome or other protective antiseptic cream or try the local cure – fresh lime juice. Avoid coral cuts by wearing shoes when walking on reefs and try not to touch coral when swimming.

Since any cut or puncture to the skin can possibly turn septic in this climate, don't hesitate to visit a doctor if you experience any sign of infection.

Bites & Stings Mosquitoes can be a real nuisance in the Cooks at certain times of year, particularly during the rainy season from around mid-December to mid-April. Use repellent, and carry some with you if you'll be tramping through the bush or in caves. Mosquito coils are available everywhere in the Cook Islands and the pyrethrin-based smoke kills mosquitoes – lighting a mosquito coil will make your room mosquito-free for several hours, or you can use insect spray. Screens on windows or mosquito nets over beds are also helpful.

The most effective insect repellent is called DEET (N,N-Diethylmetatoluamide); it is an ingredient in many commercially available insect repellents. Look for a repellent with at least a 28% concentration of DEET. DEET breaks down plastic, rubber, contact lenses and synthetic fabrics, though, so be careful what you touch after using it. It poses no danger to natural fibre fabrics. Other good repellents include Off! and Repel, which comes in a stick or a spray and will not eat through plastic the way repellents containing DEET do. Or you can mix up a half-and-half combination of Dettol (the bathroom cleaner) and baby oil, mineral oil or coconut oil. Kerosene is another effective repellent; mix kerosene with baby oil or mineral oil and rub it all over you. You'll stink to high heaven but at least you won't have to worry about being bitten by insects.

Bee, wasp, centipede and other insect stings are usually painful rather than dangerous. Large centipedes can give a painful or irritating bite but it's no more dangerous to your health than a bee or wasp sting. Large red-and-yellow wasps are easily spotted and easy to avoid. Tiny red ants have an annoying but not dangerous sting.

Calamine lotion will relieve insect bites and stings; ammonia is also effective. Ice packs or antihistamine cream will reduce the pain and swelling. Or you can reduce the itch by using a local remedy: pick a frangipani leaf and rub the white liquid oozing from the stem onto the bite. If you are allergic to bee or wasp stings, be sure to carry your medication with you.

Snakes There are no snakes in the Cook Islands.

Jellyfish & Other Sea Creatures Jellyfish are not a big problem in the Cook Islands because most swimming is done in protected lagoons, inside the coral reefs. However, on rare occasions when there have been particularly high or rough seas, jellyfish have been known to be washed into the lagoons.

Local advice is the best way of avoiding contact with these sea creatures with their stinging tentacles. Stings from most jellyfish are simply rather painful. The most effective folk remedy for jellyfish stings, used all over the world, is to apply fresh urine to the stings as soon as possible – something in the urine neutralises the jellyfish venom. Ammonia is also effective. Dousing in vinegar will deactivate any stingers which have not 'fired'. Calamine lotion, antihistamines and analgesics may also reduce the reaction and relieve the pain.

On very rare occasions someone will see a poisonous stonefish or stingray in the lagoon. Stonefish look exactly like stones, hence their name; when they are hanging around coral or stony areas, as they usually do, their natural camouflage makes it practically impossible to see them. Fortunately they usually enter the lagoons only in May when they lay their eggs, remaining outside the reef the rest of the year. If you do get stung by a stonefish, go to the hospital, where they will give you an injection.

More commonly encountered inside the lagoon is stinging coral – it's the yellow coral that looks something like a brain. Don't touch this coral. If you do, however, the sting is only bothersome, not dangerous. Applying fresh urine will neutralise the sting.

If you're out reef walking don't thrust your arm into deep tidepools, as eels sometimes lurk there.

There are no sharks in the lagoons but they do live in the open sea beyond the reefs. The sharks that live around here are not the human-eating variety so they pose no danger to divers.

Women's Health

Gynaecological Problems Poor diet, lowered resistance due to the use of antibiotics for stomach upsets and even contraceptive pills can lead to vaginal infections when travelling in hot climates. Keeping the genital area clean, and wearing skirts or loose-fitting trousers and cotton underwear will help to prevent infections.

Yeast infections, characterised by a rash, itch and white, lumpy, cottage cheese-like discharge, can be treated with a vinegar or lemon-juice douche, or by putting a few teaspoons of plain (not flavoured!) yoghurt into the vagina. The bacteria that cause the fermentation of yoghurt eat yeast; it's a very effective remedy, but only if used in the early stages of infection, if you let it get too severe then the yoghurt doesn't seem to help much. Nystatin suppositories are the usual medical prescription.

Trichomonas is a more serious infection; symptoms are a discharge and a burning sensation when urinating. Sexual partners must also be treated, and if a vinegar-water douche is not effective, medical attention should be sought. Flagyl is the prescribed drug.

Pregnancy Most miscarriages occur during the first three months of pregnancy, so this is the most risky time to travel. The last three months should also be spent within reasonable distance of good medical care, as quite serious problems can develop at this time. Pregnant women should avoid all unnecessary medication, but vaccinations and malarial prophylactics should still be taken, where possible, if you'll be travelling in an area where these are recommended. Additional care should be taken to prevent illness and particular attention should be paid to diet and nutrition.

WOMEN TRAVELLERS

It's tempting to say that the Cooks present no special problems for women travellers, and leave it at that. Most of the time and in most situations women travellers will never have a problem in the Cooks. As a visitor to the islands, you will usually be treated with courtesy and kindness.

Nevertheless, you should be aware that the threat of rape does exist. Be cautious about going alone to deserted places, such as tramping in the mountains; be cautious about swimming alone in the lagoon late at night, or even walking down some deserted stretch of beach late at night. As in other parts of the world, your best protection is to be accompanied – go with a friend, or get a group of travellers together at the place you're staying.

On Rarotonga there's a women's counselling centre, Punanga Tauturu (☎ 21-133) at Ingram House opposite Avatiu Harbour. A group of men for non-violence, Te Akapuanga, can be reached at the same phone number.

Clothing

As applies everywhere, as a woman traveller your travelling experiences will go a lot smoother if you observe the local customs of dress and don't offend people by your appearance. Fortunately this is easy to do in the Cooks by observing a few basic courtesies.

Swimming wear is for swimming; it's fine at the beach or by the pool but elsewhere you should cover up. Don't swim or sunbathe topless or in the nude, as you will cause grave offence to locals if you do. Sleeveless blouses and shorts are fine to wear anywhere, but 'short shorts' up to your bum will cause many raised eyebrows and could make you look cheap in the eyes of the locals. Wearing a pareu is fine.

If you visit the outer islands, remember that their standards of dress are more conservative than on Rarotonga and Aitutaki, which have been visited by plenty of foreign tourists.

If you go to church, be sure to wear something with sleeves, so your shoulders and upper arms are covered. Don't wear a pareu or shorts to church; a skirt or dress is best, preferably with the hemline at or below the knee. It's customary for women to wear hats in the Cook Islands Christian Church

(CICC), so wear one if you can – but don't worry about it if you don't have one; everyone understands that visitors to the islands are not usually travelling with hats! Flowers can be worn any other time, but not to church.

DANGERS & ANNOYANCES

The Cook Islands are probably safer than most places in the world, but a certain amount of precautionary common sense is still called for. In general, you will find the Cooks to be just as idyllic as the tourist brochures lead you to expect and the people to be some of the friendliest you will ever meet. As anywhere, crime does exist but with normal, minimal caution you should have no problems.

Theft

Theft has unfortunately become quite a problem on Rarotonga, though it's nothing like the levels of many other parts of the world. It's practically unheard of for anyone to be attacked or robbed, or even to be robbed sneakily from their person; it is more likely to happen if you leave things laying around. Don't leave all your money in your wallet on the beach and then go off swimming. Even theft of clothes from clotheslines at night is a problem; it's best to bring your clothes in at night, even if they're not completely dry, and hang them out again in the morning.

These things seem so obvious that you wouldn't even think to mention them in a generally more dangerous place, but it's very easy to be seduced by all the 'paradise' aspects of the Cook Islands, especially Rarotonga, and be lulled into thinking that nothing could possibly happen here – which unfortunately is not the case. It's not a bad idea to check your valuables with your hotel management, just as you would when travelling in other places, to prevent theft from your room when you're not there. It's not necessary, though, to go to the extreme of carrying your money out of sight in a money belt or under-the-clothes compartment – not yet, anyway.

The problem of theft seems to have increased markedly just in the past decade or so, especially on Rarotonga. For the first edition of this book in 1986, Tony wrote that he'd 'never seen so many cars and motorcycles standing around with their keys left in the ignition'. You don't see that anymore, at least not on Rarotonga. Even if you don't leave your keys in the ignition, motorcycles are easy to hotwire and it's conceivable that someone could take off with yours. Always be sure to remember the license plate number.

Swimming

In the sheltered lagoons swimming could hardly be safer but be very wary of the breaks in the surrounding reef. Currents are especially strong here; the lagoon waters sweep swiftly out to the open sea and often straight downwards due to the very steep drop-offs just off the reef. Rarotonga has several such passages, notably at Avana Harbour, Avaavaroa, Papua and Rutaki, and they exist on other islands as well. Danger signs for swimmers used to be posted on shore on Rarotonga, but on our last visit we found they'd all been removed. Check the Rarotonga map for the position of reef passages before you go swimming. Several unnecessary deaths have occurred when people have been swept away in these passages. Venturing outside the reef should only be done if you are fully aware of the tidal flow and currents, and then only with great care.

Check the Health section earlier in this chapter for advice on other things you should watch out for when swimming – sunburn, jellyfish, stinging coral etc.

Insects & Other Creatures

At certain times of year mosquitoes can be a real nuisance, although they are not malarial. Bring repellent. Other insects that bite or sting include bees, red-and-yellow wasps, and small red ants with an annoying sting. The insect most people fear the most is the large centipede. Though it looks very frightening – they can reach about 15 cm (six inches) long – their sting is no more dangerous than a bee or wasp sting. Jellyfish are not pleasant, either, but they are not usually found inside the lagoons, where most people swim. Stonefish are poisonous but they are rarely encountered. See the Health section earlier in this chapter for more on insects and other creatures found in the Cook Islands, their stings and what to do if you do get stung.

Not really a danger, but definitely an annoyance if there are many around, are the large cockroaches that live in the Cooks (and in the tropics all over the world). They won't hurt you, but do make sure they don't crawl over your food at night as they can spread germs. Insect spray is sold at every grocery shop. It's said that if the cockroaches are flying, it means it will rain the next day.

WORK

Tourists are prohibited from working in the Cook Islands. The government makes a concerted effort to ensure that jobs that can be done by locals, go to locals. If you get caught working on a visitor's (tourist) permit, you'll be in big trouble.

You will see a number of foreigners working, though, especially on Rarotonga. These people often have Cook Islands permanent resident status – many are married to Cook Islanders – and often they have skills to perform jobs which had to be done, could not be filled by locals (international law, for example) and thus were granted a special work permit. Others are here on various volunteer programmes – the United States Peace Corps, Australian Volunteers, the World Health Organisation and the United Nations Volunteer Programme all send volunteers to the Cooks.

In order to work legally in the Cook Islands you must obtain a work permit from the Immigration office, beside the airport on Rarotonga. Contact this office (☎ 29-363, fax 29-364, PO Box 473) to find out the current requirements for getting a work permit. However, work permits are not easy to obtain. You may have to go back to your country of origin, apply for a work permit from there, and wait for it to be granted before you can return. You may have to come up with an employment sponsor in the Cooks, who must convince the government that the job they want to give you could not be done by a local. Or you could always volunteer with one of the volunteer programmes.

ACTIVITIES

The Cook Islands are relaxed, slow and easygoing, a fine place for taking it easy. But there are plenty of more energetic activities to keep you busy if you're so inclined.

All the activities mentioned here are covered in more detail in the individual island chapters. Our purpose here is to give you an overview of what's available and to direct you to the appropriate chapters.

Swimming

Of course with all the water around, water sports are the most obvious activity in the islands, and swimming is the first water sport on most people's minds. All the islands have at least some sort of sheltered lagoon where you can swim safely, and at least some sandy beaches.

The two most visited islands, Rarotonga and Aitutaki, are great for swimming. Most other islands of the southern group are surrounded by reefs that are very close to the land, so the swimming possibilities are fewer, but even these islands have somewhere or other to swim – sometimes in caves! The various island chapters point out the best places to swim on each island.

Snorkelling & Scuba Diving

Rarotonga and Aitutaki both have excellent possibilities for snorkelling in the lagoons inside the reef, and for scuba diving outside the reef.

There are many features that make diving on Rarotonga and Aitutaki particularly attractive, especially the high 30 to 60 metre (100 to 200 foot) visibility and the variety of things to be seen down below. Another attraction is that diving and instruction prices in the Cooks are some of the lowest in the world.

Diving operators on both islands offer

daily diving trips using your gear or theirs, and if you aren't already a certified diver you can take a four-day course and receive NAUI or PADI certification that will permit you to dive anywhere in the world.

Snorkelling is enjoyable on both islands. Snorkelling gear is sold on Rarotonga and is available for hire on both Rarotonga and Aitutaki. Both islands also have lagoon cruise operators to take you to some of the best snorkelling spots. See the Rarotonga and Aitutaki chapters for more on snorkelling and diving.

There aren't as many possibilities for snorkelling on the other islands of the southern group; their reefs are so close to shore that the lagoons are narrow and shallow. If you venture to the islands of the northern group, though, be sure to bring your snorkelling gear along because most of the northern group islands have large lagoons with clear water, abundant fish and exotic shells.

Sailing, Windsurfing & Other Water Sports

The sheltered lagoons of Rarotonga and Aitutaki are also great for other water sports. On Rarotonga, head to Muri Beach where sailboats, windsurfers, outrigger canoes, kayaks, wave skis, surfboards and other water paraphernalia are available for hire. Aitutaki has less paraphernalia but an even bigger lagoon.

Lagoon Cruises

Aitutaki must be one of the best places in the world for lagoon cruises. The lagoon is large, warm, brilliantly turquoise, and full of brightly coloured tropical fish and a variety of living corals. The main island is surrounded by a number of *motus* (smaller islands) and cruises to these islands, with swimming, snorkelling and a barbecue fish lunch, stopping at some of the lagoon's best snorkelling spots on the way, operate every day except Sunday. Don't miss taking a lagoon cruise if you go to Aitutaki.

Rarotonga's lagoon is smaller, so you don't really need a boat to get around on the lagoon. An innovation on Rarotonga, though, are glass-bottom boats, operating from Muri Beach and cruising to some of the best places to see coral and tropical fish. The cruises bring along snorkelling gear, and conclude with barbecue lunches. Rumour has it that a glass-bottom boat is supposed to be going to Aitutaki soon, too.

Deep-Sea Fishing

Boats for deep-sea fishing, equipped with everything you need, are available for charter on Rarotonga and Aitutaki. If you visit some of the other outer islands, where tourism is not as organised, you might get some of the locals to take you fishing the way they do it, in outrigger canoes!

Hiking & Walking

All the islands have innumerable possibilities for walking, tramping and exploring. Rarotonga, with its craggy interior mountains, its lush valleys and beautiful white-sand beaches, has something for everyone, from challenging mountain treks to easy strolls through valleys and along beaches and streams. Even expert rock climbers can find plenty to challenge them on Rarotonga. See the Walking & Climbing section in the Rarotonga chapter.

Rarotonga is the only mountainous island in the Cooks; the other islands offer less strenuous walking possibilities. The southern group islands of Atiu, Mauke, Mitiaro and Mangaia all have caves to visit, a good reason to take off tramping through the makatea to reach them. Aitutaki, with its single small mountain Maungapu and limitless beaches and trails, is also great for walking and exploring.

Caving

Atiu, Mauke, Mitiaro and Mangaia all have interesting caves to explore. See the individual chapters for details.

Tumunu

Though the missionaries managed to stamp out the practice on most of the other Cook Islands, *tumunu*, or bush beer-drinking schools, are still held on the island of Atiu. Related to the *kava*-drinking ceremonies of Fiji and some other Pacific islands, this is about the last place in the Cooks you'll be able to experience this custom.

Tandem Skydiving

Tandem skydiving is a relatively new sport in which you go skydiving securely strapped to a professional skydiver who does all the work while you just enjoy the experience. It is a current craze in New Zealand and you can do it on Rarotonga for about the same price as in New Zealand.

Visiting Marae

History and archaeology buffs will enjoy visiting the historic marae on many of the Cook Islands. Rarotonga and Aitutaki have some particularly impressive marae, but they are found in some form on all the islands. Traditional religious meeting places associated with particular chiefs, high priests or clans, the marae are still very significant in some aspects of culture on Rarotonga and on many other islands. Although the carved wooden figures on the marae were destroyed, burned or taken away by the zealous British missionaries, the stones of many of the ancient ones are still there.

Dancing

Cook Islands dancing is some of the most famous and beautiful in the Pacific so of course you should be sure to see at least one performance while you're here. Don't forget, though, that dancing is not only performance – it is also a popular activity that you can participate in. Friday night is the big night for going out dancing, especially on Rarotonga and Aitutaki. Even the smaller islands of Atiu and Mangaia manage to have a Friday night dance. Dancing in the Cooks is lots of fun, with lots of swaying hips, quivering knees and plenty of enthusiasm.

Other Activities

On several islands tennis is a popular sport. On Rarotonga you can hire racquets at the larger resort hotels and play on their courts; there are many other courts around the island, too, which you can play on if you have your own tennis gear. Atiu has a remarkable number of tennis courts, Mangaia has courts, and in fact, if you have your own gear, you can probably play tennis one way or another on most of the islands.

On Rarotonga you can play squash at the Edgewater Resort.

Of course running can be done anywhere, but on Rarotonga you can join the Hash House Harriers, Hussies & Hoffspring for an easy fun run every Monday afternoon.

Rarotonga also now has the Top Shape Health & Fitness Centre for aerobics and body building.

Horse riding is also available on Rarotonga.

HIGHLIGHTS

Many of the highlights of the Cook Islands are listed in the previous Activities section, so we won't say too much more about them here. Everything mentioned here is covered in more detail in the individual island chapters.

Physical Beauty

The top 'highlight' of the Cook Islands would have to be the physical beauty of the islands. With their soft white-sand beaches, swaying coconut palms, turquoise lagoons replete with colourful tropical fish, their lush vegetation and flowers and their velvety-warm air – what more could anyone ask for?

Music & Dance

Be sure to attend at least one dance performance; they're held practically every night at 'island nights' on Rarotonga and at least a couple of nights a week on Aitutaki. Cook Islands music is good, too, with a variety of styles including string band music, drumming on wooden slit drums, rousing church hymn-singing and other styles.

Cultural Events

Many kinds of cultural events are held on the islands. There are public events, like Gospel Day, the Constitution Day celebrations, the

Polynesian Music Festival, the Tiare Festival Parade, and even sporting competitions, which everyone is welcome to attend – don't miss them if they happen while you're here. Then there are also a number of more family-based traditions, like hair cutting ceremonies, investiture ceremonies, weddings, funerals and so on. It's a privilege to be invited to these kinds of events so if you do get invited, take the chance to attend.

Cook Islands Cultural Village

You can probably learn more about Cook Islands culture in one day at the Cook Islands Cultural Village on Rarotonga, especially if you also take the Circle Island tour, than you will in any other day of your stay.

Food

Be sure to try some traditional Cook Islands food while you're here – preferably prepared in a traditional Maori underground oven *(umu)*. Sample some fresh tropical fruits and tasty seafood, try the raw fish in coconut sauce *(ika mata)*, taro, taro leaves *(rukau)* and breadfruit *(kuru)*, drink coconut water fresh from the coconut, or a tropical fruit juice like passionfruit or mango.

Simple Pleasures of Relaxing

Even with all the activities available in the Cooks, some of your most enjoyable times will probably be when you're just relaxing and enjoying the simple pleasures of life, like watching the sunset, lazing on the beach, lolling in the lagoon, bicycling along the back roads or talking to someone you've met. For some reason it seems easier to relax in the Cooks than in many other places.

ACCOMMODATION

Although there is no visa requirement to enter the Cooks, there is one stipulation for all visitors – you must have pre-booked accommodation when you arrive.

This isn't quite as totalitarian as it sounds. For a start, they don't say how long you have to book for – conceivably you could book for the first night only. Secondly, there's nothing to stop you changing your mind as soon as you see the place you've booked into and go looking elsewhere – some people do change their minds quite legitimately. And thirdly, often nobody really checks – you could easily walk out of the airport saying you'd booked into Hotel A or Z when you'd done nothing of the sort.

'Prior booking' is the law, however, and you will be asked to fill in a blank on your arrival form stating where you are booked to stay. If you haven't booked anywhere, they have every right to turn you away and put you back on the airplane without ever setting foot outside the airport. One traveller wrote to tell us he saw this happen to a couple who had written simply 'hostel' on their arrival form.

This rule is supposedly to stop people sleeping on beaches, camping out or staying with local people. It's also done to try to make sure that every visitor has a place to stay. Some of the more popular hotels on Rarotonga are routinely booked up months in advance; if you arrive cold and expect to find a room at these places, you will be sadly disappointed. Other hotels are not so busy. But with increasing numbers of tourists arriving on Rarotonga and only a limited number of hotel rooms, they want to be sure that visitors do indeed have a place to stay when they arrive.

People staying long-term, often rent houses locally. You can get quite a reasonable place, fully furnished with everything you need including linen and kitchenware, for around NZ$200 a week. No doubt some people stay with locals, although it probably doesn't happen much on Rarotonga. On the northern group islands where accommodation is very limited you may have to stay with local people. On some islands this is organised, arranged and prices are firmly set. On others, where visitors are few and far between, arrangements are likely to be very informal. In such a case, make certain that you do not take advantage of Polynesian hospitality – be sure to pay your way. Bringing along an ample supply of food, not only for yourself but also to share, is always appreciated.

Rarotonga is far and away the major

attraction and it has far and away the most places to stay. There's a handful of places to stay on Aitutaki and a place or two on a few of the other islands. On Rarotonga there are two major resort hotels (with another, a Sheraton, under construction), some hostel-style accommodation and pretty much everything else is motel-style, closely related to the motels in New Zealand. This is no bad thing in one way – nearly every place has some sort of kitchen or cooking facilities.

On the other hand it's a disappointment that most of the accommodation makes so little reference to the Pacific. The average Rarotongan motel could easily be in Newcastle, Australia or Palmerston North, New Zealand. A few places are trying to cultivate more of a South Pacific atmosphere.

FOOD

Rarotonga has a number of good restaurants. Elsewhere in the islands the choice of places to eat is more limited.

Fortunately most accommodation, particularly on Rarotonga, has kitchen facilities so you can fix your own food and save some money along the way. The catch here is that a lot of food is imported and is consequently expensive. There are a couple of ways of improving this situation. First of all, look for local produce. There's little in the way of local packaged food, apart from the expensive Frangi fruit juices and the terrible Vaiora soft drinks; virtually all other packaged food is imported (usually from New Zealand) and is very expensive. The price tags on anything from packaged cereal to yoghurt can be astonishing.

There are, however, plenty of locally grown fruits and vegetables. The trick is finding them – you're likely to do much better looking for them in local shops, at the Punanga Nui open market on Rarotonga, or even buying direct from the locals rather than from big supermarkets. Whereas locally grown fruits and vegetables can be very reasonably priced, in the supermarkets you often find the vegetables have come straight from New Zealand and cost several times the New Zealand or Australian prices. Bread and doughnuts are baked locally on most of the islands and are reasonablypriced.

Kuru (Breadfruit) *Artocarpus altilis* (JK)

The second way of economising on food is to bring some supplies with you. All food imports must be declared on arrival and although fresh produce is prohibited, you should have no problem with packaged goods.

Remember that just as costs on Rarotonga are higher than in New Zealand, Australia or North America, costs are also higher again on the outer islands than on Rarotonga. If you're going to the outer islands it's wise to bring some food supplies with you, both for economy and variety. If you're going to a place with no formal accommodation it's only polite to supply as much food as you eat and some more besides.

Local Food

You won't find too much local food on the restaurant menus but at 'Island Night' buffets or at barbecues you'll often find interesting local dishes. An *umukai* is a traditional feast cooked in an underground oven: food is *kai*, underground is *umu*.

Some dishes you might come across include:

arrowroot – also called manioc, manioca or tapioca, the root of this plant is often eaten as a starchy vegetable

breadfruit/kuru – spherical fruit which grows on trees to grapefruit size or larger. It is more like a vegetable than a fruit and can be cooked in various ways; eg, like french fries.
eke – octopus
ika mata – raw fish, marinated in lemon or lime juice then mixed with coconut cream and other ingredients
kumara – sweet potato
poke – pawpaw pudding
puaka – suckling pig
taro – all purpose tuber vegetable. The roots are prepared rather like potato; the leaves, known as *rukau*, can also be cooked and look and taste very much like spinach.

DRINKS

Nonalcoholic Drinks

The truly local drink is coconut water and for some reason Cook Islands coconuts are especially tasty.

Try the Atiu Island Coffee, grown and processed on Atiu. If you visit Atiu you can take a tour of the coffee plantation and factory to see how the coffee is grown and processed. The coffee is sold in half-kilo bags at various places around Rarotonga, and served in some restaurants.

The Frangi juice factory, on the main road near the Rarotonga International Airport, makes a variety of fresh juices, including orange, mango-orange, passionfruit-orange, pineapple and others. Frangi juices are sold at their factory outlet, called The Cold Shop, and at some of the small shops around the island, but not in the supermarkets.

The local soft drink bottling company is called Vaiora – they make cola, lemonade, orange and other fairly awful imitations. Apart from the drinks being flat, the bottles are notable for having labels that always fall off.

Alcohol

Cook's Lager, Rarotonga's own beer, is quite good as well as being the least expensive beer in the Cooks. It's been available since late '87 and free tours of the Rarotonga Brewery in Avarua, followed by a free beer, are given on weekdays.

A wide variety of New Zealand beers are also available, Steinlager being the favourite, plus Fosters (Australian), San Miguel (Philippines), Heineken (Dutch), Hinano (Tahitian) and Viamo (Western Samoan). They cost around NZ$2 to NZ$3 a can in bars and are cheaper from shops, where a large bottle of Steinlager costs around NZ$4.

Until independence Cook Islanders were strictly forbidden Western alcohol which was, however, permitted to *papa'a* (Europeans and other foreigners). Beer is a problem on the Cook Islands: far too much money

gets spent on it and drunkenness is a social problem.

Three liqueurs made from local products, *Coffee-Ara, Coffee-Coconut-Ara* and also *Passionfruit-Ara*, are made on Rarotonga and sold at The Perfume Factory on the back road in Avarua. They are strong (40% alcohol) and taste good either straight or mixed with juice or coffee.

Imported liquors are available in the Cooks, but are heavily taxed and thus quite expensive. The widest selection is found at Cook Islands Liquor Supplies near Avatiu Harbour on Rarotonga.

If you go to Atiu, check out a tumunu, or bush beer-drinking session. Tumunus are also held on Mauke but although there is a bar named the Tumunu on Rarotonga they are really only found on those two islands. Nowadays the tall hollowed-out coconut tree stump (the tumunu) from which the home brew used to be served has been replaced by plastic drums; you can see a couple of real old tumunus at the Cook Islands Library & Museum Society museum in Avarua. The old ritual kava ceremonies, to which the tumunu is related, were stamped out by the missionaries and are no longer found in any form.

ENTERTAINMENT

Cook Islands dancing is considered to be some of the best dancing in the Pacific and there are plenty of chances to see it at the 'island nights' held around Rarotonga most nights of the week. The island nights start off with a buffet dinner of local foods, followed by a floor show of dance, music and song. The grand finale is when the performers come out into the audience, choose unsuspecting partners and take them up on stage to have a go at Cook Islands dance. It's good fun and definitely worth doing sometime during your stay. The Cook Islands Cultural Village on Rarotonga is another good place to see Cook Islands dancing, along with many other elements of Cook Islands culture. Island nights are also held on Aitutaki on weekends.

Then there's going out dancing yourself. Cook Islanders love to dance and Friday night is the popular night for going out dancing. There's a wide variety of places to go on Rarotonga, a couple of good places on Aitutaki, and even Atiu and Mangaia manage to have a dance on Friday nights. Hips sway and shake and knees quiver like they never do back home! It's good fun.

Sports are popular in the Cooks and there's plenty of chance to see a variety of sports, with everything from sedate lawn bowls to rousing rugby or cricket games, to sailing races. (Sailing races are held at Muri Beach on Rarotonga every Saturday, starting at 1 pm.) Anytime there's a game, you're welcome to go and watch. See the *Cook Islands News* for announcements of upcoming games. There are also a number of sports you can engage in yourself, on land, in the water and in the air; see the Activities section earlier in this chapter.

The Empire Cinema in Avarua is the only one in the Cook Islands. It has two sides (Cinema 1 and Cinema 2) and each presents two films each evening (no shows on Sunday). They're often quite good; check the *Cook Islands News* for the daily schedule.

THINGS TO BUY

There are many things that you can buy as souvenirs of the Cooks, ranging from unique, very high quality handicrafts to cheap tourist products. Several islands in the Cooks have their own handicraft specialities. Most of them can be bought on Rarotonga; if you take a trip to the outer islands, though, you may find things you haven't seen on Rarotonga.

Local arts, crafts and souvenirs include:

Tangaroa Figures

Tangaroa is the squat, ugly but well-endowed figure you find on the Cook Islands' one dollar coin. The god of the sea and of fertility, Tangaroa has become the symbol of the Cooks. It's been a long-term rehabilitation though because the early missionaries, in their zeal to wipe out all traces of heathenism, did a thorough job of destroying idols wherever they found them. Poor old

Tangaroa, along with the rest of the old gods, was banned. When the Cook Islanders did start carving Tangaroa figures again they were often sexless, but now they're fully endowed once again. You can get Tangaroa figures ranging from key ring figures a couple of cm high up to huge ones standing a metre or more high and just about requiring a crane to move them. A figure about 25 cm high will cost around NZ$40.

Other Wooden & Stone Products

Carved wooden slit drums are a Polynesian specialty; you can find them in most of the crafts houses. Ukeleles, made of wood and coconut shells, are another good souvenir. You'll find them at the Women's Craft Federation on Aitutaki. The Cook Islands Cultural Village on Rarotonga also sells them, and is an excellent source of woodcarvings (including drums), woven items and other traditional crafts, as are several of the other Rarotonga arts & crafts houses.

Traditional Mangaian ceremonial stone adzes with intricately carved wooden handles or stands and sennit binding (museum pieces in some of the world's major museums) are still made on Mangaia. You can take a look at them in the museums on Rarotonga, and visit the craftspeople on Mangaia to buy one if you like them; you might also find them for sale on Rarotonga. Traditionally carved stone taro pounders are also still made and used on Mangaia.

Rito Hats

The beautiful hats which the women wear to church on Sunday are a Cook Islands speciality. These rito hats are woven of fine, bleached pandanus leaves and the best ones come from the islands of Rakahanga and Penrhyn. Prices start at about NZ$50, so they're not cheap, but they're even more expensive in Tahiti.

Baskets & Woven Pandanus Products

Some good-quality basket work is still done but look out for plastic carton strapping and other man-made materials creeping into use. Excellent-quality traditional baskets are still made on Mangaia, where you can buy them directly from the women who make them, and on several other of the outer islands.

Traditional woven pandanus products such as mats, purses and fans are now rarely made on Rarotonga, since the pandanus which used to grow on this island has mostly died off, but you can probably find something if you look around in the arts & crafts shops. On most of the other islands of the southern group, with the exception of Atiu where there is also less pandanus now than there used to be, all the traditional pandanus items are still made for everyday use. If you visit the outer islands, you can find pandanus products everywhere.

Pearls

Pearls, an important Cook Islands product, are farmed on the northern group islands of Manihiki and Penrhyn and sold on Rarotonga. Black pearls, golden pearls, white pearls, pearls embedded in their mother-of-pearl shells, and mother-of-pearl products, including fans, hats and more, are all available on Rarotonga.

Shells & Shell Jewellery

There's a lot of shell jewellery produced and also larger items like shell lamps. Some of this work is imported, principally from the Philippines, but some fine shell work is produced locally. Before you rush off to buy shells remember that something has to be evicted to provide the shell, and conservationists are worried about some species being collected to extinction. The tiny Shells & Craft shop in Muri on Rarotonga has a wide selection of unusual shells.

Tivaevae

These colourful and intricately sewn appliqué works are traditionally made as burial shrouds but are also used as bedspreads, with smaller ones for cushion covers. They're rarely seen for sale on most islands; if you do find a full-size tivaevae for sale, you'll find they cost several hundred dollars due to the enormous amount of time required to make them. Smaller wall hang-

A	E	H
B	F	I
C	F	J
D	G	K

A: (TW)
B: (TW)
C: (TW)
D: (TC)
E: (TC)
F: (TC)
G: (TC)
H: (TC)
I: (TC)
J: (TW)
K: (TW)

Tivaevaes (NK)

ings, cushion covers, or clothing using tivaevae-inspired patterns are cheaper.

The Atiu Fibre Arts Studio on Atiu is the only place in the Cook Islands where tivaevaes are commercially produced and always available. If you stop by the Tivaivai Cafe on Atiu, where the studio's products are on display, you can see a selection of tivaevaes, wall hangings, clothing and more; tivaevaes are on sale there or you can special order one, choosing the pattern and colour scheme you prefer. Tivaevaes are also sold at a few places on Rarotonga.

Gardenia *Gardenia augusta* (JK)

Other Souvenirs

There are a multitude of other things you can buy as souvenirs of the Cooks. Pure coconut oils and coconut oil-based soaps come either in their natural state or scented with local flowers, including tiare maori (gardenia), frangipani, starfruit flower and jasmine. The Perfume Factory and Perfumes of Rarotonga, both on Rarotonga, sell quality perfumes made from these local flowers for about NZ$15 a bottle, for both men and women.

Colourful pareus come in many styles and thicknesses; original tie-dyed ones of very thin material, costing about NZ$15, are the most popular and the best for the warm climate. You can also find a multitude of T-shirts in the shops around Rarotonga with logos saying Cook Islands, Rarotonga, South Pacific etc.

A kg or two of Atiu Island Coffee is another good souvenir. Liqueurs made from local fruits and coffee beans are also a popular souvenir and can be tasted and bought at The Perfume Factory in Avarua. Tangaroa-shaped ceramic bottles are also sold there, to put the liqueur in, if you like.

Rarotonga has a couple of resident artists and their paintings and other artwork are on sale, often at very reasonable prices.

On the low end of the spectrum, Tangaroa figures with spring-loaded, pop-up penises are about the most tasteless but there are plenty more where that came from. More insidious are the Cook Islands handicraft souvenirs that don't originate from the Cooks at all. A lot of the shell jewellery and wooden bowls were born in the Philippines! There are also plenty of New Zealand Maori items which the unscrupulous might try to pass off as Cook Islands Maori. In fact I'd be very suspicious of anything which could conceivably be made overseas – even supposedly indigenous items like Tangaroa figures. Fortunately the craft shops do seem to be remarkably honest and if you ask if a piece is local or made elsewhere you'll usually be given a straight answer.

Getting There & Away

Occasionally a cruise ship might call on the Cooks, and some yachts pass through, although the Cooks are nowhere near as popular for yachties as Tahiti, Fiji or Tonga. Usually, however, getting to the Cooks means flying, and since Rarotonga is the only island with an international airport, that's where you'll land. Yachties can enter the Cooks at a couple of other islands.

Travel Insurance

However you're travelling, it's worth taking out travel insurance. Work out what you need. You may not want to insure that grotty old army-surplus backpack – but everyone should be covered for the worst possible case: an accident, for example, that will require hospital treatment and a flight home. It's a good idea to make a copy of your policy, in case the original is lost. If you are planning to travel for a long time, the insurance may seem very expensive – but if you can't afford it, you certainly won't be able to afford to deal with a medical emergency overseas.

Medical care is very basic in the Cooks. Even the Cook Islanders don't depend solely on the medical care available here; their national health system provides for them to fly to New Zealand for medical treatment when necessary. As a foreigner, though, you're not covered by this same protection unless you have personal insurance.

Warning

This chapter is particularly vulnerable to change. Airfare prices, especially, are extremely volatile. There can be great variations in price depending on when you're going, which travel agent you buy with, the duration of ticket validity and many other factors. Special deals come and go, routes are introduced and cancelled, schedules change, rules are amended. The information given in this chapter was what we found when we were checking, but the details are constantly changing. By all means conduct your own investigation of options before you purchase your ticket, to find out the best deal to suit your needs. Get opinions, quotes and advice from as many travel agents and airlines as possible before you part with your hard-earned cash.

AIR

Arriving in Rarotonga

The Rarotonga International Airport is a rather simple one, by international standards. When the plane lands, a set of stairs-on-wheels is rolled up to the plane, and you get off and walk across the tarmac to the airport building. Music will be playing to greet you and there's a festive feeling in the air.

Unless you're a Cook Islander you'll be given a free 31-day visitor's permit upon arrival, which can later be extended (see the Facts for the Visitor chapter for details). You'll be asked to fill in an arrival form, including a blank for where you'll be staying in the Cooks while you're there. This is a vitally important blank, because the Cook Islands has a 'prior booking requirement' and you can be turned away and sent back to the airplane if you haven't booked a place to stay, at least for the first night of your visit (see the Accommodation section in the Facts for the Visitor chapter for details about this requirement). You'll also be asked to show an onward or return ticket.

After you've picked up your bags and passed through customs, you'll be greeted and asked where you're staying. A fleet of mini-buses and taxis is on hand to meet each flight, and you will be directed to the one going to the place you're staying, which will whisk you away in short order. See the Getting Around section in the Rarotonga chapter for more on airport transport options.

The Westpac bank at the airport is open for all arriving and departing flights. If you have New Zealand dollars you don't need to change money, as New Zealand and Cook

Aviation History

Aviation in the Cook Islands has had quite an interesting history. During WW II, airstrips were built on Penrhyn, Aitutaki and Rarotonga, and in 1945 a DC3 service operated every two weeks on a Fiji-Tonga-Western Samoa-Aitutaki-Rarotonga route. This service by New Zealand National Airways Corporation was dropped in 1952, but Tasman Empire Airways Limited had meanwhile started a monthly Solent flying boat service on the 'Coral Route' from Auckland to Papeete via Fiji and Aitutaki. See the Aitutaki chapter for more about this route.

The Solent service was increased to once every two weeks and continued until 1960. For a time there were no flights at all to the Cooks apart from infrequent New Zealand Air Force flights. In 1963 Polynesian Airways started a service from Apia in Western Samoa to Rarotonga but this was stopped in 1966 due to new regulations banning small aircraft making such long-distance flights over water. Once again the Cook Islands were left without international connections, and it was not until the new Rarotonga International Airport was opened in 1974 and big jets could fly into Rarotonga that flights resumed. ■

Islands paper money is used interchangeably in the Cooks. If you need to change money, however, you can do it here.

Airfares

Air New Zealand and Polynesian Airlines are the only international airlines stopping at the Cook Islands. Even though there are only two airlines, it still pays to take the time to do some research and compare prices and stopover options when buying your ticket to the Cooks. Travel agents often work out special package deals (airfare plus accommodation) that cost the same or even less than what you'd pay for the airfare alone.

It's also often possible to visit the Cooks either as a stopover when you're travelling across the Pacific, or as part of a Round-the-World or Circle Pacific ticket. Depending where you're coming from, it may not cost much more to visit the Cooks in combination with other destinations than it would to visit the Cooks, or the other destinations, alone.

High and low season airfares apply when flying to the Cooks, but the high and low seasons are variable, depending where you're coming from and even which airline you choose. Check your dates and options when you book your ticket; going just a day or two earlier or later can make a big difference in cost.

There are more Cook Islanders living in New Zealand than there are in the Cook Islands themselves, and many of them come home for the Christmas and summer school holiday period, beginning in mid-December and ending in January. This means there's an extra heavy demand for air seats coming from New Zealand to the Cooks in December, and going in the other direction in January. Keep this in mind when making your travel plans; if you're travelling at this time you may find many flights are full, so it's a good idea to reserve your seats as far in advance as possible. It also may not be easy to change your dates if you're flying around this time.

To/From New Zealand

Air New Zealand has four direct flights weekly between Auckland and Rarotonga; cost is NZ$1025 return in the low season, NZ$1258 return in the high season for a one-year ticket. There's also a cheaper 21-day ticket for NZ$899.

Polynesian Airlines have flights between Auckland and Rarotonga, but they don't go direct; they go via Apia, Western Samoa. Cost is NZ$1367 most of the year, NZ$1551 from 1 December to 15 January. Other stopover options on Polynesian Air include American Samoa, Tonga and Niue, at an extra cost.

If you want to visit other places around the Pacific, check out the airlines' many stopover options. You may be able to include Rarotonga as a stopover on your way to somewhere else in the Pacific, or get stopovers in other places if you're coming to or from the Cooks. For example, Air New Zealand offers a six-month return ticket from Auckland to Los Angeles, with two stopovers allowed in each direction, for NZ$1880 in the low season, NZ$1920 in the high season (December), with stopover options including Fiji, Tonga, Western Samoa, Rarotonga, Tahiti and Hawaii. Or you could get a 60-day return ticket from Auckland with stopovers at Fiji, Western Samoa, Tonga and Rarotonga for NZ$1675.

Remember that costs can be less if you buy through a discount ticket agency. STA and Flight Centres International are popular discount travel agents. STA has offices in Auckland, Hamilton, Palmerston North, Wellington, Christchurch and Dunedin; Flight Centres have dozens of offices throughout New Zealand.

Also be sure to check around with various travel agents to see what package holiday options are on offer; numerous travel agents in New Zealand offer very attractive prices in package holidays (airfare plus accommodation) to Rarotonga which can work out even cheaper than the airfare alone. Or you can get a package to include a number of Pacific destinations. For example, when we were checking, Polynesian Airlines was offering nine-night packages from Auckland to Rarotonga and Niue for NZ$1149 and 13-night packages including Rarotonga, Niue and Apia for NZ$1359.

To/From Australia

There are no direct flights from Australia to Rarotonga. Air New Zealand's flights are routed through Auckland; Polynesian Airlines' flights are routed through Apia, Western Samoa.

All the same advice applies as for if you are coming from New Zealand. Especially, be sure to check around with various travel agents for package deals – we found one that gave you two weeks of accommodation, with airfare included, for less than the airfare alone would have cost. Check the travel agents' ads in the Yellow Pages and ring around, because each seems to have its own particular deal.

When we asked the airlines their prices, Polynesian Airlines had the cheapest ticket: you could get from Sydney to Rarotonga, via Fiji and Western Samoa, for A$999 in the low season, A$1250 in the high season, valid for four months. Flights from Melbourne were the same prices, but they were routed via Noumea and Western Samoa. Air New Zealand's flights from Sydney and Brisbane, via Auckland, were A$1135, or A$1350 if originating from Melbourne. As always, airfare costs may be cheaper from discount travel agencies. STA and Flight Centres International are major dealers in cheap air fares. Both have offices in all the major cities.

To/From Asia & Japan

As in New Zealand and Australia, package holidays can be the most economical way of visiting Rarotonga if you're starting from Asia or Japan, or you may want to include the Cooks as a stopover if you're visiting other places in the Pacific.

Ticket discounting is widespread in Asia, particularly in Hong Kong, Singapore and Bangkok; Hong Kong is probably the discount air-ticket capital of the region. There are a lot of fly-by-nights in the Asian ticketing scene so a little care is required. STA, which is reliable, has branches in Hong Kong, Tokyo, Singapore, Bangkok and Kuala Lumpur.

To/From Canada

As when coming from other countries, you can get better deals on airfares by buying from discount travel agencies; also check around for package deals offered by various travel agents.

Travel CUTS, a reputable discount and student travel agency, has about 35 offices around Canada. The *Toronto Globe & Mail* and the *Vancouver Sun* carry travel agents' ads. The magazine *Great Expeditions* (PO Box 8000-411, Abbotsford BC V2S 6H1) is also useful.

Flights between Canada and Rarotonga

are usually routed through Hawaii or Los Angeles. See the following To/From the USA section; much of the same advice applies, especially as regards stopover options.

To/From the USA

Polynesian Airlines has a weekly direct flight between Los Angeles and Rarotonga. Cost is US$1023 for most of the year, rising to US$1260 in the high season from 1 December to 15 January.

Air New Zealand's flights between Los Angeles and Rarotonga are routed through either Honolulu or Tahiti; you can make a stopover in either place if you want. Cost for a three-month ticket routed either way is US$998 from April to August, US$1098 from September to March. The Air New Zealand flight from Honolulu to Rarotonga costs US$858 from April to August, US$898 from September to March. Another excellent option for travelling through the Pacific is Air New Zealand's 'Coral Route'; read on.

You may be able to do better than these straightforward fares with travel agents; ask about discounted airfares as well as about package holidays (airfare plus accommodation).

The Sunday travel sections of papers like the *Los Angeles Times*, the *San Francisco Examiner*, the *Chicago Tribune* and the *New York Times* always have plenty of ads for cheap airline tickets and there are often good deals on flights across the Pacific, especially in the west coast papers. Even if you don't live in these areas, you can have the tickets sent to you by mail.

Two of the most reputable discount travel agencies in the USA are STA and CIEE/Council Travel. STA has offices in Los Angeles, San Francisco, Berkeley, Philadelphia, New York, Boston and Cambridge. Council Travel has offices in all these cities and in about 20 others around the country.

The magazine *Travel Unlimited* (PO Box 1058, Allston, Mass 02134) publishes details of the cheapest airfares and courier possibilities for destinations all over the world from the USA.

The 'Coral Route' Air New Zealand operates a special 'Coral Route' through the Pacific, departing from Los Angeles, which has some excellent stopover options. Their basic return (round-trip) LA-Auckland-LA flight is US$798 if you fly direct with no stopovers. On the Coral Route, you pay US$898 LA-Auckland-LA with one stopover, and you can add on additional stopovers for US$100 each. You can also continue on from Auckland to Australia for an extra NZ$100, as another stopover option.

Stopover options include Honolulu, Tahiti, Rarotonga, Western Samoa, Tonga and Fiji. You can ask for as many or as few stopovers as you like, with a few restrictions on how you can organise your routing (there's no direct flight between Honolulu and Tahiti, for example). There's no limitation for how long you can stay at any stopover point, as long as you finish your entire trip in one year. They also have arrangements with other airlines whereby they can add the Solomon Islands, Vanuatu and New Caledonia as further stopover options. Check with Air New Zealand for details on these, as these fares are outside their basic Coral Route fare structure.

To/From the UK

Rarotonga is about as far away as you can get from the UK, so most travellers coming this far also visit other destinations. Compare airfares carefully; coming great distances like this is when Round-the-World airfares become especially economical compared to regular return airfares.

Straightforward economy return airfare from London to Rarotonga with Air New Zealand costs £920 from February to June, £1249 from July to January. As always, though, you can get airfares cheaper from discount ticket agencies, known as 'bucket shops' in UK parlance.

There has always been cut-throat competition among London's many bucket shops; London is an important European centre for cheap fares. There are plenty of bucket shops in London and although there are always some untrustworthy operators, most of them are fine. Look in the listings magazines *Time Out* and *City Limits* plus the Sunday papers and *Exchange & Mart* for ads. Also look out for the free magazines widely available in London – start by looking outside the main railway stations, or tubes. The Globetrotters Club (BCM Roving, London WC1N 3XX) publishes a newsletter called *Globe* which covers obscure destinations and can help in finding travelling companions.

Most British travel agents are registered with the Association of British Travel Agents (ABTA). If you have paid for your flight to an ABTA-registered agent who then goes out of business, ABTA will guarantee a refund or an alternative. Unregistered bucket shops are riskier but also sometimes cheaper.

Two good, reliable low-fare specialists are Trailfinders in west London, which produces a lavishly illustrated brochure including airfare details, and STA with a number of branches in London and around the UK.

To/From Mainland Europe

A surprising number of German tourists are turning up on Rarotonga lately; they say it's due to an especially attractive airfare originating in Frankfurt, since Air New Zealand began flying to Frankfurt. The route goes from Frankfurt to Los Angeles, with connections from there to the rest of the Pacific, including Air New Zealand's 'Coral Route' (see the earlier To\From the USA section). Straightforward Frankfurt/Rarotonga return airfare with Air New Zealand is DM1058 from April to August, DM1098 from September to March.

As usual, you can get better fares from the discount ticket agencies; also check with travel agents and compare the options on package holidays. Also compare the options for Round-the-World fares, which could work out favourably compared to a normal return fare, and compare stopover options if you want to also visit other places in the Pacific.

There are many bucket shops where you can buy discounted air tickets. STA and Council Travel, the two worldwide discount and student travel agencies, have a number of offices in various European countries. Any of their offices can give you the details on which office might be nearest you. In Amsterdam, NBBS is a popular travel agent.

Side Trips from Rarotonga

The Rarotonga travel agents, especially Stars Travel, often offer attractive package deals including airfare plus accommodation, making it easy and inexpensive to visit other nearby South Pacific islands while you're in the Cooks. Last time we were there, they were offering side trips to Western Samoa with per-person costs starting at NZ$399 for two nights, NZ$499 for five nights or NZ$585 for seven nights, with more expensive options for upgraded accommodation. Side trips to Niue were even cheaper, with five-night packages starting at NZ$399/335/325 per person for singles/doubles/triples.

Round-the-World Tickets

Round-the-World (RTW) tickets have become very popular in the last few years. The airline RTW tickets are often real bargains, and can work out no more expensive or even cheaper than an ordinary return ticket. Prices start at about UK£850, A$1800 or US$1300.

The official airline RTW tickets are usually put together by a combination of two airlines, and permit you to fly anywhere you want on their route systems so long as you do not backtrack. Other restrictions are that you (usually) must book the first sector in advance and cancellation penalties then apply. There may be restrictions on how many stops you are permitted and usually the tickets are valid for 90 days up to a year. An alternative type of RTW ticket is one put together by a travel agent using a combination of discounted tickets.

Circle Pacific Tickets

Circle Pacific tickets use a combination of airlines to circle the Pacific – combining Australia, New Zealand, North America and Asia, with a variety of stopover options in and around the Pacific. As with RTW tickets

Approximate Sample Airfares

Destination	*Fare type*	*Cost*	*Season*	*Validity*	*Airline*
Honolulu/Raro	Econ/rtn	US$858	low	3 mths	Air NZ
Honolulu/Raro	Econ/rtn	US$898	high	3 mths	Air NZ
LA/Raro	Econ/rtn	US$998	low	3 mths	Air NZ
LA/Raro	Econ/rtn	US$1098	high	3 mths	Air NZ
LA/Raro	Econ/rtn	US$1023	low	12 mths	Poly Air
LA/Raro	Econ/rtn	US$1260	high	12 mths	Poly Air
Vancouver/Raro	Econ/rtn	C$1168	low	1 mth	Air NZ
Vancouver/Raro	Econ/rtn	C$1538	high	1 mth	Air NZ
Toronto/Raro	Econ/rtn	C$1548	low	1 mth	Air NZ
Toronto/Raro	Econ/rtn	C$1998	high	1 mth	Air NZ
London/Raro	Econ/rtn	UK£920	low	12 mths	Air NZ
London/Raro	Econ/rtn	UK£1249	high	12 mths	Air NZ
Frankfurt/Raro	Econ/rtn	DM4248	low	12 mths	Air NZ
Frankfurt/Raro	Econ/rtn	DM7462	high	12 mths	Air NZ
Auckland/Raro	Econ/rtn	NZ$1025	low	12 mths	Air NZ
Auckland/Raro	Econ/rtn	NZ$1258	high	12 mths	Air NZ
Auckland/Raro	Econ/rtn	NZ$899	low	21 days	Air NZ
Sydney/Raro	Econ/rtn	A$999	low	4 mths	Poly Air
Sydney/Raro	Econ/rtn	A$1250	high	4 mths	Poly Air
Tokyo/Raro	Econ/rtn	Y204,100	low	12 mths	Air NZ
Tokyo/Raro	Econ/rtn	Y352,100	high	12 mths	Air NZ
Hong Kong/Raro	Econ/rtn	HK$12,890	low	12 mths	Air NZ
Hong Kong/Raro	Econ/rtn	HK$24,560	high	12 mths	Air NZ
Singapore/Raro	Econ/rtn	S$3600	low	12 mths	Air NZ
Singapore/Raro	Econ/rtn	S$7200	high	12 mths	Air NZ

there are advance purchase restrictions and limits to how many stopovers you can make. These fares are likely to be around 15% cheaper than RTW tickets.

Other types of tickets also allow you to visit a number of destinations in the Pacific. Air New Zealand has the 'Coral Route' if you're coming from the USA, which you can also connect with at Los Angeles if you're coming from Canada, the UK or mainland Europe. Polynesian Airlines has a variety of combination tickets also available, including the 30-day 'Polypass' for 30 days of unlimited travel on that airline (with some restrictions), with stopover possibilities at Los Angeles, Honolulu, Tahiti, Rarotonga, Niue, Tonga, Western Samoa, American Samoa, Fiji, New Caledonia, Auckland, Sydney and Melbourne. Cost is US$999 for all ports excluding Los Angeles, or NZ$1299 for all ports including Los Angeles (children half fare).

Buying a Plane Ticket

The plane ticket will probably be the single most expensive item in your budget, and buying it can be an intimidating business. There is likely to be a multitude of airlines and travel agents hoping to separate you from your money, and it is always worth putting aside a few hours to research the current state of the market. Start early: some of the cheapest tickets have to be bought months in advance, and some popular flights sell out early. Talk to other recent travellers – they may be able to stop you making some of the same old mistakes. Look at the ads in newspapers and magazines (not forgetting the press of the ethnic group whose country you plan to visit), consult reference books and watch for special offers. Then phone around travel agents for bargains. (Airlines can supply information on routes and timetables; however, except at times of inter-airline war they do not supply the cheapest tickets.) Find out the fare, the route, the duration of the journey and any restrictions on the ticket. (See under Restrictions in the Air Travel Glossary.) Then sit back and decide which is best for you.

You may discover that those impossibly cheap flights are 'fully booked, but we have another one that costs a bit more...' Or the flight is on an airline notorious for its poor safety standards and leaves you in the world's least favourite airport in mid-journey for 14 hours. Or they claim only to have the last two seats available for that country for the whole of July, which they will hold for you for a maximum of two hours. Don't panic – keep ringing around.

Use the fares quoted in this book as a guide only. They are approximate and based on the rates advertised by travel agents at the time of going to press. Quoted airfares do not necessarily constitute a recommendation for the carrier.

If you are travelling from the UK or the USA, you will probably find that the cheapest flights are being advertised by obscure bucket shops whose names haven't yet reached the telephone directory. Many such firms are honest and solvent, but there are a few rogues who will take your money and disappear, to reopen elsewhere a month or two later under a new name. If you feel suspicious about a firm, don't give them all the money at once – leave a deposit of 20% or so and pay the balance when you get the ticket. If they insist on cash in advance, go somewhere else. And once you have the ticket, ring the airline to confirm that you are actually booked onto the flight.

You may decide to pay more than the rock-bottom fare by opting for the safety of a better-known travel agent. Firms such as STA, who have offices worldwide, Council Travel in the USA or Travel CUTS in Canada are not going to disappear overnight, leaving you clutching a receipt for a non-existent ticket, but they do offer good prices to most destinations.

Once you have your ticket, write its number down, together with the flight number and other details, and keep the information somewhere separate. If the ticket is lost or stolen, this will help you get a replacement.

It's sensible to buy travel insurance as early as possible. If you buy it the week before you fly, you may find, for example, that you're not covered for delays to your flight caused by industrial action.

Air Travellers with Special Needs

If you have special needs of any sort – you've broken a leg, you're vegetarian, travelling in a wheelchair, taking the baby, terrified of flying – you should let the airline know as soon as possible so that they can make arrangements accordingly. You should remind them when you reconfirm your booking (at least 72 hours before departure) and again when you check in at the airport. It may also be worth ringing round the airlines before you make your booking to find out how they can handle your particular needs.

Airports and airlines can be surprisingly helpful, but they do need advance warning. Most international airports will provide escorts from check-in desk to plane where needed, and there should be ramps, lifts, accessible toilets and reachable phones. Note, however, that the Rarotonga International Airport has none of these things, so plan accordingly. Aircraft toilets, on the other hand, are likely to present a problem; travellers should discuss this with the airline at an early stage and, if necessary, with their doctor.

Guide dogs for the blind will often have to travel in a specially pressurised baggage compartment with other animals, away from their owner; though smaller guide dogs may be allowed in the cabin. All guide dogs will be subject to the same quarantine laws (six months in isolation etc) as any other animal when entering or returning to countries currently free of rabies, such as Britain and Australia.

Deaf travellers can ask for airport and in-flight announcements to be written down.

Children under two travel for 10% of the standard fare (or free, on some airlines), as long as they don't occupy a seat. They don't get a baggage allowance either. 'Skycots'

Air Travel Glossary

Apex Apex, or 'advance purchase excursion', is a discounted ticket which must be paid for in advance. There are penalties if you wish to change it.

Baggage Allowance This will be written on your ticket: usually one or two items to go in the hold, with a total weight not to exceed 20 kg, plus one item of hand luggage. If your route goes through the USA, however, the baggage allowance is greater – usually two pieces of checked luggage, each piece not to exceed 32 kg, plus one item of hand luggage. Be sure to check with the airline if you're in doubt, as the fees charged for overweight or excess baggage can be amazingly high.

Bucket Shop An unbonded travel agency specialising in discounted airline tickets.

Bumped Just because you have a confirmed seat doesn't mean you're going to get on the plane – see Overbooking.

Cancellation Penalties If you have to cancel or change an Apex ticket there are often heavy penalties involved. Insurance can sometimes be taken out against these penalties. Some airlines impose penalties on regular tickets as well, particularly against 'no show' passengers.

Check In Airlines ask you to check in a certain time ahead of the flight departure (usually 1½ hours on international flights). If you fail to check in on time and the flight is overbooked, the airline can cancel your booking and give your seat to somebody else.

Confirmation Having a ticket written out with the flight and date you want doesn't mean you have a seat until the agent has checked with the airline that your status is 'OK' or confirmed. Meanwhile you could just be 'on request'.

Discounted Tickets There are two types of discounted fares – officially discounted (see Promotional Fares) and unofficially discounted. The lowest prices often impose drawbacks like flying with unpopular airlines, inconvenient schedules, or unpleasant routes and connections. A discounted ticket can save you other things than money – you may be able to pay Apex prices without the associated Apex advance booking and other requirements. Discounted tickets only exist where there is fierce competition.

Full Fares Airlines traditionally offer first class (coded F), business class (coded J) and economy class (coded Y) tickets. These days there are so many promotional and discounted fares available from the regular economy class that few passengers pay full economy fare.

Lost Tickets If you lose your airline ticket an airline will usually treat it like a travellers' cheque and, after inquiries, issue you with another one. Legally, however, an airline is entitled to treat it like cash and if you lose it, it's gone forever. Take good care of your tickets.

No Shows No shows are passengers who fail to show up for their flight, sometimes due to unexpected delays or disasters, sometimes due to simply forgetting, sometimes because they made more than one booking and didn't bother to cancel the one they didn't want. Full fare passengers who fail to turn up are sometimes entitled to travel on a later flight. The rest of us are penalised (see Cancellation Penalties).

On Request An unconfirmed booking for a flight, see Confirmation.

should be provided by the airline if requested in advance; these will take a child weighing up to about 10 kg. Children between two and 12 can usually occupy a seat for half to two-thirds of the full fare, and do get a baggage allowance. Push chairs can often be taken as hand luggage.

Bicycles can travel by air. You *can* take them to pieces and put them in a bike bag or box, but it's much easier simply to wheel your bike to the check-in desk, where it should be treated as a piece of baggage. You may have to remove the pedals and turn the handlebars sideways so that it takes up less space in the aircraft's hold; check all this with the airline well in advance, preferably before you pay for your ticket.

SEA

There are no regularly scheduled passenger ships to the Cooks. The occasional luxury liner cruise ship passes through, stopping for only a day or two, but this is very infrequent. If you're coming by sea, it usually means you'll be coming on a private yacht.

The Cook Islands are not a major Pacific yachting destination like French Polynesia, Tonga or Fiji. Nevertheless, a steady trickle of

Open Jaws A return ticket where you fly out to one place but return from another. If available, this can save you backtracking to your arrival point.
Overbooking Airlines hate to fly empty seats and since every flight has some passengers who fail to show up (see No Shows) airlines often book more passengers than they have seats. Usually the excess passengers balance those who fail to show up but occasionally somebody gets bumped. If this happens guess who it is most likely to be? The passengers who check in late.
Promotional Fares Officially discounted fares like Apex fares which are available from travel agents or direct from the airline.
Reconfirmation At least 72 hours prior to departure time of an onward or return flight you must contact the airline and 'reconfirm' that you intend to be on the flight. If you don't do this the airline can delete your name from the passenger list and you could lose your seat. You don't have to reconfirm the first flight on your itinerary or if your stopover is less than 72 hours. It doesn't hurt to reconfirm more than once.
Restrictions Discounted tickets often have various restrictions on them – advance purchase is the most usual one (see Apex). Others are restrictions on the minimum and maximum period you must be away, such as a minimum of 14 days or a maximum of one year. See Cancellation Penalties.
Standby A discounted ticket where you only fly if there is a seat free at the last moment. Standby fares are usually only available on domestic routes.
Tickets Out An entry requirement for many countries – including the Cook Islands – is that you have an onward or return ticket, in other words, a ticket out of the country. If you're not sure what you intend to do next, the easiest solution is to buy the cheapest onward ticket to a neighbouring country or a ticket from a reliable airline which can later be refunded if you do not use it.
Transferred Tickets Airline tickets cannot be transferred from one person to another. Travellers sometimes try to sell the return half of their ticket, but officials can ask you to prove that you are the person named on the ticket. This is unlikely to happen on domestic flights, but on an international flight tickets can easily be compared with passports.
Travel Agencies Travel agencies vary widely and you should ensure you use one that suits your needs. Some simply handle tours while full-service agencies handle everything from tours and tickets to car rental and hotel bookings. A good one will do all these things and can save you a lot of money but if all you want is a ticket at the lowest possible price, then you really need an agency specialising in discounted tickets. A discounted ticket agency, however, may not be useful for other things, like hotel bookings.
Travel Periods Some officially discounted fares, Apex fares in particular, vary with the time of year. There is often a low (off-peak) season and a high (peak) season. Sometimes there's an intermediate, or shoulder season, as well. At peak times, when everyone wants to fly, not only will the officially discounted fares be higher but so will unofficially discounted fares or there may simply be no discounted tickets available. Usually the fare depends on your outward flight – if you depart in the high season and return in the low season, you pay the high-season fare. ■

yachts do pass through the islands, except during the December-to-April hurricane season. Official entry points are Rarotonga and Aitutaki in the southern group and Penrhyn and Pukapuka in the northern group. Many yachties only visit the practically uninhabited atoll of Suwarrow – illegally if they haven't already officially entered the country. Yachties are under the same entry and exit regulations, including the departure tax, as those who arrive and depart by air.

It doesn't happen often but there's a remote chance that you might be able to catch a yacht sailing from the Cooks to other nearby destinations like Tonga, Samoa, Fiji, French Polynesia or New Zealand. Check with the Waterfront Commission at Avatiu Harbour on Rarotonga, and on its downstairs bulletin board, as yachties sometimes use this as a message board.

In the unlikely event that a yacht is looking for crew, of course they'd prefer to take on experienced crew members. However, it's not very likely that fully qualified and experienced crew members are hanging around the Cook Islands waiting for a yacht to happen by and pick them up. Being able to pay for your own food and even part of the passage costs, being personable, flexible, uncomplaining, a fast learner, an eager worker, a good cook and so on, are all assets in your favour. If you're really serious about catching a yacht, though, you'll do better to try your luck at some of the other Pacific islands more on the main sailing routes.

LEAVING RAROTONGA

There's a NZ$20 departure tax when you fly out of Rarotonga; for children aged two to 12 it's NZ$10, and it's free for children under two.

The Westpac bank at the airport is open for all arriving and departing flights. Remember that Cook Islands money, both bills and coins, can only be changed in the Cook Islands so if you don't change it before you leave, it will only be good for a souvenir when you arrive somewhere else.

Getting Around

There are basically just two ways of getting from island to island around the Cooks (if you don't own your own yacht). In the southern group you can fly with Air Rarotonga or you can take the inter-island cargo ships, two of which carry passengers in addition to freight. If you want to go to the northern islands, Penrhyn, Manihiki and Pukapuka are the only ones with airports, and the flights are long and expensive. Otherwise the only way to reach the northern group islands is by freighter ship.

AIR

Air Rarotonga, with a fleet of three 18-passenger Bandeirante turbo-prop planes, is the only commercial inter-island air service in the Cooks. Flights go several times a day between Rarotonga and Aitutaki, several times a week between Rarotonga and the other southern group islands, and only once or twice a week between Rarotonga and the northern islands. There are no flights on Sunday on any of Air Rarotonga's routes.

One-way fares (double for return) are:

Route	*Cost*	*Flying Time*
Rarotonga-Aitutaki	NZ$142	50 minutes
Rarotonga-Mangaia	NZ$127	40 minutes
Rarotonga-Atiu	NZ$127	45 minutes
Rarotonga-Mitiaro	NZ$142	50 minutes
Rarotonga-Maukc	NZ$142	50 minutes
Rarotonga-Manihiki	NZ$500	3½ hours
Rarotonga-Penrhyn	NZ$550	4 hours
Rarotonga-Pukapuka	NZ$550	4¼ hours
Manihiki-Pukapuka	NZ$165	1½ hours
Manihiki-Penrhyn	NZ$145	1 hour

On flights between Rarotonga and other southern group islands there's a special 'Super Saver' fare available only if you book and purchase your ticket locally, in cash.

Flying in the Cooks

Flying among the various Cook Islands is done in 18-passenger Bandeirante turbo-prop planes. With people travelling back and forth among the islands for many different reasons, there's often quite a motley collection of passengers on any flight.

Around December and January there are large numbers of people flying to and from the outer islands, as relations living on Rarotonga, New Zealand, Australia and other places overseas return to the outer islands to spend the Christmas holidays at home. If you are travelling at this time, book a seat as early as possible; despite additional flights being scheduled at this time, it can still be a struggle to find an available seat.

The tradition of giving *eis* whenever people arrive and depart is alive and well in the outer islands. It's still practiced on Rarotonga, too, but much more so in the outer islands where, to many people, it would be inconceivable for a guest to arrive or depart without being garlanded with flowers. Sometimes, as in the case of important figures, so many eis are draped around the neck that the recipient seems to be practically buried in flowers. The small airplanes sometimes feel like mobile florist shops, and the aroma can be almost overpowering! ■

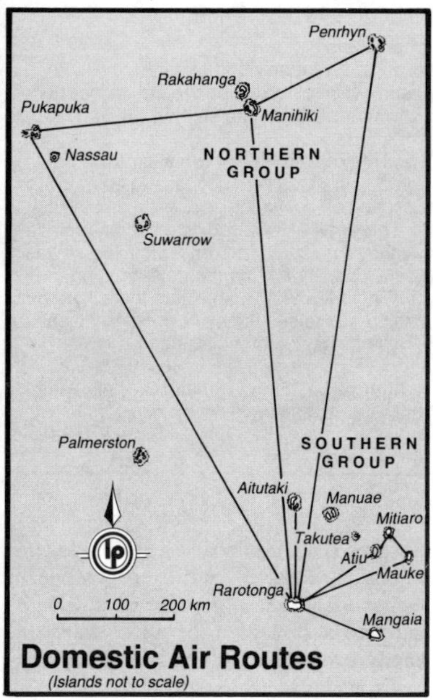

Domestic Air Routes
(Islands not to scale)

Super Saver fares from Rarotonga to Aitutaki, Mauke or Mitiaro are NZ$198 return; from Rarotonga to Atiu or Mangaia they're NZ$180 return. The Super Saver fares between Rarotonga and Aitutaki apply only on the last flight of the day from Rarotonga to Aitutaki, or the first flight of the day from Aitutaki to Rarotonga.

If you're going to more than one of the southern group islands, you can get a 30-day Paradise Island Pass for NZ$96 per sector. Note that there are no longer any direct flights between Atiu and Mauke, so if you want to fly between those two islands it requires two sectors (Atiu to Mitiaro, then Mitiaro to Mauke, or vice versa).

All the Rarotonga travel agents offer package tours to the southern group islands which include airfare plus accommodation. You can visit just one island this way, or several; a popular combination is to visit Atiu, Mitiaro and Mauke all in one go, since the flights from Atiu to Mitiaro and from Mitiaro to Mauke take only 10 minutes each. Plans are also in the works for a northern group tour to include Manihiki, Penrhyn and Pukapuka.

Another option is to charter a plane through Air Rarotonga, but of course this works out to be more expensive than going on the scheduled flights. You can charter a plane to any licensed airport in the Cook Islands, including the islands of the northern group, and even internationally. The standard charter plane is a Beechcraft Baron 58, accommodating up to five passengers (plus one pilot); larger aircraft are available subject to schedule commitments. The normal charter fare includes the pilot, but if you have a pilot's licence, you can bring in your logbook and see about flying the plane yourself if you wish. Ask at Air Rarotonga for details.

Air Rarotonga has an office at the Rarotonga International Airport (☎ 22-888, fax 20-979) where tickets are sold and bookings are made. They also have an administration office (☎ 22-890) near the Air Rarotonga hangar, about 500 metres west along the main road, which is where you go for scenic flights and tandem skydiving.

Outer-Island Day Tours

One-day tours to Aitutaki depart from Rarotonga Airport daily at 8 am and return to Rarotonga by about 7.30 pm. See the Day Tours section of the Aitutaki chapter for details.

A one-day tour to include both Atiu and Mauke in one go is scheduled to begin soon. Ask Air Rarotonga or the Rarotonga travel agents if it's started yet.

All the day tours can be booked through any travel agent or directly with Air Rarotonga.

BOAT

Shipping services have had a colourful history in the Cooks: companies have come and gone, ships have run onto reefs, fortunes have been made but more often lost. Despite the increasing use of air services, shipping is still vital to the islands. Most of the northern

Why the Shipping Services Don't Run to Schedule

In Aitutaki we met a group of marine geologists from Fiji, a woman off to Manihiki to research musical instruments and other associated artefacts, and a man off on a loop around the northern islands. Supposedly two days out from Rarotonga towards Manihiki, the ship was already four days behind schedule.

Day one was lost at Mauke when it was too rough and they had to wait for conditions to improve before unloading. Day two was lost because although the ship was not supposed to be going to Aitutaki in the first place it had been diverted there because of the marine geologists and all their equipment. Then because of the day lost at Mauke the ship arrived at Aitutaki on a Sunday instead of a Saturday. Since no work gets done on a Sunday they couldn't unload and another day was lost. On Sunday night a ferocious wind blew up (some yachties told us the next morning they recorded wind speeds of 50 knots) and continued all day Monday – so again there was no unloading. The marine geologists spent the day climbing hills to see if they could spot the ship, with their equipment, offshore. It had moved round to the other side of the island to shelter from the wind.

On Tuesday we flew back to Rarotonga, leaving them all wondering whether they would get their gear off that day and if the ship would be continuing north that night.

Tony Wheeler

islands can only be served by ship and throughout the islands, ships are necessary to bring in commodities and export produce.

Shipping services in the islands face two major problems. Firstly, there are simply too few people and they're too widely scattered to be easily and economically serviced. From the ship owners' point of view, shipping between the islands is only feasible with a government subsidy. From the islanders' point of view, it's difficult to produce export crops if you can't be certain a ship will be coming by at the appropriate time to collect them.

The second problem is that the islands generally have terrible harbours. The south sea image of drifting through a wide passage in the reef into the clear sheltered waters of the lagoon doesn't seem to apply to the Cooks. In the northern atolls the reef passages are generally too narrow or shallow to allow large ships to enter. In the southern volcanic islands the passages through the fringing reefs are usually too small to let a ship enter and dock. Even Rarotonga's main harbour, Avatiu, is too small for large ships – or even too many small ones. All this means that ships have to anchor outside the reef and transfer passengers and freight to shore by lighters. At some of the islands even getting the lighters through the narrow reef passages is a considerable feat. Unless conditions are ideal it's not even possible to anchor offshore at some of the Cook Islands, and freighters have to be under way constantly, even while loading and unloading.

If you plan to explore the outer islands by ship you need to be flexible and hardy. Schedules are hard to pinpoint and unlikely to be kept to – weather, breakdowns, loading difficulties or unexpected demands can all put a kink in the plans. At each island visited, the ship usually stays just long enough to discharge and take on cargo. Travellers thus get the chance to spend a few hours visiting each island before taking off again. Outside of Rarotonga, only the northernmost island of Penrhyn has a wharf; at all the others, you have to go ashore by lighter or barge.

On board the ships, conditions are cramped and primitive: these are not luxury cruise liners. They're also small and the seas in this region are often rough. If you're at all prone to seasickness you'll definitely spend some time hanging your head over the side. See the Health section in the Facts for the Visitor chapter for suggestions on what to do for motion sickness.

Despite the discomforts, though, travelling by ship through the Cook Islands does have its romantic aspects. This may be one of the last places in the world that you can sleep out on the deck of a South Pacific island freighter, savouring the wide horizon, chatting with your fellow passengers and the captain and crew, watching the moon rise up out of the ocean and the stars above you in the velvety-warm air.

Fortunately the distances are not too far; travel throughout the southern islands usually involves setting off in the late afternoon or early evening, sleeping on the way and arriving at the next island early in the morning. Trips from Rarotonga to the northern islands naturally take longer; travel time can be about three days to reach the northern group but the round-trip time may be extended by visiting several islands, or by taking longer to load and unload cargo, since sailings to the northern islands are less frequent than around the southern group. Typically, a northern group trip, departing Rarotonga and visiting a couple of the northern islands, often with a stop at Aitutaki on the way, might take about 10 days or so before getting back to Raro.

The Avatapu & Marthalina

Two ships, the *Avatapu* and the *Marthalina*, both based at Rarotonga's Avatiu Harbour, provide inter-island cargo and passenger services for the Cooks. Both have offices there at the harbour where you can get more information, check schedules and make bookings. The *Avatapu* (☎ & fax 22-369, PO Box 131) has its own office; business for the *Marthalina* is handled at the Waterfront Commission office (☎ 21-921, fax 21-191, PO Box 84).

The *Avatapu* has two classes of passenger service: deck and bunk. Deck passengers sleep out on deck. Bunk passengers are in a dormitory-style compartment with five upper bunks and five lower bunks. The bunks are very small and indoor facilities somewhat cramped; if the night is warm and still, it's more pleasant to sleep out on deck. On the other hand, if a tropical downpour suddenly starts you'll wish you had a bunk! Fresh-water shower and toilets are available to all. Cabins are not available.

Bunk passengers have the option of buying a 'bunk only' ticket, or 'bunk plus food', including three meals a day. Deck passengers normally bring their own food, but they can eat aboard at a specified cost per meal. Passengers may not use the ship's galley or refrigerator.

In early 1994 the *Avatapu*'s prices were:

	Deck	*Bunk*	*Bunk & Food*
Rarotonga to 1st Southern Group Island	NZ$25	NZ$40	NZ$70
Rarotonga to 2nd Southern Group island	NZ$30	NZ$55	NZ$100
Rarotonga to 3rd Southern Group island	NZ$35	NZ$70	NZ$125
Rarotonga to 3 or 4 islands and back	NZ$70	NZ$100	NZ$140
Rarotonga–Aitutaki–Manihiki	NZ$120	NZ$180	NZ$270

The *Marthalina* is larger than the *Avatapu* but it's a different type of vessel, transporting petrol as well as cargo. It takes deck passengers only, but not all the time – it's principally a tanker and cargo ship. Still, it never hurts to ask if they're taking passengers at the time. Passenger prices are not as organised as on the *Avatapu*, so you just have to check for details at the time you want to go.

HITCHING

Hitching is never entirely safe in any country in the world, and we don't recommend it. Travellers who decide to hitch should understand that they are taking a small but potentially serious risk. However, many people do choose to hitch, and the advice that follows should help make their journeys as fast and safe as possible.

Hitchhiking is not the custom in the Cooks and it's quite likely that you'll never see anyone do it. However, it's not illegal, only rather cheeky, and if you do hitchhike you'll probably get a ride in short order. You may have better luck if you flag down a vehicle rather than sticking your thumb out pointing skyward, which we've been told can be interpreted as a rude gesture in the Cooks.

LOCAL TRANSPORT

On Rarotonga there's a bus service, lots of taxis, and you can hire cars, Jeeps, minibuses, motorcycles and bicycles. On Aitutaki there are taxis plus rental cars, motorcycles and bicycles. On Atiu and Mauke the small hotels have motorcycles to rent. Mangaia has only one pick-up truck and a couple of motorcycles to rent, but several of the small places to stay are thinking of expanding into the rental motorbike business. Elsewhere you can walk. See the individual island chapters for more information.

TOURS

There are various interesting tours you can take in the Cooks. On Rarotonga the 'Circle Island' tours provide a good introduction to the island and its history, culture, people, agriculture, economy and more.

One-day tours are available from Rarotonga to the islands of Aitutaki, Atiu and Mauke. Of course it's better if you can stay longer but these tours do give a fine introduction to these islands and if time is limited, they do enable you to at least get a taste of these islands. Air Rarotonga is planning to start tours of the northern group islands, too.

The Southern Islands

Rarotonga and Aitutaki are the best known of the southern islands and 99% of visitors to the Cook Islands get no farther than these two islands. A trickle do continue to the other islands of the southern group, fewer still to the northern group.

The southern group of islands are larger in terms of both size and population than the northern islands. These volcanic islands are also economically better off than the coral atolls of the northern group.

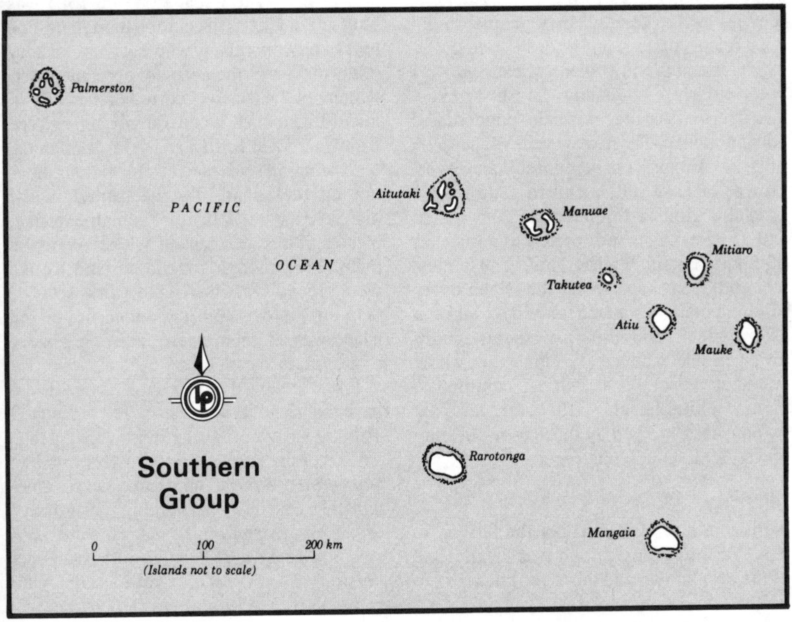

Palmerston
Aitutaki
PACIFIC
OCEAN
Manuae
Mitiaro
Takutea
Atiu
Mauke
Rarotonga
Mangaia
Southern Group
0 100 200 km
(Islands not to scale)

Rarotonga

Population: 10,886
Area: 67.2 sq km

Rarotonga is not only the major island and population centre of the Cook Islands – it's also, like Tahiti in French Polynesia, virtually synonymous with the whole island chain. Nobody goes to the Cook Islands – they go to Rarotonga. Many people do not even realise there is anywhere else to go.

The island is extravagantly beautiful – it's spectacularly mountainous and lush green. The interior is rugged, virtually unpopulated and untouched. The narrow valleys and steep hills are simply too precipitous and overgrown for easy settlement. In contrast, the coastal region is fertile, evenly populated and as neat, clean and 'pretty' as some sort of South Pacific Switzerland. You almost feel somebody zips round the island every morning making sure the roads have all been swept clean and the flowers all neatly arranged and watered. Fringing this whole Arcadian vision is an almost continuous, clean, white beach with clear, shallow lagoons and, marked by those ever-crashing waves, a protective outer reef.

HISTORY

Numerous legends touch upon the early existence of Rarotonga, which was clearly one of the best known and most important of the Polynesian islands.

Ancient oral histories relate that the first person to discover the island was Io Teitei, also called Io Tangaroa, who was from Nuku Hiva in the Marquesas Islands, now part of French Polynesia. He came by canoe about 1400 years ago, but didn't stay; he went back to Nuku Hiva and never returned to Rarotonga.

Back in Nuku Hiva, Io Tangaroa's younger brother, Tongaiti, followed Io Tangaroa's directions and came to Rarotonga. Later, Io Tangaroa's eldest son, To'u Ariki, came. They, too, both went back to Nuku Hiva and never returned to Rarotonga, but To'u Ariki's first-born son, Tumutoa, who had been with his father when they came to Rarotonga and returned to Nuku Hiva, later did return to Rarotonga.

Though Rarotonga had definitely been visited and even settled beforehand, then – the Ara Metua inland road, also called Te Ara Nui O Toi ('The Great Road of Toi') was built around the 11th century, though no-one today knows precisely who Toi was – history often states that the definite, permanent settlement of the island occurred in the early or mid-13th century, when Tangiia-nui arrived from Tahiti and Karika arrived from Samoa, both bringing settlers to establish communities on the island. Tangiia settled in the district that still bears his name today, Ngatangiia; Karika settled where Avarua is today. Even though Tangiia-nui and Karika were probably not the island's first settlers, their arrival to establish communities on the island was an important event in the history of the island's settlement.

In one version of history it was Tongaiti who gave the island its first name: Te Ou Enua O Tumutevarovaro. Tumutevarovaro means 'source of the echo' *(tumu* = source; *te* = the; *varovaro* = echo); the entire name means something like 'the misty land of Tumutevarovaro' or 'the mist rising from Tumutevarovaro' *(te* = the; *ou* = mist; *enua* = land; *o* = of). In another version, it was Tu-te-rangi-marama who named the island Tumutevarovaro; other traditions say it could have been others who gave the island its name.

There are also a variety of stories relating to how the island got its present name of Rarotonga. *Raro* = under or down; *tonga* = south, so the name means something like 'down south' or 'under the south'. In another version, *raro* in the ancient language of eastern Polynesia meant the direction the tradewinds came from, that is, west; so Rarotonga could then mean 'south-west'. From the point of view of the early discoverers and navigators from the Marquesas and Society islands, Rarotonga was certainly to the south-west. The giving of the name Rarotonga has been credited to a number of the early figures in the island's history including Tongaiti, Iro from Tahiti, Tangiia and Karika.

Eventually the island was settled and the land divided among six tribes, each headed by a tribal king, or ariki. There were three districts on the island: Te Au O Tonga on the north side of the island, Ngatangiia on the east and south-east side and Puaikura on the west. Conflicts and wars over land and other issues were frequent among the tribes, and the people did not live on the low coastal plain as they do today; they lived at the higher elevations where they could more easily defend themselves from attack, only venturing down to the sea in armed groups, for fishing. Inland they practiced agriculture and raised livestock including pigs.

In around 1350 AD, Rarotonga was the island from which seven canoes from the 'great migration' to settle New Zealand, departed. Fourteen canoes, coming from various Polynesian islands including Rarotonga itself, assembled at Avana Harbour in the Ngatangiia district and took off from there to sail to New Zealand or, as it was known to them in those days, Aotearoa ('land of the long white cloud'). They followed the sailing directions of Kupe, an early Polynesian navigator who had discovered and named Aotearoa around 900 AD, explored it, then returned and told about the land and how to get there. Seven of the 14 canoes completed the trip. The people on these canoes became the great ancestors of several New Zealand Maori tribes, with the tribes taking the names of the canoes the ancestors arrived on as their tribal names (eg, the Tainui tribe, the Te Arawa tribe etc).

European Discovery

Surprisingly, considering its historic importance and also that it is the largest and most populous of the Cook Islands, Rarotonga was one of the later islands to be discovered by Europeans. The first discovery can probably be credited to the mutineers on the *Bounty*, who happened upon Rarotonga after they had returned to Tahiti and were searching for a remote island where they could hide from the British navy. This was probably sometime in late 1789, but, and this is hardly surprising, the mutineers didn't come forward to tell about their important discovery.

In any case, the mutineers did not set foot upon Rarotonga; nor did the crew of Captain Theodore Walker's *Endeavour* who sighted the island in 1813. A piece of sandalwood floating in the sea, however, was picked up by the *Endeavour* and taken to Australia. The idea that the island might have sandalwood – a valuable commodity – led to the formation of a sandalwood company in Australia and to the next European visitor. Philip Goodenough, captain of the *Cumberland*, showed up in 1814 and spent three months on Rarotonga – three less than harmonious and peaceful months. Unable to find any sandalwood the crew of the *Cumberland* decided to take back *nono* wood instead. This was an unsuccessful gamble as nono wood turned out to be of negligible value.

During their stay at Ngatangiia the crew managed to get themselves involved in a number of local squabbles which resulted in the deaths of a number of the crew, including Goodenough's female companion, Ann Butcher, the first European woman to come to the island, and also of numerous Rarotongans. Eventually the *Cumberland* left Rarotonga in some haste, but two local women and a man were taken with them and left at their next stop, Aitutaki. William Gill later described the *Cumberland's* visit to Rarotonga as a 'continued series of rapine, cruelty, vice and bloodshed'. Understandably, Goodenough did not go into great detail about his adventures so Rarotonga remained comparatively unknown. In the following years a number of vessels visited Rarotonga but only stayed for short periods.

In 1821 Papeiha, the Polynesian missionary, or 'teacher', from Raiatea in the Society Islands, was landed on Aitutaki by the English missionary John Williams. In 1823 Williams returned to Aitutaki to see how successful he had been. Papeiha had done remarkably well so Williams and Papeiha set

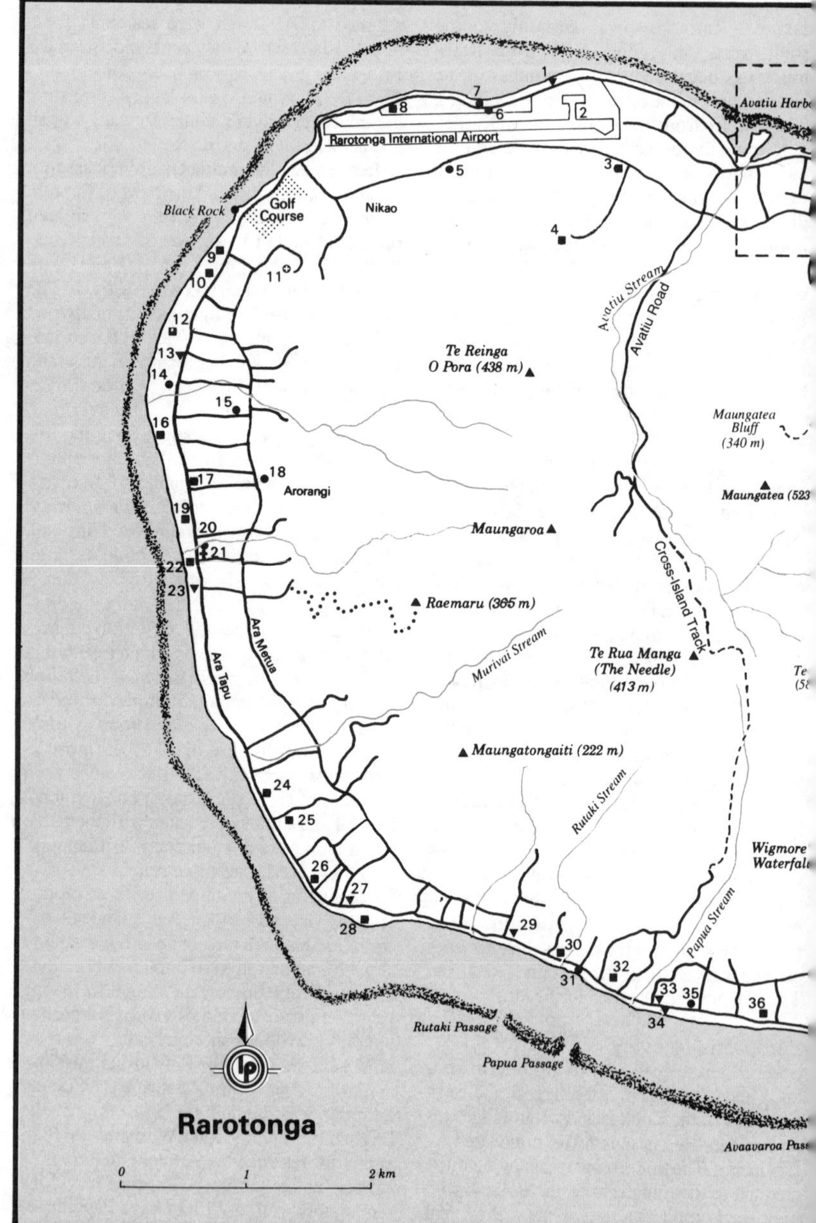

Avatiu Harb
Rarotonga International Airport
Black Rock
Golf Course
Nikao
Avatiu Stream
Avatiu Road
Te Reinga O Pora (438 m)
Maungatea Bluff (340 m)
Maungatea (523
Arorangi
Maungaroa
Cross-Island Track
Raemaru (365 m)
Murivai Stream
Te Rua Manga (The Needle) (413 m)
Ara Tapu
Ara Metua
Maungatongaiti (222 m)
Rutaki Stream
Papua Stream
Wigmore
Waterfal
Rutaki Passage
Papua Passage
Avaavaroa Pass
Rarotonga
0
1
2 km

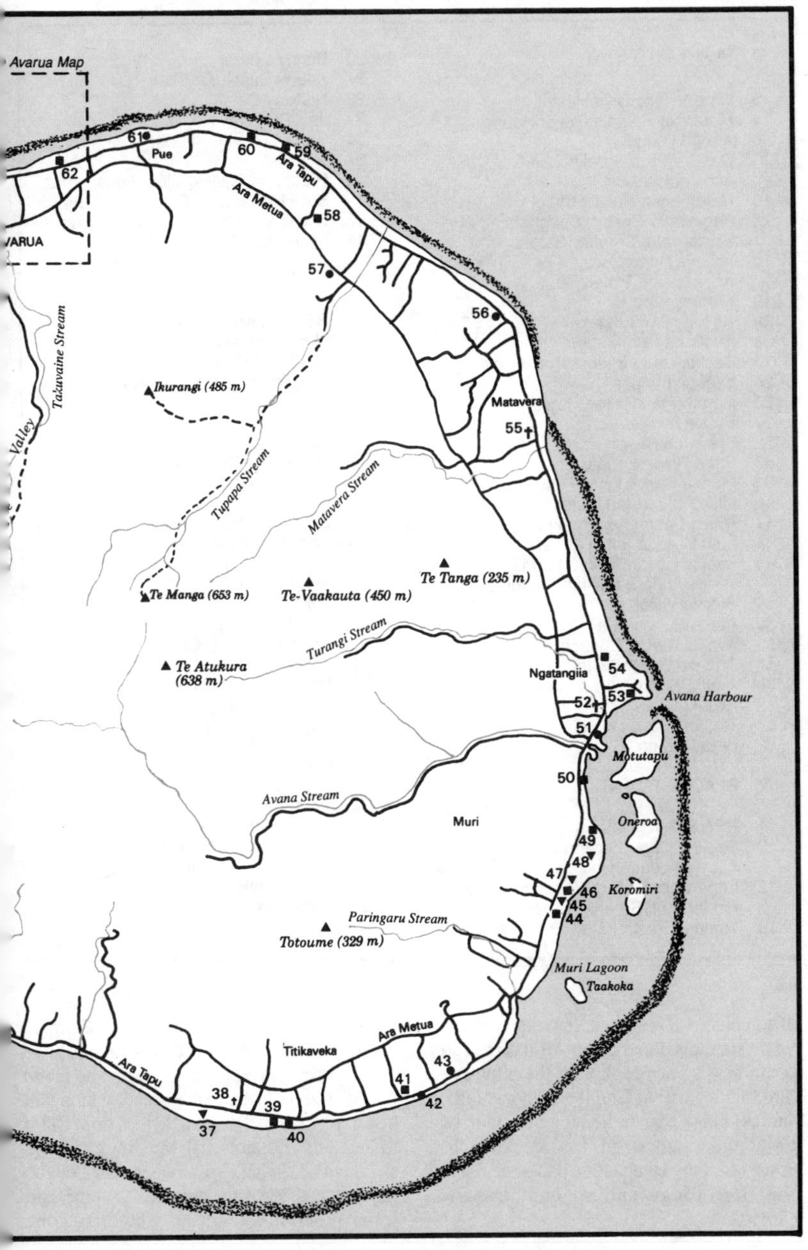
Avarua Map
VARUA
Pue
Ara Tapu
Ara Metua
Takuvaine Stream
Valley
Ikurangi (485 m)
Tupapa Stream
Matavera Stream
Matavera
Te Manga (653 m)
Te-Vaakauta (450 m)
Te Tanga (235 m)
Turangi Stream
Te Atukura
(638 m)
Ngatangiia
Avana Harbour
Motutapu
Avana Stream
Muri
Oneroa
Koromiri
Paringaru Stream
Totoume (329 m)
Muri Lagoon
Taakoka
Titikaveka
Ara Metua
Ara Tapu
37
38
39
40
41
42
43
44
45
46
47
48
49
50
51
52
53
54
55
56
57
58
59
60
61
62

■ PLACES TO STAY

3 Tiare Village Dive Hostel
4 Matareka Heights Guest House
8 Airport Lodge
9 Oasis Village Steakhouse & Accommodation
10 Rarotongan Sunset Motel
12 Edgewater Resort, Spaghetti House Restaurant, Serenity Studio
16 Manuia Beach Hotel
17 Are - Renga Motel
19 Arorangi Lodge
22 Ati's Beach Bungalow
24 Puaikura Reef Lodge
25 Backpackers International Hostel
26 Lagoon Lodges
28 Rarotongan Resort Hotel
30 Rutaki Lodge
32 Sheraton Resort
36 Palm Grove Lodge
39 Moana Sands Hotel
40 Little Polynesian Motel
41 Raina Beach Apartments
44 Muri Beachcomber Motel
46 Pacific Resort, Cook Islands Windsurfing & Sailing School
49 Sokala Villas
50 Aroko Bungalows
53 Avana Marina Condos
54 Sunrise Beach Motel
58 Ariana Bungalows & Hostel
59 Kii Kii Motel
60 Tamure Resort Hotel
62 Paradise Inn

▼ PLACES TO EAT

1 RSA & Citizens Club
9 Oasis Village Steakhouse & Accommodation
12 Edgewater Resort, Spaghetti House Restaurant, Serenity Studio
13 Tumunu Restaurant/Bar
23 Bunny's Diner
27 Kaena Restaurant
29 Halfway Cafe
33 Just Burgers
34 Liana's Restaurant/Bar
37 Jam Hut
45 Rarotonga Sailing Club, Aquasports, Sails Restaurant, Boardwalk Cafe
47 Shells & Craft, Lizzie's Takeaways
48 Flame Tree Restaurant

OTHER

1 RSA & Citizens Club
2 Airport Terminal
5 Tereora College & National Stadium
6 Air Rarotonga Hangar, Adventure Centre
7 Parliament
11 Hospital
12 Edgewater Resort, Spaghetti House Restaurant, Serenity Studio
14 Dive Rarotonga
15 Cook Island Divers
18 Cook Islands Cultural Village
20 Tinomana Palace
21 Arorangi CICC Church
31 Piri's Place
35 Wigmore's Supermarket
38 Titikaveka CICC Church
42 Beach Cargo
43 Marineland Pacific Divers
45 Rarotonga Sailing Club, Aquasports, Sails Restaurant, Boardwalk Cafe
46 Pacific Resort, Cook Islands Windsurfing & Sailing School
47 Shells & Craft, Lizzie's Takeaways
51 Vaka Village
52 Ngatangiia CICC Church
55 Matavera CICC Church
56 Perfumes of Rarotonga
57 Arai-Te-Tonga
61 Outpatient Clinic

off to convert Rarotonga, leaving two other Polynesian missionaries on Aitutaki to carry on the work. They took with them the three Rarotongans whom Goodenough had left on Aitutaki nine years earlier, together with two Rarotongan fishermen whose canoe had blown off course when they had gone fishing from Rarotonga and so had made for Aitutaki.

Despite having Rarotongan passengers on board, the island proved elusive, and after a week's futile search they gave up and made for the island of Mangaia instead, which had been charted by Captain Cook. The Mangaians did not rush out to greet the arrival of Christianity with open arms; on the day the mission ship arrived, Papeiha and some other missionaries who had gone ashore were attacked and felt lucky to have escaped with their lives, so the missionaries hastily sailed on.

Their next stop was Atiu, the main island of the group known as Nga Pu Toru ('The Three Roots') which also includes Mauke and Mitiaro. Here Williams, Papeiha and Tamatoa Ariki, an Aitutakian ariki (chief) who was also with them, convinced Rongomatane, a notorious cannibal king, to embrace Christianity. This was achieved in a remarkably short time and the neighbouring islands of Mauke and Mitiaro were converted with equally amazing rapidity due to Rongomatane's assistance. As a finale Rongomatane, who had never been to Rarotonga, gave Williams sailing directions which turned out to be spot on.

As he had been on Aitutaki, Papeiha was left on Rarotonga to convince the islanders to give up their religion and take on the new one. And, as on Aitutaki, he succeeded with thoroughness and surprising speed. Four months later additional Polynesian missionaries were landed to assist Papeiha and in little more than a year after his arrival Christianity had taken firm hold.

The first permanent London Missionary Society (LMS) missionaries were Charles Pitman and John Williams who came to Rarotonga in 1827, followed a year later by Aaron Buzacott. Between them these three men translated the entire Bible into Maori, and Buzacott also established the village of Arorangi which was to be a model for new villages on the island. The missionaries wished to gather the previously scattered population together in order to speed the propagation of Christianity.

Cannibalism may have been stamped out, but the arrival of Christianity was not all peace and light. The indigenous culture was all but destroyed and missionaries also brought epidemics of previously unknown diseases: dysentery, whooping cough, mumps and measles were just some of them. From an estimated 6000 to 7000 people on Rarotonga when Christianity arrived the population had fallen to 2800 in 1848 and in another 20 years to less than 2000.

Although the missionaries tried to exclude other Europeans from settling, more and more whalers and traders visited the island. In 1850 to 1851 more than 20 trading ships and 60 whalers paused at Rarotonga, and Buzacott's wife lamented that men of 'some wealth and little religious principle' were settling on the island. The Rarotongans had been firmly warned to beware of the French, however, who had taken over Tahiti in 1843. The dangers of Papism were a major worry for the London Missionary Society!

In 1865 the Rarotongan ariki, frightened by rumours of French expansionary intent, requested British protection for the first time. This request was turned down. In the following years the missionaries' once absolute power declined as more Europeans came to the island and trade grew. Finally in 1888 a British protectorate was formally declared over the southern islands and Rarotonga became the unofficial capital of the group.

What to do with the islands next was a subject of some controversy but eventually in 1901 they were annexed to newly independent New Zealand and the close relationship between the two countries, that continues to this day, was established.

GEOLOGY & GEOGRAPHY

Rarotonga is the only high volcanic island on the Tahiti model in the Cook Islands. The inland area is mountainous with steep valleys, razorback ridges and swift-flowing streams. Most of this area is covered with dense jungle. Rarotonga is the youngest of the Cook Islands: the volcanic activity which thrust it above sea level occurred more recently than on any of the other islands. The major mountains of the island are the remains of the outer rim of the cone. The cone is open on the north side and Maungatea rises in the very centre.

The narrow coastal plain with its swampy area close to the hills is somewhat akin to the raised, outer coral fringe, or makatea, of several other islands in the southern group, though on Rarotonga the coastal plain is fertile, sandy loam rather than the jagged razor-sharp coral of true makatea. On Rarotonga the plains are far more fertile than on islands like Mitiaro, Mauke, Atiu or Mangaia.

The lagoon within Rarotonga's outer reef is narrow around most of the island but it widens out around the south side where the beaches are also best. Muri Lagoon, fringed by four motu, or small islands – three sand cays and one volcanic islet – is the widest part of the lagoon, although even here it is very shallow in most places. There are few natural passages through the reef and the main harbour at Avatiu has been artificially enlarged. Yachts also anchor at Avarua and at Avana Harbour.

ORIENTATION

Finding your way around Rarotonga is admirably easy – there's a coastal road around the edge (the Ara Tapu), another road about 500 metres inland (the Ara Metua) going most of the way around the island, and a lot of mountains in the middle. Basically it's that simple. A number of roads connect the Ara Tapu to the Ara Metua and there are a few roads leading into inland valleys. If you want to get all the way into the middle, or cross the island from one side to the other, you have to do it on foot.

INFORMATION

Tourist Office

The Cook Islands Tourist Authority (☎ 29-435, fax 21-435) has an office on the main road, right in the middle of Avarua. They have the usual sort of tourist office information and can help you with everything from accommodation, Rarotonga nightspots and 'island nights', to inter-island shipping services and flights. They also hand out free copies of *What's On in the Cook Islands*, an excellent annually produced information-and-adverts booklet guide to Rarotonga and Aitutaki, and *Jason's*, a fold-out advertisement sheet with good maps of both islands. The office is open Monday to Friday from 8 am to 4 pm.

Money

The two principal banks on Rarotonga, Westpac and ANZ, both have offices in Avarua. The Westpac office is easy to spot on the main road, beside the Foodland supermarket; the ANZ office is tucked away in the rear of the big white three-storey building between Foodland and the police station. Both banks are open weekdays from 9 am to 3 pm and you can change travellers' cheques and major currencies in cash at either one. They also give cash advances on the Visa, MasterCard and Bankcard credit cards.

Travellers' cheques and major currencies in cash can also be changed at some of the larger hotels, but you'll get a better rate of exchange at the bank. Most of the larger stores, hotels, rental car companies etc accept Visa, MasterCard and Bankcard.

Post & Telecommunications

The central post office is just inland from the traffic circle in central Avarua. It's open from 8 am to 4 pm on weekdays, closed on weekends. Poste Restante is handled here; they will receive and hold mail for you for 30 days. It should be addressed to 'Your Name, c/o Poste Restante, Avarua, Rarotonga, Cook Islands.

The post office also has branches in Arorangi and Titikaveka, plus several postal 'depots' at small shops around the island where you can buy stamps, and post and receive letters.

International and inter-island telephone, telegram, telex and fax services are handled at the Telecom office on Tutakimoa Rd in Avarua, a couple of blocks inland from Cook's Corner. You can make an international collect phone call from any phone on the island, but if you want to pay for the call yourself, you must either find someone who will allow you to do it on their telephone or come in and place it here. You can also receive faxes here. The Telecom office is open 24 hours, seven days a week.

A card-operated public telephone is outside the central post office in Avarua. Phone cards, costing NZ$10 or NZ$20, can be purchased at the post office or at Telecom. Local, inter-island and international phone calls can all be made on the card phone. Another card phone is on the grassy strip separating the lanes of the coast road opposite the police station in central Avarua.

Foreign Representatives

New Zealand and France both have representatives in Avarua. See the Visas & Embassies section of the Facts for the Visitor chapter for details.

Travel Agencies

Rarotonga travel agencies include:

Hugh Henry & Associates
Betela (☎ 25-320, fax 25-420, PO Box 440)
Island Hopper Vacations
Avarua (☎ 22-026, fax 22-036, PO Box 240)
Matina Travel
Avarua (☎ 21-780, fax 24-780, PO Box 54)
Stars Travel
Avarua (☎ 23-669, 23-683, fax 21-569, PO Box 75)

Bookshops

The largest selection of books about the Cook Islands – history, literature, legends, poetry, arts & crafts, politics, culture etc – are found at three places in Avarua: the University of the South Pacific (USP) centre, the Cook Islands Library & Museum Society opposite USP, and at the Cook Islands Trading Company (CITC) department store in the centre of Avarua. The USP centre sells the complete selection of books published by USP at prices lower than anywhere else. CITC has a wide selection of other general-interest paperback books as well, including children's books.

The Bounty Bookshop in the large white three-storey building between Foodland and the police station has a selection of foreign magazines, plus the *New Zealand Herald* newspaper and the *Cook Islands News*. They also have a small selection of books, including books on the Cook Islands and other Pacific destinations. Island Crafts, next to the Westpac bank, and Pacific Supplies, on the main road in Avarua heading out towards the airport, also have books about the Cook Islands.

You can have access to all the books at the Cook Islands Library & Museum Society, including the Pacific Collection, by simply signing up for a Temporary Borrower's Card. The National Library also allows visitors to borrow books. At both you pay a refundable deposit and a small library fee.

Maps

The Survey Department produces topographical maps of the Cook Islands, with excellent maps of Rarotonga, Aitutaki and most of the other islands. The 1:25,000 Rarotonga map shows all the roads, a number of walking trails, the reefs and the villages, with a separate enlargement of Avarua. The Survey Department maps are available for about NZ$7 at many shops in Avarua – check at CITC, Bounty Bookshop, Island Crafts, Pacific Supplies, and even at some of the rental car companies and travel agents. Or you can buy them at the Survey Department office (☎ 29-434, fax 27-433), which is situated beside the airport at this writing but is scheduled to be shifting to the main road near the golf course in Arorangi sometime soon.

The Tourist Authority office in Avarua has the Survey Department map plus a couple of free publications containing good maps: *Jason's* has a large fold-out map of Rarotonga and Aitutaki, and the *What's On* booklet also contains maps. *Rarotonga's Mountain Tracks and Plants* by Gerald McCormack & Judith Künzle contains detailed maps for a number of walking tracks.

Police

The National Police Headquarters (☎ 22-449) is on the main road in the centre of Avarua. Come here to obtain your Cook Islands driver's licence and for other police matters.

Medical Services

Rarotonga's hospital (☎ 22-664) is on a hill up behind the golf course, west of the airport. A sign on the main road marks the turn-off. There's also an Outpatient Clinic (☎ 20-065) on the main road at Tupapa, about one km east of Avarua. You can go to either one.

Emergency
Emergency phone numbers are:

Police ☎ 999
Ambulance & Hospital ☎ 998
Fire ☎ 996

Photography
Film sales and one-hour colour print services are available at the CITC Pharmacy (☎ 29-292) and at Cliff's Photo Service (☎ 20-555), both in Avarua. Cliff's also develops colour slides and does other specialised work including photography for weddings and special occasions.

Laundry
Snowbird Laundromat (☎ 21-952), behind the Empire Theatre building in Avarua, has a few washers and dryers. Prices are NZ$3.50 per washload, including soap and softener, NZ$4.50 for every 10 minutes to dry. If you want to just drop it off and pick it up later, wash-dry-fold is NZ$9/17/24 for one/two/three loads. It's open weekdays from 8 am to 5 pm, Saturday until 3 pm.

There's another Snowbird Laundromat in Arorangi village (☎ 20-952) with the same prices and opening hours; the sign is easy to spot on the main road.

Health & Fitness Centre
The Top Shape Health & Fitness Centre (☎ 21-254) has three aerobics classes each weekday (both high and low impact), a weights room, a massage clinic and a hairdresser. It's open weekdays from 6.30 am to 8.30 pm, Saturday from 8 am to noon, closed Sunday. Visitors are welcome.

AVARUA
Avarua, the capital of the Cook Islands and Rarotonga's main town, lies in the middle of the north coast stretch, a couple of km to the east of the airport. Until quite recently it was just a sleepy little port, very much the image of a south seas trading centre. The town had quite a facelift, though, to spruce it up for the international Maire Nui festival in October '92. Two new lanes were added to the road along the waterfront and many of the buildings were remodelled. Other buildings were built, including the National Auditorium, National Museum and National Library. More and more businesses are opening in the town and though it's still just a small town, there seems to be more activity than just a few years ago.

Avarua doesn't demand a lot of your time but it does have all the basic services (post office, banks, supermarket and other shops, restaurants etc) and some interesting places to visit. If you're looking for nightlife, Avarua is probably where you'll find it.

For places to stay and eat in Avarua, see those sections further on in this chapter.

Orientation
Finding your way around Avarua is no problem; there's only one main road, the Ara Maire Nui, and it's right along the waterfront with a grassy strip down the middle with plenty of shady trees.

The most obvious landmark you can use to orient yourself in town is the traffic circle, which is on the main road near the Takuvaine Stream and the Avarua Harbour entrance. People often give directions in relation to the traffic circle.

If you're standing at the traffic circle, on the east side of it you'll see a group of seven tall coconut trees, arranged in a circle. This is called the 'Seven-in-One Coconut Tree'. Look inland and you'll see the post office on the right side of the road; the Philatelic Bureau and the New Zealand High Commission are in the two-storey building beside the post office. Heading inland down this road past the post office brings you to the turn-off for Rarotonga Breweries and, farther on, to the road heading up the Takuvaine Valley.

A number of interesting sights are in the couple of blocks to the east of the traffic circle. They include the Para O Tane Palace, the Beachcomber Gallery, inland from the gallery the Avarua CICC church with its distinctive surrounding graveyard, and just inland from the church, the University of the South Pacific (USP) centre and opposite it the Cook Islands Library & Museum

Society. From this corner where the University and the Library & Museum Society face each other, one block inland is the Takamoa Theological College and one block to the east is the Sir Geoffrey Henry National Culture Centre, where the National Auditorium, the National Library and the National Museum are found.

The main commerical centre of town is in the blocks just west of the traffic circle. The Banana Court Bar which you can see from the traffic circle, with the Blue Note Cafe on the verandah, is a long-time Rarotongan institution. Next door, just past the little Pearl Hut and Perfumes of Rarotonga shacks, is the Tourist Authority visitor information office, with an 'i' sign hanging out front on the footpath. The large CICC department store is on the corner, there's a petrol station on the opposite corner, and just a few doors inland from this corner is Cook's Corner Arcade, with the town's bus stop out front. Keep heading inland down this road if you want to reach the Telecom office or the Perfume Factory.

Heading west from this corner is the main commercial strip of Avarua, with the police station, the banks, supermarket, shops, cafes, travel agencies and so on. A couple of long blocks down, on the seaward side of the road, is the Punanga Nui open-air market with fruit and vegetable stalls, arts & crafts and clothing stalls, takeaway food caravans and the Women's Development Craft Centre. Just past this is Avatiu Harbour, where the inter-island passenger freighter ships are based. The airport is a few km farther west.

Seven-in-One Coconut Tree

Just to the east of the traffic circle is a group of seven tall coconut trees growing in a perfect circle. Tradition has it that they are really all one tree! Supposedly in the distant past an amazing coconut with seven sprouts was found on the island of Takutea, near Atiu, and brought here to be planted. The locals swear it is true, and the tree has become a famous landmark.

Papa Tangaroa Kainuku, oral historian of Rarotonga and *tumu korero* (speaker) of Kainuku Ariki, told us a different story about the trees, however. Apparently his grandfather, Frederick Goodwin, brought seven coconuts (not one!) from Manihiki when he returned to Rarotonga sometime around 1900, and planted the seven trees in a circle here to commemorate the birth of his daughter, Papa Tangaroa's mother, Te Ariki Vaine Akakino Ia E Te Vaa Tangata I Taputapuatea, who was born on 6 November 1898 while Goodwin was away in Manihiki. The circle of trees marked the boundary between Kaviri on the east, belonging to Makea Nui Ariki, and Tura'i on the west, belonging to Karika Ariki.

Philatelic Bureau

Cook Islands stamps, coins and bank notes are all international collector's items. The Cook Islands Philatelic Bureau, next door to the post office just inland from the traffic circle, sells uncirculated mint and proof sets of coins and bank notes, plus collector editions of Cook Islands stamps. It's open weekdays from 8 am to 4 pm.

Rarotonga Breweries

Rarotonga Breweries, founded in 1987, produces the Cook Islands' own beer – Cook's Lager. Free half-hour brewery tours operate Monday to Friday at 2 pm, followed by a free glass of the amber liquid. To get to the brewery, take the road heading inland from the traffic circle past the post office, take the first right turn where you see the sign and continue around to the large two-storey warehouse-style building.

Para O Tane Palace

Half a block east of the traffic circle on the inland side is the Para O Tane Palace and Taputapuatea, the palace area of Makea Takau. She was the ariki, or chief, of this district in 1888 when the London Missionary Society withdrew to the sidelines and the British Government officially took control of the Cook Islands (or at least the southern group), forestalling any possibility of a French takeover from Tahiti. The palace, once a grand edifice, was destroyed in the

■ PLACES TO STAY

35 Paradise Inn

▼ PLACES TO EAT

7 Punanga Nui Open-Air Market
10 Ronnie's Restaurant/Bar, Reefcomber Cabaret
18 Foodland Supermarket, Mama's Cafe, Island Hopper Vacations
22 Cook's Corner Arcade
25 Banana Court Bar, Blue Note Cafe
27 Breez'n Cafe
28 Trader Jack's Restaurant/Bar
30 Metua's Cafe, Browne's Arcade
32 Top Shape Health & Fitness Centre, Staircase Restaurant/Bar
34 Priscilla's Restaurant
37 Portofino Restaurant
42 Uncle Rima's Takeaways

OTHER

1 Cook Islands Liquor Supplies
2 CITC Wholesale Supermarket & Hardware Store
3 Tere's Bar
4 *Avatapu* Office
5 Waterfront Commission, *Marthalina* Office
6 Cliff's Photos
7 Punanga Nui Open-Air Market
8 Women's Handcraft Centre
9 June's Boutique, June's Pearls, South Seas International, Pacific Supplies
10 Ronnie's Restaurant/Bar, Reefcomber Cabaret
11 Budget Rent-A-Car
12 Meatco Supermarket
13 JPI Department Store
14 The Dive Shop
15 Linmar's Department Store
16 Island Crafts
17 Westpac Bank
18 Foodland Supermarket, Mama's Cafe, Island Hopper Vacations
19 ANZ Bank, Bounty Bookshop, Stars Travel
20 Police Station
21 Petrol Station
22 Cook's Corner Arcade
23 CITC Department Store, Pharmacy & Duty Free
24 Tourist Authority Office, Avis Rent-A-Car, The Galerie
25 Banana Court Bar, Blue Note Cafe
26 Post Office, Philatelic Bureau, New Zealand High Commission
29 T-Shirt Factory
30 Metua's Cafe, Browne's Arcade
31 TJ's Nightclub
32 Top Shape Health & Fitness Centre, Staircase Restaurant/Bar
33 Beachcomber Gallery
36 Empire Theatre
38 Are Tiki Shop
39 Snowbird Laundromat
40 Rarotonga Bowling Club
41 Prime Minister's Office
43 Para O Tane Palace
44 Avarua CICC Church
45 National Museum
46 Rarotonga Breweries
47 Cook Islands Library & Museum Society
48 University of the South Pacific (USP) Centre
49 National Auditorium
50 National Library
51 The Perfume Factory
52 Telecom
53 Takamoa Theological College

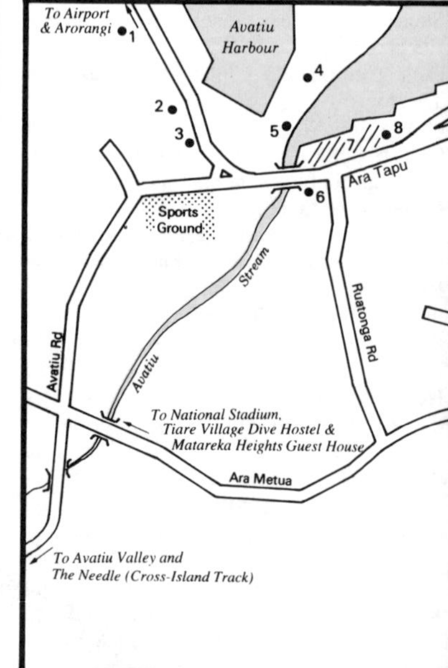

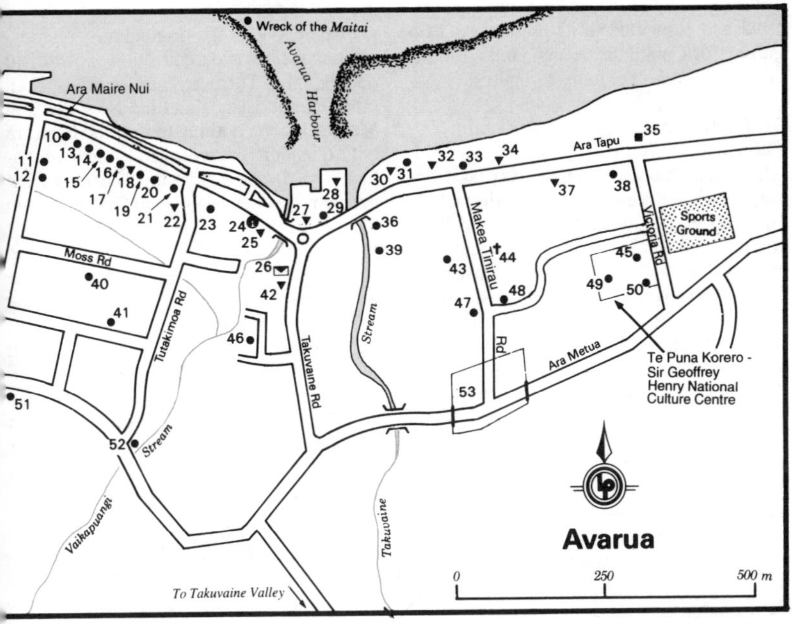

hurricane of 1942 and remained a ruin for many years. It was restored in the early '90s and renamed the Para O Tane Palace, though its original name was Beritani (Rarotongan for 'Brittania'). It is the residence of Makea Takau's descendent, Makea Nui Teremoana Ariki, and is not open to the public.

This whole area where the church and palace were built was once the location of the largest and most sacred marae (religious meeting ground) on Rarotonga. The missionaries wanted to take over and replace the old religion, however, and so they destroyed the old marae; today nothing remains of it.

Beachcomber Gallery

One long block east of the traffic circle on the sea side of the main road, facing the CICC church, the Beachcomber Gallery occupies a building constructed in 1845 by the London Missionary Society for their Sunday school. The building, which had been worn down to a ruin, was restored in

Makea Takau, *Ariki* of Avarua District at Time of Annexation

1992 and converted to its present use as a gallery for Cook Islands arts, crafts, jewellery, pearls and other items of interest.

CICC Church

The CICC church in Avarua is a fine, old, white painted building made of coral, from very much the same mould as other CICC churches in the Cooks. It was built in 1853 when Aaron Buzacott was the resident missionary. The interesting graveyard around the church is worth a leisurely browse. At the front you'll find a monument to the pioneering Polynesian 'teacher' Papeiha. Just to the left (as you face the church) is the grave of Albert Henry, the first Prime Minister of the independent Cook Islands – you can't miss it, it's the one with a life-size bronze bust wearing a pair of spectacles! Other well-known people buried here include author Robert Dean Frisbie.

You're welcome to attend services; the main service of the week, as at all five of Rarotonga's CICCs, is Sunday at 10 am. See the Religion section in the Facts about the Country chapter for advice about the customs of attending a CICC church.

Library & Museum Society

Inland behind the Para O Tane Palace, the small Cook Islands Library & Museum Society with its friendly staff has a collection of rare books and literature on the Pacific locked away which, if you enquire, you may be able to inspect and read – but only on the premises. There's also an extensive Pacific Collection, as well as other general interest books, all of which can be checked out. You can get borrowing privileges even if you're only visiting the island: visitors staying up to three months can get a library card for NZ$10 a month plus a NZ$25 deposit which is refunded when you go. If you stay for over three months the cost is just NZ$15 for a year's membership.

The small museum has an interesting collection of ancient and modern artefacts – basketry, weaving, musical instruments, wooden statues of various old gods, adzes, shells and shell fishhooks, spears, tools and other historical items, a beautiful old outrigger canoe, one of the original missionaries' printing presses and a collection of historical photographs. There are also exhibits from other Pacific islands and the New Zealand Maoris. It costs nothing to visit the museum but a donation is appreciated – make a donation, it's a fine little museum! The library and museum are open Monday to Saturday from 9 am to 1 pm.

If you're going to Atiu, check out the large tumunu pots here in the museum. You can read more about tumunu ceremonies in the Atiu chapter, and attend a modern tumunu if you visit that island. But the only place you'll see a real tumunu pot is right here.

And no, the large iron pot on the verandah wasn't used in cannibal rites – it's an old whaling pot, used for boiling down blubber to make whale oil. When people were eaten in the Cooks, they were baked in ovens!

University of the South Pacific (USP)

The University of the South Pacific (USP), based in Suva, Fiji, has its Cook Islands Centre in the building opposite the library. The centre was established on Rarotonga in 1975 and moved into this building a few years later. Most classes are taught externally from the main campus. A wide selection of books on the Cook Islands and other parts of the Pacific, published by the university, are on sale in the office. If you're planning a lengthy stay in the Cooks, you might want to ask here about classes for learning the Cook Islands Maori language.

Takamoa Theological College

Just inland from the Library & Museum Society and USP is the Takamoa Theological College, built in 1842. One of the earliest mission compounds on the island, it is in its original condition and still in use. It was established to train locals for the ministry and from here missionaries were sent out to many parts of the Pacific. Today it still educates CICC ministers for work in all of the Cook Islands; those wishing to do international missionary work must study further in New Zealand.

Wreck of the *Yankee*

On 24 July 1964 the brig *Yankee* broke her mooring line in a gale and ran onto the reef at the eastern end of Avarua. The *Yankee* was a much-recorded vessel; not only did she lay on the reef just off Avarua in various stages of disintegration for almost 30 years, becoming something of a local legend, but during her heyday she was once operated by the *National Geographic* magazine, appearing in numerous articles in the 1950s.

The *Yankee* had a long and interesting history before her ignominious end. The 30 metre (97 foot), 117 ton, steel-hulled vessel was built in 1912 in Germany but was taken by the British as a war prize after WW I. She served as the North Sea pilot vessel *Duhnen* until she was bought by Irving and Electra Johnson in 1946. Overhauled and re-rigged as a brigantine in Devonshire, she carried 723 sq metres (7775 sq feet) of sail when fully rigged and circled the world no less than seven times before finally being sold to Miami-based Windjammer Cruises in 1957. Earlier that year she had visited the Cooks with the Johnsons and she returned with her new owners in 1961.

On her third visit in 1964 she was in sorry condition and, say the pundits, her crew was too busy partying on with some Rarotongan bar-girls that had come on board to handle a sudden storm when it blew up in the middle of the night, blowing the vessel onto the reef. At that time there was no regular air service to the Cook Islands and it took a long time to ship her irate American passengers out.

When Tony Wheeler wrote the first edition of this book in 1986, the wreck of the *Yankee*, though quite rusty, was still largely intact, out on the fringe of the reef roughly behind where Metua's Restaurant is today. When Nancy Keller came to update the book in 1988, Hurricane Sally and various other storms in the meantime had ravaged the shipwreck, stripping it down to a rusty skeleton and pushing it all the way up onto the beach, between where the Beachcomber shop and Priscilla's Restaurant are today. Returning in 1993 she discovered the wreck was completely gone, having been removed in the effort to spruce up Avarua for the Maire Nui festival in October '92. ■

National Culture Centre

One block inland from the Paradise Inn is the large new Sir Geoffrey Henry National Culture Centre. Conceived by Prime Minister Sir Geoffrey Henry, the complex was formally opened on 14 October 1992. The centre is home to the National Auditorium, the National Museum, the National Library, the Conservatory & National Archives and the Ministry of Cultural Development.

The National Auditorium is the venue for large-scale concerts and other events.

The National Museum is a small museum with a selection of Cook Islands and South Pacific artefacts. It's open Monday to Friday from 9 am to 3 pm; admission is free, with donations appreciated.

The small National Library is open weekdays from 9 am to 4 pm, later (until 8 pm) on Monday and Wednesday. Visitors can get borrowing privileges by paying a NZ$50 refundable bond plus a monthly NZ$2 library fee.

Wreck of the *Maitai*

West of the traffic circle and directly offshore from the centre of Avarua is the wreck of the SS *Maitai*, a 3393-ton Union Steam Ship vessel which used to trade between the Cook Islands and Tahiti. She ran onto the reef, fortunately without loss of life, on 24 December 1916. Her cargo included a number of Model T Fords. All that remains today is her rusted boiler, just off the edge of the fringing reef. In the '50s a couple of enterprising New Zealanders brought up one of the ship's bronze propellers.

The Galerie

Artist Jillian Sobieska operates The Galerie on the main road in the centre of Avarua. You can find her here painting island scenes, flowers and portraits Monday to Friday from 9 am to 2 pm, Saturdays from 10 am to noon.

The Perfume Factory

The Perfume Factory is easy to spot on the Ara Metua road just behind town, heading west. Here you can buy perfumes, colognes and pure coconut oil, all scented with local flowers, including frangipani, starfruit, gardenia and jasmine. Handmade coconut oil soap, lotions, shampoos, and many imported French and other perfumes are also available. You can also taste and buy some locally produced liqueurs, including Passionfruit-Ara, Coffee-Ara and Coffee-Coconut-Ara. The Perfume Factory has been enormously successful since its opening in 1981 and it now exports its products. It's open from 8 am to 4.30 pm Monday to Saturday, closed Sunday.

Punanga Nui Outdoor Market

On the main road and beside the waterfront near Avatiu Harbour, Punanga Nui is an outdoor market with a collection of stalls selling fresh fruits and vegetables, clothing, handicrafts and takeaway foods.

Avatiu Harbour

This small harbour on the west end of Avarua is Rarotonga's principal harbour. An international freighter or two, the two inter-island passenger freighters serving the Cooks, a collection of fishing boats and yachts and the occasional visiting ship of one kind or another are all often seen here.

AROUND THE ISLAND

Most island attractions are on or near the coastal road that encircles Rarotonga. The coast road, the Ara Tapu ('Sacred Road') is a wide, well-surfaced route, paralleled by a second road, the Ara Metua ('Ancient Road') which is slightly inland.

This second road, the Ara Metua – called 'the back road' by locals – follows the path of an ancient road originally built of coral blocks around 1050 AD. Historically it was known as Te Ara Nui O Toi ('The Great Road of Toi'), although who, exactly, Toi was has been lost in history. None of the old road remains in an original state; most of it was surfaced or built over during WW II and a road improvement campaign in the early 1990s took care of the rest.

Prior to the arrival of missionaries the Rarotongans lived inland near the plantations and gardens they tended. The missionaries moved them down to the coast and concentrated them in villages centred around churches to make them easier to control. If you hire a vehicle or take a circle island tour and go around the island on the Ara Metua, you'll see another side to the island – swamp taro fields, white goats and black pigs grazing in pawpaw patches, citrus groves, men on ancient tractors or even digging out entire fields with shovels, and graves of the ancestors off to one side of the houses.

The following description moves around the island anti-clockwise, starting from Avarua; km distances from the centre of Avarua are indicated.

Airport (2.5 km)

The Rarotonga International Airport was officially opened in 1974 and tourism in the Cooks really started at that time.

Behind the airport is the National Stadium, where many of Rarotonga's big sporting events are held. The first international stadium to be built in the Cook Islands, it was constructed in 1985 for the South Pacific Mini Games. Beside it is Tereora College.

Cemetery (2.5 km)

Opposite the airport terminal is a small graveyard known locally as the 'brickyard'. A controversial Australian cancer-cure specialist Milan Brych (pronounced 'brick') set himself up on Rarotonga after being chucked out of Australia. When his patron, Cook Islands Prime Minister Sir Albert Henry, was run out of office in 1978, Brych was soon run out of the country as well. Cancer patients who died despite his treatment are buried in the graveyard.

Tom Neale, the hermit of Suwarrow atoll, is also buried opposite the airport. He died in 1977 and his grave is in the front corner of the Retired Servicemen's Association (RSA) cemetery. You can enter through the gates

Top: Park on the east side of Rarotonga (TC)
iddle: Muri Beach, Rarotonga (TC)
ttom: Sunset at Arorangi, Rarotonga (TW)

Top: Tie-dying with breadfruit leaves (NK)
Left: Coconut palm tree (TC)
Right: Lagoon, southern coastline, Rarotonga (NK)

with the 'Lest We Forget' sign to see his grave.

Parliament (3.5 km)
The Cook Islands Parliament is opposite the Air Rarotonga terminal. The building was erected in 1973 to '74 as a hostel for the New Zealand workers that came to work on the construction of the airport. The Prime Minister's and other ministers' offices are in the former bedrooms, with a few walls rearranged.

Parliament meets at various times throughout the year, according to need; it's usually in session from around August to January, but there is no fixed schedule. Stop by or ring the Parliament building (☎ 26-500) to find out when Parliament will be in session. You are welcome to watch the proceedings from the public gallery, so long as you're properly dressed; taking photos is not permitted. If you happen to wander in when Parliament is not in session, one of the staff will give you a short tour of the building.

Golf Course (5.5 km)
The Rarotonga Golf Club (☎ 27-360) welcomes visitors to play on its nine-hole course. A round (or two to make it 18 holes) costs NZ$10 for the green fee and you can hire a set of clubs for NZ$10 a half day. The golf course is open Monday to Friday from 8 am to 4 pm; Saturday is for members only and it's closed on Sunday.

Black Rock (6.5 km)
Just beyond the golf course and down on the beach is Black Rock, where Papeiha is supposed to have swum ashore, clasping the Bible over his head. Actually he was rowed ashore in a small boat! This is also the departure point from where the spirits of the dead are supposed to commence their voyage back to the legendary homeland of Avaiki. If you follow the road up behind the hospital there are good views (see the Walking & Climbing section later in this chapter).

Arorangi (8 km)
On Rarotonga's west coast, Arorangi was the first missionary-built village and was conceived of as a model village for all the others on the island. There are a number of popular places to stay and eat in Arorangi. Along the road there are numerous small shops.

The main place of interest in Arorangi is the 1849 CICC church – a large white building which still plays an important role in village life. The missionary Papeiha, the first to preach the Christian gospel on Rarotonga, is buried here, right in the centre front of the church; a huge monument to him has been raised by his many descendants.

To the left of the church is the old Tinomana Palace, built for the last local ruler by the British. The name of the palace is *Au Maru*, meaning 'the Peace brought by Christianity'.

Interestingly, Tinomana, the chief who first accepted the message of Christianity from Papeiha, is not buried in the church graveyard although he is honoured by a memorial plaque inside the church. He later became Papeiha's father-in-law when the missionary married one of his daughters and he gave the land that the church is built upon, but he is buried on the hill behind Arorangi, near his old marae. Did he have second thoughts about his adopted religion?

The Serenity Art Studio (☎ 20-238) is in Arorangi beside a brown A-frame house right on the beach, on the north side of the Edgewater Resort's tennis courts. Clare Higham, the artist who runs the studio beside her home, is now in her 70s and her watercolours and line-and-wash depictions of local Rarotongan scenes and flowers are much appreciated both on Rarotonga and in New Zealand. Prices are in the NZ$50 to NZ$100 range. You'll find this friendly artist here from April to November; the rest of the year she lives in Mt Maunganui, New Zealand.

Rising up behind Arorangi is the flat-topped peak of Raemaru. See the Walking & Climbing section later in this chapter for details of the climb to the top, and the Aitutaki chapter for the story of why the mountain is flat-topped and what happened to the rest of it!

Cultural Village (7 km)
The Cook Islands Cultural Village on Arorangi's back road is a delightful experience; you'll learn more about traditional Cook Islands culture in one day here than you probably will for the rest of your stay.

Guided tours through the village, beginning at 10 am, visit a number of traditional huts and include information and demonstrations of many aspects of Cook Islands culture, including history, Maori medicine, ancient fishing techniques, weaving, coconut husking, woodcarving, traditional firemaking and cooking, costume making and dancing. The tour is followed by a feast of traditional foods, with your tour hosts and the people from the various huts all getting together for a rousing show of traditional music, dance and chants, lasting until about 1.30 pm.

Cost for the tour is NZ$31, plus NZ$2 for transport if you need it, with discounts for children 14 and under. Ring (☎ 21-314, after hours 22-225, fax 25-557) to make bookings and to arrange transport.

In the afternoon, the Cultural Village offers a Circle Island Tour around Rarotonga (see Organised Tours under Other Activities later in this chapter). You can visit the Cultural Village and do the Circle Island Tour all in one day (NZ$45) or on two separate days (NZ$50).

South Coast (from 12 km)
The south coast of Rarotonga from the Rarotongan Hotel right round to Muri Lagoon has the best beach and the best swimming possibilities. The reef is much farther out and the sea bottom is relatively free from rocks and sandier than the other beaches. There are lots of good places to stop for a swim, particularly from around the 16 to 20 km mark. At 16.5 km you can pull off the road beside the beach and park: the beach is very fine here.

Wigmore's Waterfall (15 km)
On the eastern edge of the Sheraton Resort complex, a road leads inland to Wigmore's waterfall, a lovely little waterfall dropping into a fresh, cool, natural swimming pool. You can drive all the way up to the waterfall, though the last stretch of road is quite rugged and is probably most suitable for 4WD vehicles or sturdy motorbikes. Otherwise it makes a pleasant walk from the coast road up to the waterfall and back. If you do the Cross-Island Trek you will come to the waterfall near the end of your journey.

Titikaveka (19 km)
There's another picturesque CICC church at Titikaveka with some interesting old headstones in the graveyard. The church was built in 1841 of coral slabs, hewn by hand from the reef at Tikioki and passed to the site at Titikaveka hand-to-hand in a human chain.

Muri Lagoon (22 to 25 km)
The reef is farther out from the shore on the south side of the island. Muri Beach, on Muri Lagoon on the south-east side of the island, is a particularly beautiful stretch of beach. The shallow water has a sandy bottom dotted with countless sea cucumbers, and some coral formations making it interesting for snorkelling. Out towards the reef are four small islands, or motu: Taakoka, Koromiri, Oneroa and Motutapu. Taakoka is volcanic, the other three are sand cays.

The beach by the Pacific Resort, on the coast side of Koromiri motu, is especially

Motu Rori

Sea cucumbers are an oriental delicacy and many people around Muri find their lagoon's abundant sea cucumber *(motu rori)* population delicious. The creature's internals look rather like spaghetti and around here a reference to eating spaghetti probably means rori rather than pasta. Rori are best cooked with butter, garlic and spices but the locals are equally happy to eat them raw. It's not uncommon to see someone pick one up in the lagoon, tear the skin open, squeeze the guts out as if from a tube of toothpaste, toss the black skin away and eat the 'spaghetti' on the spot. ■

›opular and at low tide you can easily wade ›ut to Koromiri. Hermit crabs scuttle around n the forested undergrowth while offshore ›n the reef is the rusted hulk of a Japanese una fishing boat, the *Iwakuni Maru No 1*, vhich washed up onto the reef in the early 60s. You can wade out to the wreck; the hull ıas now broken.

ɫarotonga Sailing Club (23 km)
'he Rarotonga Sailing Club on Muri Beach velcomes visitors. Upstairs the *Sails* restau-ant/bar has a great view of the lagoon, as oes the *Boardwalk Cafe* downstairs. norkelling gear, Sunburst sailboats, cata-ıarans, windsurfing boards, kayaks, utrigger canoes, wave skis and so on can be ired from the Aquasports desk downstairs. Vindsurfing lessons, novice 'resort course' cuba dives in the lagoon and lagoon cruises ı a glass-bottom boat are also available. A ıiling race is held at the club every Saturday fternoon, starting at 1 pm. All the same 'ater toys, and even another glass-bottom oat, are also available for hire at the Pacific esort, just a few doors down the beach.

vana Harbour & Vaka Village (25 km)
eside Motutapu, the northernmost of the ›ur Muri Lagoon islands, is the compara-vely wide and deep reef passage into Avana arbour, also sometimes called Ngatangiia arbour since it's in the Ngatangiia district. 's a popular mooring spot for visiting ıchts and small fishing boats.

This harbour is historically significant as e departure point for the Maori canoes hich set off around 1350 AD on the great ›yage which resulted in the Maori settle-ent of New Zealand. In the grassy park ›posite the big white Ngatangiia CICC ıurch, a circle of seven stones with a histor-al plaque commemorates this event. Each the seven stones stands for one of the ınoes that completed the journey. On the ›int of land to your left as you gaze out rough the harbour passage is the large well-eserved marae where the mariners were ven their blessing for the journey and where human sacrifices were made to the gods.

Vaka Village is a collection of shelters and traditional thatch-roofed huts in a large clear-ing near the harbour, constructed for the 1992 Maire Nui festival.

Matavera (27.5 km)
The old CICC church at Matavera, also made of coral, is beautiful anytime, but especially lovely at night when the outside is all lit up. The scenery inland of the stretch of road between Matavera and Avarua is particularly fine.

Perfumes of Rarotonga (28.5 km)
Perfumes of Rarotonga, on the main road in Matavera, makes its own perfumes and colognes from local flowers, plus coconut oil soap from the local coconuts, and other craft work. Prints and paintings by Rick Welland, one of Rarotonga's foremost artists until he

Original Painting by Rick Welland

went vagabonding a couple of years ago (he was painting in Mexico, last we heard) are also displayed and sold here.

Arai-Te-Tonga (30 km)
Just before you arrive back in Avarua a small sign points off the road to the most important marae site on the island. Marae were the religious ceremonial gathering places of pre-Christian Polynesian society; the koutu, similar in appearance, were political meeting grounds where ariki, the great chiefs of pre-missionary Rarotonga, held court. Ceremonial offerings to the ancient gods were collected on the koutu before being placed upon the marae.

A small sign on the coast road marks the turn-off for Arai-Te-Tonga. A great marae is on your right as you go down the small road heading inland towards Arai-Te-Tonga. When you meet the Ara Metua there's a stone-marked koutu site in front of you; walk down the Ara Metua to your left and you'll see on your right (the inland side) yet another ceremonial ground. This whole area was a gathering place and the remains of the marae, the koutu and other meeting grounds are still here.

Arai-Te-Tonga has the remains of an oblong platform four metres long that was at one time over two metres high. At one end stands the 'investiture pillar', a square basalt column two metres high which extends an equal distance down into the ground. Don't walk on the marae; it's still a sacred site.

Inland Drives
Two inland drives on the north side of the island give you an opportunity to see the lush fertile valleys of Rarotonga, with mountains towering above on every side. Both go along streams and both are in areas historically populated by the Rarotongan people before the missionaries came.

The drive along Avatiu Stream begins at Avatiu Harbour – just turn inland at the harbour and keep going straight ahead. The road extends about 3.5 km inland; at the end of the road is the beginning of the Cross-Island Trek, which must be continued on foot past this point.

The other drive is up into the Takuvaine Valley, reached by going inland on the road past the post office in Avarua and continuing inland. It's a wonderfully peaceful place. The Happy Valley Road extends inland for about two km; a walking track continues inland and climbs up to the summit of Te Ko'u mountain.

WALKING & CLIMBING

You don't have to get very far into the interior of Rarotonga to realise the population is almost entirely concentrated along the narrow coastal fringe. The mountainous interior is virtually deserted and can be reached only by walking tracks and trails.

Rarotonga's Mountain Tracks and Plants by Gerald McCormack & Judith Künzle (Cook Islands Natural Heritage Project, 1994, paperback) is an excellent booklet if you plan to walk any of the mountain tracks. The same authors also publish a separate colour-illustrated booklet, *Rarotonga's Cross-island Walk* (Cook Islands Natural Heritage Project, 1991, paperback) about the

cross-island walk alone. We recommend their books as they give much more interesting detail about each walk, together with its geology, plants, animals and other natural features, than we have space to include here. Much of what follows is based on their detailed knowledge of the inland areas.

The Cook Islands Conservation Service publishes a leaflet titled *A Guide to Walks & Climbs* with brief details on a number of interesting walks, but don't rely on it too heavily; the leaflet was made over 20 years ago and it is quite out of date.

The valley walks are easy strolls suitable even for older people or young children and the scaling of the hill behind the hospital is also easy and short, although a bit steep. Most of the mountain walks are hard work, often involving difficult scrambling over rocky sections. Apart from the cross-island track by the Needle and the ascent of Raemaru behind Arorangi village, both of which we've included directions for here, most of the mountain walks are a cross between scaling Everest and hacking your way through the Amazon jungle.

The interior of Rarotonga is surprisingly mountainous with some steep slopes and sheer drops. It's wise to keep an eye out for these drops as you can stumble across them quite suddenly. Although the trails are often difficult to follow, Rarotonga is too small for you to get really lost. You can generally see where you're going or where you've come from. If you do get lost, the best thing to do is to walk coastward on a ridge crest. Streams often have sprawling hibiscus branches, making progress very slow.

Walking will generally be easier if you follow the ridges rather than trying to beat your way across the often heavily overgrown slopes. Rarotonga has no wild animals, snakes or poisonous insects (except for centipedes, wasps and annoying red ants) but the valleys and bushy inland areas do have plenty of very persistent mosquitoes, so be sure to bring repellent. Shorts are cool and easy for walking, but you may want to wear some sort of leg or ankle protection as you can easily get badly scratched if you lose the track and have to force your way through fern or scrub. Wear adequate walking shoes or boots, not thongs or sandals (jandals), as the trails can often be challenging. They can also be quite muddy and slippery after rain; don't underestimate the danger of this when you're on a steep incline going up or downhill. Be sure to carry plenty of drinking water with you; hiking on Rarotonga can be thirsty work.

Most important, be sure to observe the basic tramping safety rules of letting someone know where you're going and when you expect to return, and *don't go alone*. There have been numerous instances of trampers getting injured or lost in the mountains. If you slip and injure yourself, it could be a very long time before anyone would accidentally happen along to find you. Don't be paranoid, but do take sensible precautions.

Walking times quoted are for a complete trip from the nearest road access point and do not allow for getting lost – which on most trails is a distinct possibility.

Cross-Island Trek (3½ to four hours)
The trek across the island via 413-metre Te Rua Manga ('the Needle') is the most popular walk on the island. It can also be done as a shorter walk from the north end to the Needle and back again, rather than continuing all the way to the south coast. It's important that you do the walk in a north-south direction, as there are many more possibilities for taking a wrong turn if you try it from the other direction. Be sure to wear adequate shoes and to take enough drinking water with you. There are several places on this walk that get extremely slippery, and therefore dangerous, when there's been wet weather.

The road to the starting point runs south from Avatiu Harbour. If you're driving, continue on the road up the Avatiu Valley until you reach a prominent sign stating that this is the beginning of the walk and that vehicles cannot be taken past this point. After this point a private vehicle road continues for about a km.

A footpath takes off from the end of the

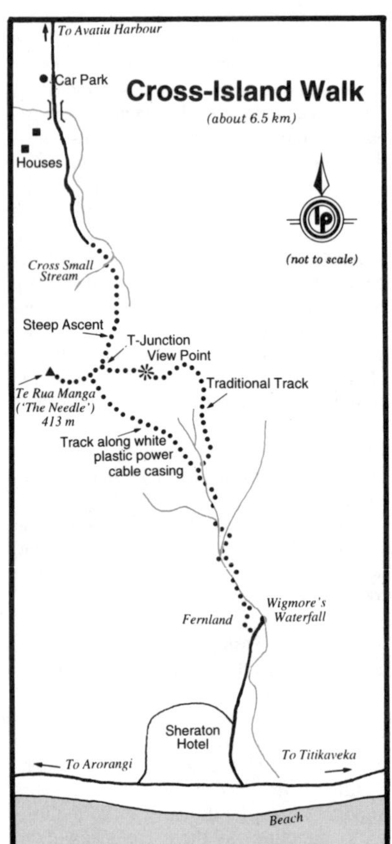

vehicle road. It is fairly level for about 10 minutes, then it drops down and crosses a small stream. Avoid following the white plastic power cable track up the valley; instead pick up the track beside the massive boulder on the ridge on your left, after the stream crossing.

From here the track climbs steeply and steadily all the way to the Needle, about a 45-minute walk. If it wasn't for the tangled stairway of tree roots the path would be very slippery in the wet (which it often is). The roots make the climb easy but also tiring. At the first sight of the Needle there's a convenient boulder right in the middle of the path, where you can rest and admire the view.

A little farther on is a very obvious T-junction. Te Rua Manga ('the Needle') is a 10-minute walk to the right; Wigmore's Waterfall is a 90-minute walk to the left. Up to now you've been ascending a ridge running in a north-south direction; at this junction it intersects with another ridge, running in an east-west direction. This is an important junction and you will return to it after you visit the Needle.

Actually climbing the Needle is strictly for very serious rock climbers – it's high and sheer. You can, however, scramble round the north side to a sheer drop and a breathtaking view from its north-western corner. From here you can look back down the valley you've ascended or look across north-west to the flat peak of Raemaru. You can also see the south coast from the Needle and there are fine views across to Maungatea and Te Ko'u to the east. Take care on this climb though, the ledge is very narrow and there's a long and unprotected drop which would be fatal if you slipped. Do *not* try to climb round to the southern side of the Needle, as there is no view from that side and it's extremely dangerous.

Retrace your steps back to the T-junction from where the left fork takes off heading east. Just before you reach the T-junction you'll come to a path leading off to the right (south), following a white plastic electric cable casing which was put there around 1990. Some guides take this way, as the traditional track is slightly more difficult. If you take this way, however, you will miss the most spectacular view of the Needle on the entire track, visible from the peak just east of the T-junction.

From the T-junction, the traditional track drops slightly, then climbs to a small peak that gives you the best view of the Needle you're going to find. From here the track leads down a long, slippery ridge for about half an hour's walking time. Despite the helpful tree roots, this long descent can be annoyingly slippery, and positively treacherous in wet weather.

After about 30 minutes the track meets the Papua Stream and follows it down the hill, zigzagging back and forth across the stream several times. After about 45 minutes of following the stream, the track emerges into fernland. Here the track veers away from the stream to the right, passing clearly through the fernland. Be sure to stick to the main track; there are several places where newer, minor tracks seem to take off towards the stream but don't take these, as they will bring you out at dangerous spots upstream from the waterfall. After about 15 minutes the main track turns back towards the stream, bringing you to the bottom of the beautiful Wigmore's Waterfall. If you're hot, sweaty and muddy by this time, the pool under the fall is a real delight.

A rough dirt road comes from the south coast up to Wigmore's Waterfall. Walking down this road brings you to the coast road in about 15 minutes, passing alongside the eastern edge of the large Sheraton Resort complex.

The public bus will drop you at Avatiu Harbour, from where you can begin the walk inland, and you can flag the bus down when you reach the coast road again at the end of the track. Note, however, that on Saturday the last daytime bus departs from Avarua at 1 pm, and there are no more buses until the night bus schedule starts at 6 pm. There is no public bus on Sunday. If you come on an organised trek across the island, hotel transfers are provided at both ends; see Organised Walks, further on in this section.

Raemaru (two to 2½ hours)

Raemaru (365 metres) is the flat-topped peak rising directly behind Arorangi village on Rarotonga's west coast. From the coast road you can easily see the route to the top running up the northern ridge line, before it crosses to the southern ridge to approach the rock face on the south-west side of the summit, which you ascend to reach the summit. See the Aitutaki chapter for the legend explaining why this mountain, unlike all the other mountains on Rarotonga, is flat-topped.

Turn off the coast road onto Akaoa Road, about 200 metres south of the Arorangi Cook Islands Christian Church, and then turn right (south) onto the Ara Metua. Immediately there is a small road on the left; park on the Ara Metua and walk up this small road,

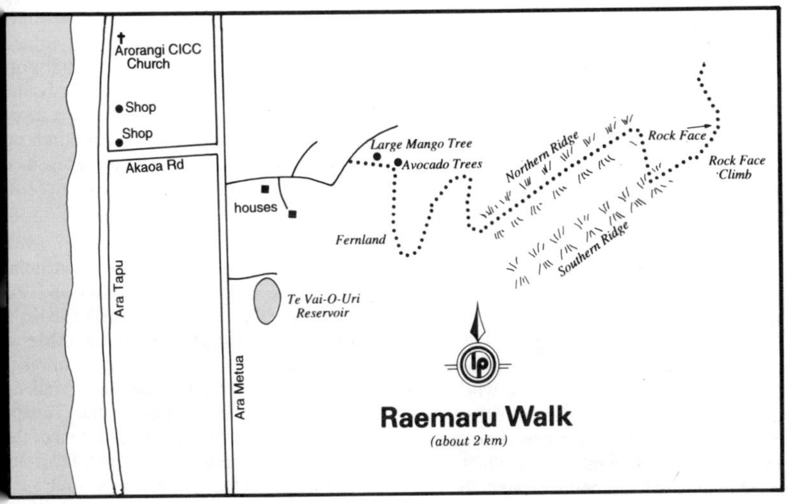

passing the gate leading to the house on the hill to your right, veering to the right and then following the road as it makes a sharp left turn.

About 50 metres past this turn, find the walking track leading off to the right. You will pass a large mango tree on your left, then walk uphill through a grove of avocado trees. The track then veers off to the right, into fernland, and doubles back and forth across the hill a couple of times as it heads uphill. The clay is very slippery when wet – be careful.

Before long the track meets the ridge and proceeds uphill very clearly along the spine of the ridge. Be careful, as the steeper sections can be slippery even in dry weather; they are positively hazardous when wet.

At the top of the ridge the track veers to the right (south) and crosses over to the southern ridge, then turns left and follows this ridge uphill to the rock face. The place where you scale the rock face is about 15 metres high. Safety ladders are planned for the rock face at around the time of this book's publication, making it easy to climb, but you must still be careful on the ascent.

Finally you emerge onto an open grassy area which slopes gently to the top. From the far end you can look down across a valley to Maungaroa (509 metres) and Te Rua Manga (413 metres), the easily recognised peak known as 'the Needle'. Looking back you can see along the coast all the way from south of Arorangi to the airport runway in the north.

Other Mountain Tracks

There are several other good mountain tracks on Rarotonga. We've given instructions for only the easier ones here; look for the *Rarotonga's Mountain Tracks and Plants* book mentioned earlier if you want to do some real mountain trekking.

The Cook Islands Natural Heritage Project, publisher of the book, is working in concert with the Cook Islands Conservation Service to upgrade and maintain Rarotonga's inland tracks. Several tracks which were once overgrown are being cleared and consistently maintained, so you can now actually find them. A few signs are also being posted, to clarify the tracks. Particularly difficult spots – going up vertical rock faces, for example – are being made safer with the help of ladders or ropes, as there's not much point in having a steady stream of hikers injured in the same predictable places on the tracks.

Good mountain tracks on Rarotonga include:

Maungatea Bluff Maungatea (523 metres) is the peak behind that impressively sheer cliff face directly overlooking Avarua. The climb brings you to the top of the 340-metre bluff at the top of the cliff face, not to the top of the mountain itself, which is very difficult to reach and affords no great view once you get there. The bluff, on the other hand, offers a great view over Avarua and the north coast. The track is muddy and extremely slippery when wet. The track begins from the Ara Metua (the inland road) behind Avarua, beside the Tauvae Store. The return walk takes three to four hours.

Te Ko'u Te Ko'u (588 metres) is more or less in the centre of the island and is interesting because there is a volcanic crater at the top which you can traverse. The walk offers spectacular views of Rarotonga's inland mountains and of the south coast. It starts off with an easy one-hour walk up the Takuvaine Valley behind Avarua, followed by a more challenging 1½ hour long, steep climb up the mountain which is treacherous when wet. The return walk takes about five hours.

Ikurangi The ascent of Ikurangi (485 metres) is a vigorous walk to a spectacular view of the north coast, Avarua and the Takuvaine Valley. It's easier than the Te Ko'u walk. The track starts from the Ara Metua just to the east of Arai-Te-Tonga and takes about four hours return – a half-hour walk up the Tupapa Valley following the Tupapa Stream, followed by a 1½ hour ascent of the mountain. A couple of small rock faces are encountered on the way to the summit.

Te Manga Rarotonga's highest mountain Te Manga (653 metres) is probably the most difficult climb on the island – the long, strenuous climb has several sections which are difficult and very steep. Starting at the same place as the Ikurangi walk, the return walk to Te Manga takes about six hours, with a one-hour walk up the valley following the Tupapa Stream followed by a two-hour ascent up the mountain.

Hospital Hill

About the easiest way to climb up to a good viewpoint is to drive up the hill to the hospital, just behind the golf course, park in the parking lot there and continue up the hill on foot. It's an easy walk which even children and elderly people can do without a struggle. For those in good shape, the walk to the top takes about five minutes. The view from the top is beautiful and unobstructed, with the airport on one side, a lush agricultural valley stretching inland from there between mountain ridges and, on the other side, the village of Arorangi, pushing from the coast up to the sides of the mountains. The different colours of water in the lagoon, much deeper blue out past the reef, the wide vista of ocean stretching off into the distance and the fresh breezes blowing by up on the top of the hill, all make it a refreshing change from the lowlands.

Valley & Beach Walks

The mountain walks on Rarotonga are hard work. If you want something easier consider the valley walks, such as the stroll along the Avana stream from Ngatangiia. You can drive quite a distance up the road beside the stream and then follow the trail, repeatedly crossing the stream until you reach a pleasant picnic spot at the water intake. A similar walk follows the Turangi stream a little north of Ngatangiia. Matavera stream makes another good walk. Be prepared for mosquitoes on these walks.

Two other beautiful valleys are Takuvaine, behind Avarua, and Avatiu, inland from Avatiu Harbour. See details on these under Inland Drives. They also have walking tracks extending up into the valleys beyond where the roads end. The road heading inland from Avatiu Harbour ends at the start of the Cross-Island Track.

Any beach on Rarotonga is pleasant for strolling. Start at Muri Beach, for example, and walk towards Titikaveka for fine views of the motus on the edge of the lagoon.

Organised Walks

The popular Cross-Island Trek is regularly organised through local travel agents and private guides. All the organised walks across the island include hotel transfers on both ends and a light lunch along the way. They only go in fine weather, as the track is very slippery when wet. If you'll only be staying on the island for a short time and you want to do a guided cross-island walk, it's wise to do it as soon as you can upon arriving, so you don't find yourself planning to do it on your last day and then it turns out to be raining.

Several guides do the cross-island walk. They include BK Services (☎ 20-019, 21-861) who go several times a week for NZ$20 per person, Russ (☎ 26-500 work, Monday to Friday 8 am to 4 pm, or ☎ 21-488 home) who leads the walk on Sunday at 10 am for NZ$25 per person, and Hugh Henry & Associates (☎ 25-320, fax 25-420) who go every day except Sunday for NZ$25 per person. Pa (☎ 21-079), a big, friendly dreadlocked fellow, leads a group across most days of the week for NZ$30 per person. For the same price Pa also leads a less strenuous nature walk up the Matavera Stream, and will guide other walks by arrangement.

WATER SPORTS & ACTIVITIES

Muri Lagoon is the best place for a variety of water sports including windsurfing, sailing, kayaking, outrigger canoeing, and of course it's great for swimming, too. Sailing races are held every Saturday at 1 pm from the Sailing Club on Muri Beach. Muri Beach is also the departure point for glass-bottom boat tours, with snorkelling and barbecue options (read on).

Snorkelling gear and other watersports equipment can be hired at two places on Muri

Beach: Aquasports (☎ 27-350, fax 20-932) at the Rarotonga Sailing Club, and the Cook Islands Windsurfing & Sailing School at the Pacific Resort (☎ 20-427, fax 21-427). Both have a variety of watersports equipment for hire including snorkelling gear, reef shoes, windsurfing boards, Sunbursts (dinghies with sail), small catamarans, outrigger canoes, kayaks, rowboats and wave skis. They also give sailing and windsurfing lessons, and three-hour scuba diving novice 'resort courses' in the lagoon. Prices are about the same at either place, though it never hurts to compare.

All the scuba diving operators will take snorkellers along on their diving trips outside the reef if there's room on the boat; cost is NZ$10 to NZ$20, with snorkelling gear included. They also hire snorkelling gear. A few accommodation places also have snorkelling gear available for their guests, so be sure to ask at the place you're staying before you spend money to hire it. If you want to buy your own snorkelling gear, try The Dive Shop in the centre of Avarua.

Snorkelling

Snorkelling in the lagoon is wonderful, with lots of colourful coral and tropical fish. The lagoon is shallow all the way around but the south side, from the Rarotongan Hotel to Muri Lagoon, has the best snorkelling. The lagoon roughly in front of the Raina Beach Apartments, the Little Polynesian Motel and Moana Sands Hotel is said to have the best snorkelling on the island.

Glass-Bottom Boat & Snorkelling Tours

The same two places on Muri Beach, Aquasports at the Rarotonga Sailing Club and the Cook Islands Windsurfing & Sailing School at the Pacific Resort, also operate glass-bottom boat tours of the lagoon every day except Sunday, starting at 11 am; Aquasports also has a Sunday tour, starting at 1 pm. The tours depart from Muri Beach and cruise out to some fine snorkelling spots; snorkelling gear is included on all the tours. The snorkelling tours last about 1½ to two hours and cost around NZ$25 (children NZ$15). Or you can continue on to Koromiri motu for a barbecue after the cruise, lasting until around 3.30 pm; cost is NZ$35 for the whole day.

Scuba Diving

Scuba diving is good outside the reef. There's coral, canyons, caves and tunnels and the reef drop-off goes from 20 to 30 metres right down to 4000 metres! Most diving is done at three to 30 metres where visibility is 30 to 60 metres (100 to 200 feet) depending on weather and wind conditions; it's seldom less than 30 metres (100 feet).

In addition to the brilliant visibility, other special features of diving on Rarotonga include the largely unspoiled reef with several varieties of colourful living coral and the very short boat trip to reach the diving grounds. The fact that Rarotonga is a small, round island means that regardless of where the wind is coming from there's practically guaranteed to be good diving somewhere around the island. For the novice or beginning diver, the sheltered lagoon makes an excellent learning and practising ground. A further attraction is that scuba diving prices in the Cook Islands are among the lowest in the world.

Rarotonga has several diving operators. Cook Island Divers (☎ 22-483, fax 22-484), Dive Rarotonga (☎ 21-873) and Marineland Pacific Divers (☎ 22-450, 20-427, fax 21-427) all do daily diving trips outside the reef. Cost is NZ$60 to NZ$70 for a one-tank dive using their gear, about NZ$10 cheaper if you have your own gear, and about NZ$10 more for night dives. They will take snorkellers along for NZ$10 to NZ$20, gear included, if there's enough room in the boat. Cook Island Divers (NAUI) and Dive Rarotonga (PADI) offer four-day diving courses leading to internationally recognised NAUI or PADI certification for NZ$425.

Resort courses – three-hour 'introduction to diving' courses designed to give an initial feel for diving – are offered by Aquasports (☎ 27-350, fax 20-932) at the Rarotonga Sailing Club, the Cook Islands Windsurfing & Sailing School at the Pacific Resort

(☎ 20-427, fax 21-427) and Marineland Pacific Divers. Cost is NZ$60.

Deep-Sea Fishing

Deep-sea fishing is excellent right off the reef and with the steep drop-off there's no long distance to travel out to the fishing grounds. World-class catches are made of many fishes including tuna, mahi mahi, wahoo, barracouta, sailfish and marlin. Yellowfin tuna, dogtooth tuna, big eye tuna and mahi mahi are found in Rarotonga's waters all year-round; seasonal catches include wahoo and barracouta (July to November), marlin and sailfish (November to March) and skipjack tuna (December to May).

There are several boats available to take you deep-sea fishing; prices vary so it pays to compare. Ask if lunch is included, and if you can keep your fish; on some boats the fish is divided among the passengers but on others the boat operators keep the fish themselves, or sell your fish back to you at a per-kg rate.

Motorised yachts making deep-sea fishing trips include the MV *Seafari* (☎ 20-328) and Pacific Marine Charters (☎ 21-237). They can take four to six passengers; cost is around NZ$85 to NZ$95 per person for a five-hour trip. They provide lunch but if you catch any fish, the fish stays with the boat. Another motorised vessel, the *Angela II*, costs NZ$60 per person for a three to four-hour trip, and the first fish you catch is yours; ring Bill Kavana at Metua's Cafe (☎ 20-850) for details.

Brent's Fishing Tours (☎ 23-356) goes on a three to four-hour tour around the island on a nine-metre (26-foot) catamaran, fishing as you go, so it's a scenic tour as well as a fishing trip. Cost is NZ$55 per person, there's a maximum of four or five passengers, and any fish caught are shared among the passengers. Beco Game Fishing Charters (☎ 21-525, 24-125) also do catamaran fishing tours; cost is NZ$75 per person for a four-hour trip, you bring your own lunch, and if you catch any fish they stay with the boat.

The Cook Islands Game Fishing Club (☎ 21-419) is a popular hangout for fishing folk; they can help you to arrange fishing trips.

Surfing

Surfing on Rarotonga isn't exactly world class, but you often see a scattering of surfers trying their luck on the waves at Avarua, right in front of the traffic circle. Other surfing spots include Avana Harbour, Black Rock and Matavera (near the Matavera School). Aquasports at the Rarotonga Sailing Club on Muri Beach is thinking of adding a surf shop to its watersports operations.

Reef Walking

Walking on the reef to see the colourful coral, crabs, shells, starfish and other creatures is always fascinating but make sure you wear strong shoes as the coral is very sharp and coral cuts can be nasty and take a long time to heal. An old pair of running shoes is much better than thongs. Listen for the clicking sounds made by tiny hermit crabs as they clamber and fall across the rocks. Walk gently, try not to damage the coral, and if you turn anything over to see what is beneath remember to turn it back again.

OTHER ACTIVITIES

At the Rarotongan and Edgewater hotels, **tennis** courts and hire gear are available. There are many other public tennis courts dotted around the island which you can use for free if you have your own gear. The Edgewater Hotel has **squash** courts and you can usually find a **volleyball** game going on at the net on the beach at the Rarotongan Hotel. There's a nine-hole **golf** course just south of the airport, and a mini-golf course on the main road in Arorangi. **Lawn bowling** is held at the Rarotonga Bowling Club in Avarua most Saturdays and there's an annual tournament.

The Hash House Harriers meet every Monday at 5.30 pm for an easy **fun run** somewhere around the island. Look for the announcement in the *Cook Islands News* each Monday, or phone David Lobb (work

☎ 22-000, home ☎ 27-002) to find out where the run will be. In the Cooks the Hash House Harriers have a couple of other branches – Hash House Harriers, Hussies and Hoffspring!

Horse Riding
Horse riding tours are offered by Aroa Pony Trek (☎ 20-048, 21-415). Rides lasting 1½ to two hours depart from near the Rarotongan Resort Hotel, go down the beach, inland up to Wigmore's Waterfall for a swim, then back again. Cost is NZ$27.50 (children half price).

Scenic Flights & Tandem Skydiving
Scenic flights and tandem skydiving operate from the Adventure Centre (☎ 29-888) at the Air Rarotonga hangar, about a km west of the main airport terminal. The trips operate all day every day with the exception of Sunday morning. If a pilot and plane are available they'll take you on a drop-in basis, but it's best to book ahead.

Scenic flights cost NZ$49 per person and they can take three passengers at a time; they're great for working out exactly where those mountain trails go and where the good diving spots are.

Tandem skydiving gives you a chance to experience skydiving with no instruction needed; you're securely attached to a skydiving master who operates the parachute, while you simply go along to enjoy the ride. Cost is NZ$200 per person, the same as in New Zealand, where tandem skydiving has become enormously popular.

Visit an Artist
Clare Higham at the Serenity Studio in Arorangi (☎ 20-238) and Jillian Sobieska at the Galerie in Avarua (☎ 21-079) welcome visitors. Also don't forget the Women's Handcraft Centre (☎ 28-033) and other arts & crafts stalls in the Punanga Nui outdoor market in Avarua, where you can often find artists and woodcarvers at work.

Organised Tours
Circle Island Tours Do a Circle Island Tour sometime during your stay on Rarotonga. A couple of excellent tours, interesting and informative, are offered. They provide insight into many aspects of Rarotongan history and culture, both ancient and modern, that you'll never learn if you simply go around on your own.

'Pa Ariki' - Maree Pa, High Chief of Takitumu at Her Coronation in 1991. Original painting by Jillian Sobieska.

The Cook Islands Cultural Village (☎ 21-314, after hours 22-225, fax 25-557) operates a Circle Island Tour which starts off at the Cultural Village with an island-style lunch and a show of legends, song and dance at 12.45 pm, followed by a circle island tour featuring history, agriculture, culture and many other aspects of Rarotongan life, ending at around 5 pm. Cost is NZ$20 (children NZ$12), including transfers to and from your hotel.

If you like, you can combine the Cultural Village Circle Island Tour with their morning Cultural Village Tour. (See under Cultural

Village in the Around the Island section, earlier on.) If you do both tours in one day the cost is NZ$45; if you do them over two days, the cost is NZ$50. Transfers, the lunch and show are included either way.

The Circle Island Historical Tours are all operated by Hugh Henry & Associates (☎ 25-320, 25-321, fax 25-420). The fascinating tour, lasting from 9.30 am to 2 pm on weekdays, focuses on the history and culture of Rarotonga, with many stops at historical sites. Cost is NZ$24.

Tipani Tours (☎ 25-266, fax 23-266) also does Circle Island Tours; they last around three hours and cost NZ$18 per person (children NZ$9).

Outer Island Tours Tours to the outer islands, lasting one day or longer, can be booked through any of the Rarotonga travel agents. See the introductory Getting Around chapter for details.

Other Tours

See the Snorkelling & Diving section for details on snorkelling & diving tours, the Walking & Climbing section for walking tours, and the Horse Riding section for horse riding tours, all found earlier in this section.

PLACES TO STAY

Rarotonga has a wide variety of places to stay in every budget range. It also has an official policy that every arriving visitor must be booked in advance into a place to stay, before arriving on the island. See the Accommodation section in the Facts for the Visitor chapter for details on this requirement.

In large part this advance booking policy is designed to discourage people from camping on the beach, which is highly illegal – don't even think about camping on the beach because this will get you deported immediately. It's also designed to make sure everyone has a place to stay. There are only about 700 hotel rooms on Rarotonga and some of the hotels are routinely booked up months in advance.

Most of the places to stay on Rarotonga have some sort of kitchen or cooking facilities where guests can do their own cooking – obviously a great convenience, not only for all the obvious reasons (being able to eat what you want, when you want to, much more cheaply than if you eat at restaurants) but also because the places to stay and the restaurants all tend to be scattered around the island, meaning a lot of travelling to restaurants if you must eat out, unless you want to constantly eat out at the same place. The large resort hotels and a few other hotels don't have kitchens in the rooms and so eating out will be an extra expense if you stay at one of these.

If you're looking for the most beautiful beach on the island, choose one of the places to stay on Muri Beach. The beaches along the south and west sides of the island are all good for swimming – but not those on the north and east sides, where the reef is too close to shore, making the beaches rocky and the lagoon too narrow for swimming. If you want to see the sunset from your hotel then of course you must stay on the west side of the island.

Places to Stay – bottom end

Tiare Village Dive Hostel (☎ 23-466, 21-874, PO Box 719), a comfortable backpackers' haven, is about three km from the centre of Avarua in a rather remote location, off the Ara Metua back road out behind the airport. You'll probably like it best if you plan to hire a motorcycle or other transport, as you are off the bus line here and it's a long walk into town. The staff will take you into town and help you get oriented, hire a bike etc the first day you arrive, and they provide free transfers to and from the airport.

The hostel consists of one large house with three triple rooms and one double room, all sharing a common sitting area, kitchen and bathroom, plus three separate self-contained A-frame chalets, each with one double bedroom and two single rooms. There's also a TV lounge, board games and a library for entertainment on rainy days. Snorkelling gear is hired for NZ$5 per day. Fresh fruits and vegetables are in abundance here, which you are welcome to eat, and the place is famous for its hospitality. Nightly cost is NZ$16 per person, with discounts for weekly stays. Bring a mosquito coil as you are inland here.

The *Matareka Heights Guest House* (☎ 23-670, fax 26-672, PO Box 587) is up the hill from the Tiare Village Dive Hostel – take the same turn-off from the Ara Metua back road and continue past the Tiare Village up to the very top of the hill. The hostel occupies the two houses at the top of the steep hill overlooking the airport. It's not bad if you have your own transport, but quite inconvenient otherwise, though they will hire you a 21-speed mountain bike, making it easier to get around and to get up that hill. It's pleasantly quiet up here, with spacious well-maintained grounds and a sweeping view over the sea.

The top house is a big three-bedroom house, each bedroom having its own bathroom and sleeping three to four people, with a large communal kitchen and lounge area. The lower house has three twin or double rooms, again with a shared kitchen and sitting area. Nightly cost is NZ$15 per person; bicycle hire is an extra NZ$10 per day or NZ$50 per week. Several travellers have written to say what a great place this is and how friendly Hugh and Joanna Baker, the owners, are. Bring mosquito coils.

The *Airport Lodge* (☎ 20-050, fax 26-174, PO Box 223) is on the main coastal road, near the end of the airport runway and opposite the radar station and the beach, about five km west of Avarua. It consists of six duplexes, each with two self-contained one-bedroom units. Each unit sleeps two people except the one, with two triple rooms, which can sleep six. Nightly cost is NZ$25/40/45 for singles/doubles/triples.

The *Are-Renga Motel* (☎ 20-050, fax 26-174, PO Box 223) is on the main road in Arorangi, about eight km from Avarua. Each of the 23 units is a comfortable little self-contained one-bedroom apartment, with separate bedroom and kitchen areas. Cost is NZ$25/40/45 for singles/doubles/triples, or there's a share rate of NZ$15 per person. Laundry facilities are available. The apartments are rather basic, but if you're looking for a low-priced motel you may well find them ideal. Be sure to check out the four hectares (10 acres) of tropical gardens in the rear, with a variety of fruit trees you are welcome to pick.

Arorangi Lodge (☎ 21-773, fax 26-174, PO Box 51), on the beach side of the main road in Arorangi, has eight self-contained units facing a garden, with grounds extending right down to the beach. Nightly cost is NZ$30/40 for singles/doubles if you want the unit all to yourself, or NZ$15 per person if you share with others. Discounts are given when it's not busy. Phone for free pick-up from the airport when you arrive.

Backpackers International Hostel (☎ & fax 21-847, PO Box 878) is in Kavera, not far from the Rarotongan Resort Hotel. Formerly called the Dive Rarotonga Hostel, this is an old favourite backpackers' hostel. It has seven twin rooms, one double room and one single room; nightly cost is NZ$15 per person, or NZ$25/30 for single/double rooms. Features include a large communal kitchen, comfortable indoor and outdoor lounge areas, and a large yard. Look for the sign pointing inland at the Kavera bus stop; the hostel is the first two-storey house on your right.

Rutaki Lodge (☎ 22-115, fax 21-847, PO Box 878) is on the coast road beside the Rutaki Store in Rutaki, on the south side of the island. It's a six-bedroom house with one single room, the rest are doubles and twins; nightly cost is NZ$25/30 for singles/doubles, or NZ$15 per person on a share basis. Here, too, there's a comfortable shared kitchen and sitting room.

The *Sunrise Beach Motel* is a straightforward motel but in addition to its regular motel units it also has two budget units at NZ$25 per person. See the 'lower middle' category for details.

The *Ariana Bungalows* and *Ariana Hostel* (☎ 20-521, fax 26-174, PO Box 925) are about 200 metres inland from the coast road, three km east of Avarua. The buildings are spaced around a lush, green garden with fruit trees ripe for the picking and a peaceful, quiet atmosphere. There is also a swimming pool, a barbecue area, a volleyball court, a recreation room with pool table, TV and video, a small shop and a self-service laundry. Pushbikes (NZ$6 per day) and motorcycles (NZ$16 per day) are available for hire, and free airport transfers are provided.

The Ariana has nine self-contained bungalows, each sleeping three persons and having a fully equipped kitchen, separate bedroom and private balcony; cost is NZ$48 for one or two people, NZ$53 for three. Two other buildings operate as hostels, with shared kitchen and bathroom facilities. One house has two bedrooms; cost is NZ$18 per person. A larger house has four bedrooms, but the panelled walls come only part way up to the ceiling; cost in this 'dorm house' is NZ$15 per person.

Places to Stay – lower middle

The *Paradise Inn* (☎ & fax 20-544, PO Box 674) is the closest hotel to the centre of town, just a short walk on the main road. Although the beach is rocky and shallow here, not good for swimming, the amenities are good, with a large lounge area, video movies, board games, library, informal bar and a barbecue area on the seafront patio. Most of the units are townhouse-style and spacious, with a double bed in the ample sleeping loft and sitting room/kitchen/bath areas downstairs. These cost NZ$60/66/77 for singles/doubles/triples. A larger family unit sleeping five costs NZ$82, though they don't accept children under 12; there are also a couple of budget single rooms for NZ$39.

The *Kii Kii Motel* (☎ 21-937, fax 22-937, PO Box 68) is about three km east of Avarua. This 24-room motel is on the beachfront, with a beachfront swimming pool since the beach here is not good for swimming. There's a choice of studio and one-bedroom units, all with kitchen; singles/doubles are NZ$54/67 in the budget rooms, NZ$68/87 in the standard rooms, NZ$86/108 in the premium-deluxe rooms, or NZ$92/114 in the rooms overlooking the sea.

Ati's Beach Bungalow (☎ 21-546, fax 25-546, PO Box 693) is on the beachfront in Arorangi, on the west side of the island, on the main road near the CICC church. It's on a good stretch of beach, with a view of the sunset. Four beachside studio bungalows are priced at NZ$105; a larger deluxe two-bedroom beachfront family unit sleeping up to six people costs NZ$235. Five small self-contained studio units in the house by the main road, with no view, are NZ$70. This is one of Rarotonga's newer places to stay and several travellers have highly recommended it.

Aroko Bungalows (☎ 29-312, after hours 21-625; PO Box 850) has one of the most tranquil and beautiful settings on Rarotonga, on the shore of Muri Lagoon with a view across to Oneroa and Motutapu motus. It's a very simple place with just three small but cosy and attractive self-contained bungalows, each sleeping two; cost is NZ$60 in the two beachfront bungalows with verandahs overlooking the lagoon, NZ$50 in the other one.

Sunrise Beach Motel (☎ 20-417, fax 22-991, Postal Depot 8, Ngatangiia), on the east side of the island just north of Avana Harbour, has eight small self-contained bungalow units, some right on the beach with an ocean view. The lagoon here is very narrow so swimming is not so good, but there's a tiny swimming pool and it's not too far to walk to Muri Lagoon. Nightly cost is NZ$85 for one or two people, additional people NZ$15, NZ$5 for children under five. A couple of 'budget units' are NZ$25 per person.

Places to Stay – middle

The *Tamure Resort Hotel* (☎ 22-415, fax 24-415, PO Box 483) is about 2.5 km east of Avarua. It's right on the waterfront but the beach here is not good for swimming, so there's a waterfront swimming pool. Nightly cost is NZ$110 and the rooms have no kitchens. This 35-room hotel is best known for its 'Island Night' entertainment, at least two nights per week.

Oasis Village (☎ & fax 28-214, PO Box 2), on the west side of the island near the beach and just south of the golf course, has three small free-standing one-room studio cabins, all with air-conditioning and private bath, tea and coffee-making equipment but no kitchens. They face the Oasis Village Steakhouse, which is a good restaurant, but unfortunately all the restaurant patrons can see right into the sliding glass doors of your room unless you close the curtains! The cabins don't face the beach but they're not far from it, and there's beach access. The cost of NZ$120 per night seems rather high for what you get, compared to other places on the island.

The *Rarotongan Sunset Motel* (☎ 28-028, fax 28-026, PO Box 377), on the beachfront on the west side of the island about six km west of Avarua, has 20 self-contained studio units with the usual motel-style mod cons including well-equipped kitchen facilities and private verandah. There's also a guest laundry and a freshwater pool. Twelve of the rooms can be interconnected. Cost is NZ$150 in the 11 garden rooms, NZ$185 in the nine beachfront rooms. It's a good idea to book ahead here, as it's often booked up months in advance.

The *Puaikura Reef Lodge* (☎ 23-537, fax 21-537, PO Box 397) on the south-west side of the island has 12 modern well-equipped units. Each has a kitchen and dining area; the family units are great if you're with children as the main sleeping area has a concertina door which you can slide across to shut off the living area. Cost is NZ$135 in these one-bedroom units, and there are also some studio units at NZ$110. There's a swimming pool, with a barbecue off to one side. The beach, narrow but pleasant and with good swimming, is only a few steps away on the other side of the road.

Lagoon Lodges (☎ 22-020, fax 22-021, PO Box 45) is on the coast road, opposite the beach, 400 metres from the Rarotongan Hotel. It stretches back from, rather than along, the road, so there's little traffic noise, and it's safe for children. There are 14 spacious bungalows set around a large 1.6 hectare (four acre) garden grounds, with a tennis court, trampoline, barbecue and swimming pool.

In addition to six studio units, several of the bungalows are larger one or two bedroom units – very spacious with a kitchen and living room area, a large verandah and virtually your own private garden. If you have children these larger units are amongst the best on the island. Prices are NZ$130 in the studio units (sleeping three), NZ$145 in the one-bedroom units (sleeping four), NZ$160 in the two-bedroom units (sleeping seven), or NZ$300 in a large three-bedroom executive lodge.

The *Palm Grove Lodge* (☎ 20-002, fax 21-998, PO Box 23) on the south side of the island is a pleasant place with a variety of free-standing self-contained bungalows, a small swimming pool and large grassy grounds, beside a fine stretch of beach good for swimming and snorkelling. Five beachfront studio units, each sleeping two, cost NZ$185 per night; two one-bedroom garden villas, each sleeping up to four people, also cost NZ$185, and there are six garden studio units, each sleeping three, at NZ$140.

The *Moana Sands Hotel* (☎ 26-189, fax 22-189, PO Box 1007) in Titikaveka on the south-east side of the island has a two-storey block of rooms, 12 in all, each with a verandah facing directly onto the beach. It's a fine beach here, with kayaks, canoes and snorkelling, and a barbecue area. Other activities can also be arranged, with the help of the very friendly and helpful staff. The rooms have no kitchens but they do have fridges, tea/coffee making facilities, toaster and electric frypan; apart from your own limited cooking facilities there is also a restaurant and bar. Six of the rooms can be interconnected. Cost is NZ$170 per night.

The *Little Polynesian* (☎ 24-280, fax 21-585, PO Box 366), not far from the Moana Sands, is also on the same fine stretch of beach. Its nine self-contained units, all with full kitchen facilities, include six studio units, two one-bedroom units and one separate 'honeymoon' unit – standing alone, presumably so the occupants can make more noise! Nightly cost is NZ$147 in the regular units, NZ$177 for the honeymoon bungalow. Features include a swimming pool, a barbecue hut, picnic tables, hammocks stretched under the palms and a trampoline. Snorkelling is good in the lagoon here; snorkelling gear, canoes, motorcycles and bicycles are available for hire. Children under 12 are not accepted, except by prior arrangement.

Raina Beach Apartments (☎ 26-189, fax 22-189, PO Box 1007), a curious looking three-storey concrete structure, is on the south-east side of the island, opposite a beach excellent for snorkelling. Two one-bedroom family units downstairs can sleep up to seven people each. The upstairs units are smaller, without the separate bedroom, but they have the same lounge area, kitchen facilities and so on. Prices are NZ$170 per apartment. The top floor has a two-bedroom penthouse suite (price on application). Up on the rooftop there's a garden, sunbathing and barbecue area with an honesty bar. All the units were completely refurbished in early 1994.

The *Muri Beachcomber* (☎ 21-022, fax 21-323, PO Box 379), a popular beachfront motel, is pleasantly situated on Muri Beach. It has 10 self-contained beachfront studio units, plus a couple of larger poolside garden units with separate bedrooms; singles/doubles are NZ$135/160. Children under 12 are accepted in the garden units, but not in the beachfront units. There's a swimming pool, children's pool, barbecue area and laundry facilities. The whole place is modern, well kept and well run. Booking in advance is generally a must.

The Muri Beachcomber also has a large four-bedroom house known as *The Lodge* that can sleep up to seven people; nightly cost is NZ$300 for two people, plus NZ$50 for each additional person (free for children under two).

Places to Stay – top end

Rarotonga has some excellent places to stay in the top end range. Three of them – the Pacific Resort, Sokala Villas and Avana Marina Condos – are on Muri Lagoon, two of them right on Muri Beach.

The *Pacific Resort* (☎ 20-427, fax 21-427, PO Box 790), right on Muri Beach, is probably Rarotonga's most attractive medium-sized resort. The 49 self-contained units all have kitchens, one or two bedrooms, sitting rooms, private verandahs and good views of the beach, garden, pond or swimming pool. Nightly cost is NZ$230 for one or two people in the 28 one-bedroom garden units, NZ$240 in the eight two-bedroom garden units, NZ$255 in the six beachside units, NZ$315 in the four beachfront units, and NZ$495 in the three luxury Pacific Villas. Interconnecting suites are available. All guests have free use of the watersports equipment (canoes, kayaks, wave skis, windsurfers, snorkelling gear etc). The resort's intimate *Barefoot Bar*, right on the beach, has a lovely view; for dining there's the open-air *Sandals Restaurant*.

Sokala Villas (☎ 29-200, fax 21-222, PO Box 82) is an assortment of seven natural-wood, one-bedroom self-contained villas right on Muri Beach. Each villa is different; five have their own private swimming pool, four are right on the beachfront, three are one-storey and four are two-storey with loft bedrooms. All are elegant and excellently appointed. It's especially popular for couples and honeymooners; children under 12 are not accepted. Prices range from NZ$160 to NZ$315 per villa.

The *Avana Marina Condos* (☎ 20-836, fax 22-991, PO Box 869) are on Muri Lagoon, overlooking Avana Harbour with a view across to Motutapu. The condos have their own jetty and each of the six units comes with its own boat; there's good swimming here, and a private beach. Five of the six units have two bedrooms and sleep up to five people; there's also one three-bedroom unit. Children are welcome. Cost is NZ$350 per night, with three days of car hire free for every seven-day stay.

The *Manuia Beach Hotel* (☎ 22-461, fax 22-464, PO Box 700), in Arorangi on the west side of the island, is described by its American owner, Michael Smith, as a 'boutique hotel' and the most expensive place to stay on Rarotonga. All of the 20 units are studio units, without separate bedrooms and without kitchen, but they do have mini-bars and tea and coffee-making equipment.

Nightly cost is NZ$375 in the garden units, NZ$465 in the beachfront units, but cost may be less if you come on some sort of airline package holiday. Children under 12 are not accepted.

The lagoon here is very shallow and the coral is not so good but it's OK for splashing around and lackadaisical snorkelling. The white sandy beach is just fine and offers excellent sunsets. You can always swim in the beachfront swimming pool; beside this there's a hot spa pool. The thatched-roof, open-air, sand-floor *Right-On-The-Beach Restaurant & Bar* is attractive. Barbecues and 'Island Night' buffets are held weekly.

Large Resorts Rarotonga has only two large resorts – the *Rarotongan* and the *Edgewater*. (The *Sheraton* may also open eventually.) Their 'rack rates' – the prices you'll pay if you walk in off the street – are high, but most of their business comes from airline and travel agents' package holidays, which make the room rates cheaper.

The *Rarotongan Resort Hotel* (☎ 25-800, fax 25-799, PO Box 103), on the south-west corner of the island, has 151 guest rooms and it's the only 'international standard' hotel in the Cook Islands. It has everything including a souvenir shop, a travel centre, tennis courts, its own beach with a beachfront swimming pool and plenty of beach activities, a bar, two restaurants, and car, motorcycle and pushbike rental. There's also a business centre with secretarial, photocopying, telex and fax services and even a conference centre.

The Rarotongan underwent major renovations and upgrading in 1992. There are four standards of rooms; the differences are principally whether you face the garden or the beach and some variation in equipment levels, though none of the rooms have kitchens. Prices are NZ$160 for singles/doubles in garden rooms, NZ$190 in non-renovated beachfront rooms, NZ$240 in renovated beachfront rooms, NZ$210 in non-renovated paradise rooms, NZ$290 in renovated paradise rooms and NZ$430 in suites. There is no extra charge for children under 16 if they occupy the same room as their parents.

Even if you are not staying at the Rarotongan, you can still come to partake of the many activities. 'Island Night' buffets and dance performances take place two evenings a week – if you don't want the buffet you can come around 9 pm and pay a cover charge of NZ$5 to see the dancing, featuring some of the best troupes on the island. The resort beach has kayaks, outrigger canoes, snorkelling gear, volleyball, badminton, windsurfers and so on. A sign announces that all 'furniture and equipment is for hotel guests only,' but no-one seems to check. An activities list at the front desk describes the various events being held each day.

The *Edgewater Resort* (☎ 25-435, fax 25-475, PO Box 121), on the beachfront at Arorangi on the west side of the island, has 180 rooms, making it the biggest resort in the Cook Islands. The rooms are quite straightforward with the three different categories differing mainly in their views (garden, partial beach view or beachfront) and furnishings. The rooms have air-conditioning, TV and in-house movies, but no kitchens. Prices are NZ$165 for the garden rooms, NZ$195 for the superior rooms, NZ$220 for the beachfront rooms, NZ$300 for the executive suites and NZ$350 for the VIP/honeymoon suite. Children under 12 are free. If you come on a package tour, as most guests do, prices are cheaper.

The resort has a beachfront swimming pool, a tennis centre with tennis and squash courts, cars, motorcycles and pushbikes for hire, and a travel desk where you can book a variety of activities around the island.

The huge 191-room *Sheraton Resort* complex on the south side of the island (☎ 28-850, fax 28-860, Private Bag) was started in 1989 but as of this writing, five years later in 1994, construction was still at a standstill. Funding problems have plagued the project and construction has been halted twice so far. Now they are saying it's due to resume, and they're hoping for an opening date around the time of this book's publication.

Places to Stay – renting a house
One of the best deals, especially if you're staying on the island for a while, is to rent a house by the week. A fully equipped two-bedroom house sleeping four or five people usually costs around NZ$200 per week.

The challenge is to find one. The only real estate agent that handles houses on Rarotonga is the Cook Islands Commercial Realty Brokers Ltd (☎ 23-840, fax 23-843, PO Box 869), whose office is above Beco on the main road just east of the traffic circle in Avarua. They have houses for rent by the week but you must take it for a minimum of five weeks.

Also check the classified section of the *Cook Islands News*, where one or two houses are usually listed. The Tourist Authority may also be able to help you turn up something. And it never hurts to simply ask around; there are plenty of houses available that are not advertised.

PLACES TO EAT

The widest choice of eating places is found in Avarua, although there is also a scattering of places right around the island. Some of the places to stay have restaurant facilities although many visitors opt to fix their own food for at least some meals. The majority of places to stay have some sort of cooking facilities. See the Places to Stay section in this chapter and the introductory Food section in the Facts for the Visitor chapter.

One pleasant surprise with Rarotongan eating is the quality of the local ingredients. Of course a lot of the raw materials (steaks for example) arrive frozen or airfreighted from New Zealand, but the local seafood, fruits and vegetables are excellent.

Avarua

Snacks & Takeaways *Mama's Cafe*, near the Foodland supermarket right on the main drag in central Avarua, is a popular cafe with inexpensive meals and snacks, plus an ice-cream counter. Around the corner, the *Hacienda Cafe* in Cook's Corner is another popular hangout with basic cafe food, including omelettes for breakfast and a variety of sandwiches, burgers, steaks etc for lunch. A separate bar and beer garden are off to one side. Outdoors in the patio of the Cook's Corner arcade, *Simone's Bistro* specialises in steaks and pizzas.

A fine place to catch a breeze, have a coffee, lunch or snack and watch the world go by is the *Blue Note Cafe* on the verandah of the Banana Court, near the traffic circle. The menu here is a bit more imaginative than the usual Rarotongan cafe fare and features selections like croissants, pita bread sandwiches, nachos, grilled meats, desserts, espresso and cappuccino.

Nearby on the beach side of the traffic circle, the *Breez'n Cafe* serves basic takeaways like burgers, fish & chips etc, and is probably most notable for its long opening hours of 7 am to 10 pm Monday to Thursday, 7 am to 3 am on Friday, 7 am to midnight on Saturday, and 6 pm to midnight on Sunday. On the inland side of the traffic circle just past the post office, *Uncle Rima's Takeaways* is another place open long hours with basic takeaways, including Chinese food, burgers and fish & chips.

Nearby, *Metua's Cafe* is an open-air seaside restaurant (see Restaurants in this section) but in the daytime it's also a pleasant hideaway for an inexpensive meal or snack or for lingering over a coffee or beer.

On the west side of Avarua, *Punanga Nui*, the outdoor market, has a number of outdoor food caravans selling basic takeaways like burgers, fish & chips, steak & chips and so on, with picnic tables where you can relax and eat. Fresh fruits and vegetables are sold in the marketplace stalls.

Restaurants *Trader Jack's* (☎ 26-464, 25-464), on the seafront near the traffic circle in the centre of Avarua, is one of the island's most popular bar-and-grill restaurants. The indoor tables, as well as those out on the deck over the sea, all have a great sea view. The lunch and dinner menus are ample and varied; specialties include seafood, pastas and charcoal-grilled steaks. Lunch is served from Monday to Saturday, dinner every night. The bar, popular with Rarotonga's up-market crowd, features live music for dancing on Friday nights.

A couple of doors east of Trader Jack's, *Metua's Cafe* (☎ 20-850), hidden away in Browne's Arcade, is also pleasantly situated on the waterfront. It's a good, inexpensive open-air restaurant/bar with some tables under cover and others out in the open. The food is good and varied, with plenty of selections for all meals. Monday, Tuesday and Wednesday nights are 'roast nights' with roast meat dinners at just NZ$11. Wednesday, Friday and Saturday nights feature a live band for dancing under the stars. It's open Monday to Saturday, starting at 7.30 am and staying open till 10 pm Monday to Thursday, till 2 am Friday and till midnight Saturday. Food is served straight through, from opening till closing time.

Priscilla's (☎ 23-530) on the main road a long block east of the traffic circle, features authentic Indian cuisine, with some Chinese and European selections. A good meal of curry, rice, vegetables, roti and salad is just NZ$9.50 if you dine in, NZ$8.50 for takeaway. It's open for lunch Monday to Friday, dinner Monday to Saturday.

A little farther east on the main road, you'll find the *Staircase Restaurant/Bar* (☎ 22-254) upstairs behind the Top Shape Health & Fitness Centre. It is a small family restaurant open for dinner Monday to Friday from 6.30 pm. It features barbecue meals, with a choice of meats plus a salad-bar buffet, for NZ$12.50 to NZ$14.50. There's live entertainment nightly with soloist Mann Short singing and playing the guitar.

Across the road is *Portofino* (☎ 26-480) where the food is Italian and the accent is nautical. It's all carried off with some flair and ability; in fact this restaurant is one of the best on the island and is so popular that reservations are recommended. The restaurant has an indoor air-conditioned section and an outdoor patio dining area, all with romantic candlelight, and a bar with an extensive and reasonably priced winelist. The fresh fish of the day, the big fisherman's platter, the pasta and pizzas are all very good and so are the desserts. It's open for dinner Monday to Saturday from 6.30 to 9.30 pm.

On the airport side of Avarua, *Ronnie's* (☎ 20-824) is a pleasant restaurant-bar-cafe with a moderately fancy indoor restaurant plus a garden cafe and bar. There's quite a variety on the menu, with reasonably priced meals and bar snacks. You can dress up or come as you are. Late in the evening there's a lot of back-and-forth to the Reefcomber Cabaret behind the restaurant. On Friday nights Ronnie's is very crowded, having become the 'in' place to go; the rest of the time it's quite peaceful. It's open Monday to Saturday from 11 am to midnight.

Around the Island

Snacks & Takeaways There are very few places around the island where you can get basic cheap takeaway-style food (burgers and the like); all of these places have tables so you can dine there, or take the food away.

Bunny's Diner in Arorangi has basic breakfasts, burgers, sandwiches etc, besides being a small grocery shop. It's open long hours: Monday to Thursday from 7 am to 10 pm, Friday and Saturday until 2 am, and Sunday from 6 to 10 pm.

Just Burgers on the main road in Vaima, on the south side of the island, makes inexpensive 'American-style' hamburgers, french fries, milk shakes and the like. It's open Monday to Saturday from 9.30 am to 9 pm, Sunday from 1 to 9 pm.

At Muri Beach, the pleasant *Boardwalk Cafe* on the downstairs deck at the Rarotonga Sailing Club, overlooking the beach and lagoon, serves inexpensive light meals, snacks and desserts, plus drinks from the upstairs bar. It's open every day from 9 am to 6 pm, Sunday from 11 am to 6 pm.

Other places for basic takeaway include the *Halfway Cafe* in Rutaki and *Lizzie's Takeaways* in Muri, both on the coast road. The *Jam Hut* near the CICC church in Titikaveka is a small but pleasant restaurant-bar-cafe.

The *RSA & Citizens Club* opposite the airport is a pub and social club where visitors as well as locals are welcome. It's open Monday to Saturday from 11 am to midnight; lunch is served from noon to 2 pm, dinner from 6 to 8 pm, and usually features a steak & salad meal. Beer is inexpensive and there are pool tables, darts and a band for dancing on Friday and Saturday nights.

PJ's Cafe in Arorangi, was one of the most popular eateries on Rarotonga until it was destroyed by fire in December 1993. They say they're planning to rebuild.

Restaurants Restaurants tend to be scattered at distances around the island, with more on the west than on the east side. Since you'll probably have to travel at least some distance to get to any of them, and most of them are quite small, reservations are a good idea. We'll mention them here in an anticlockwise direction, starting from Avarua.

The *Oasis Village Steakhouse* (☎ 28-214) in Arorangi is one of Rarotonga's best new restaurants. The open-air decor is simple but pleasant; the food is delicious and brings raves from practically everyone who eats there. The chef's special, Chateaubriand for two with baked potatoes, a selection of vegetables and Hollandaise sauce, is NZ$45; other selections include grilled steak & salad bar for NZ$18, spaghetti and other pastas for NZ$10. Lunch is served Monday to Friday from noon to 2 pm, dinner Monday to Saturday from 6 to 9 pm.

The *Spaghetti House* (☎ 25-441) in Arorangi at the turn-off to the Edgewater Resort has an extremely Spartan decor but good spaghetti and other pastas, both meat and vegetarian. Main course pastas are around NZ$12.50 for vegetarian selections, NZ$14.50 with meat; pizzas, a fish 'catch of the day' and seafood or minestrone soups are also good. It's open for dinner every night from 5 to 10 pm.

The *Reef Restaurant & Bar* at the Edgewater Resort (☎ 25-435), one of the biggest restaurants on the island, has a weekly schedule of 'Island Night' buffets, theme dinners, a 'dining under the stars' night out on the beachfront terrace – all around NZ$25 to NZ$33 – and a couple of a la carte nights. There's a continental breakfast buffet every morning, and a menu of light meals and snacks (nachos, burgers, salads etc) served every day from 11.15 am to 9.15 pm. There's entertainment every evening except Friday, when there's a theme dinner followed by a nightlife tour.

The *Tumunu Bar & Restaurant* (☎ 20-501), next to the Edgewater Resort, has a pleasant outdoor barbecue area and an indoor restaurant/bar with lots of attractive Polynesian touches. Seafood and steaks are the speciality here; dinner for two could easily come to around NZ$100 with soup, dessert and a bottle of wine. You'll feel right at home whether you dress up or go casual. There's a friendly weekly darts competition with a carton of beer as the prize, and a roast pork dinner on Sunday. The bar is open from 4 pm to midnight; dinner is served every night from 6 pm.

The *Right-on-the-Beach Restaurant & Bar* (☎ 22-461) at the Manuia Beach 'boutique hotel', yes indeed right on the beach, is open-air with a high thatched roof and sand for the floor; it's a lovely, relaxed place with a great view of the sunset. There's a Swiss chef and the specialties of the house are fresh home-made pasta and other Italian and Swiss dishes.

The *Kaena Restaurant* (☎ 25-432, 25-433), 50 metres north of the Rarotongan Hotel, specialises in a variety of steaks and seafoods. Put together a meal for two including all the house specialties – seafood chowder, fish of the day and a delicious banana crepe for dessert – and your bill will come to about NZ$55. There's also an extensive wine, beer and bar list. The Kaena looks rather plain from the outside but it's attractive inside. It's open every night from 6 pm.

The Rarotongan Resort Hotel (☎ 25-800) has the *Mana Terrace* poolside restaurant for breakfast and lunch, and the *Whitesands Restaurant* for dinner with a different theme buffet every night: an Italian night, a 'fish market' night, an Asian night and a barbecue night, are all NZ$31 per person. Wednesday and Saturday are 'island nights', with a buffet of island food cooked in an underground oven (umu) and a variety of entertainment. On Sunday the *Mana Terrace* serves an excellent Sunday brunch from noon to 3 pm followed by a poolside barbecue from 6.30 to 9 pm.

Liana's Restaurant & Bar (☎ 26-123), a couple of km beyond the Rarotongan Hotel, specialises in seafood, steaks, curries and Chinese dishes. The decor is pleasantly Polynesian, with lots of bamboo and Gauguin prints about. It's open for dinner every night from 6.30 pm.

Muri Beach has three fine restaurants. *Sails* (☎ 27-350, 27-349), upstairs at the Rarotonga Sailing Club, has an excellent view over Muri Lagoon, especially lovely around full moon when the moon seems to rise up out of the lagoon. It's open every day from 11 am to 4 pm for light meals and snacks, and for candlelight dinner every evening from 6.30 pm. Dinner main dishes include seafood, steak and so on; specialties of the house are the seafood chowder (NZ$7.50) and seafood pasta (NZ$18).

Nearby at the Pacific Resort, the *Sandals Restaurant* (☎ 20-427, 21-156) serves a continental buffet breakfast every morning and dinners nightly from 6.30 pm. Most nights there's an a la carte menu with steaks, seafoods etc, but they also have theme nights including an island night buffet, a carvery night and a weekly barbecue, each for NZ$30. Lunch is served in the beachfront *Barefoot Bar*, with both patio and indoor tables.

Finally, down near the end of Muri Beach, the *Flame Tree* (☎ 25-123 after 3 pm) is widely known as one of the best restaurants on Rarotonga, with delicious food, an elegant atmosphere and artistic decor. The international menu features dishes from India, Thailand, China, Japan, Singapore and other places, with spicy and non-spicy selections. There are plenty of vegetarian dishes, plus seafood, steak, lamb and other meats. Appetisers are NZ$9 to NZ$14, soups NZ$6.50 and main courses NZ$18 to NZ$29. It's open for dinner Monday to Saturday from 6.30 pm; reservations are recommended.

Markets & Supermarkets

The Foodland supermarket in the centre of Avarua has a good selection of foods. If you have a lot of food shopping to do, it can be worth taking a trip into town to do it here. Packaged and imported food is often cheaper here than at the tiny local grocery shops dotted around the island; for produce, you may find a better selection elsewhere, especially at the Punanga Nui open-air market stalls. Other large supermarkets in Avarua include Meatco a few doors inland from Budget Rent-A-Car and the CITC Wholesale Store opposite Avatiu Harbour.

The Punanga Nui open-air market has many stalls with a selection of fresh fruits and vegetables. Early in the morning you can often buy whole fresh fish. There's also a variety of takeaway food caravans and some stalls selling pareu, clothing and handicrafts. Punanga Nui is open every day except Sunday.

On the south side of the island, Wigmore's Supermarket has a good selection of foods, good prices, and fresh produce from Wigmore's farm. Many locals on the south side of the island who used to go into town to shop now do their shopping here.

There are many small shops dotted around the island. They are convenient and are open longer hours than the supermarkets, but like 'convenience stores' in other countries, their prices are often higher.

Alcoholic Beverages

The government-run Cook Islands Liquor Supplies on the main road on the airport side of Avarua has a wide selection of alcoholic beverages. It's open Monday to Friday from 9 am to 4.30 pm and Saturday from 8 am to noon.

Locally made liqueurs are sold at The Perfume Factory shop on the back road in Avarua; they're not too expensive (NZ$15 to NZ$20 per bottle) and they're quite tasty. The Rarotonga Brewery, making the local Cook's Lager beer, is also in Avarua.

ENTERTAINMENT

Island Nights

Cook Islands dancing is reputed to be the best in Polynesia, superior even to the better-known dancing of Tahiti. There are plenty of chances to see it at the 'island nights' that seem to be on virtually every night of the week. The prices hotels quote for their island nights – around NZ$35 – include buffet 'island meals'. You can get in for only a NZ$5 cover charge, though, if you turn up after the buffet and only want to watch the show; usually about 9 pm.

The *Rarotongan, Edgewater, Tamure* and *Manuia Beach* hotels all hold island nights at least once or twice a week. They also hold barbecues and buffets which may include live entertainment. Sunday, when most other restaurants are closed, is the big day for hotel barbecues and brunches.

The Tourist Authority office hands out a free printed leaflet with up-to-date information on all the island nights being held around the island.

Bars, Discos & Dancing

Avarua There's quite a selection of places where you can go out dancing; Cook Islanders love to dance and Friday night is the big dancing and partying night. Almost all the dancing places are in Avarua; once you get into town you can easily walk from one to another and see which one captures your fancy. They tend to attract different crowds – one place might attract young people in their early 20s, another an older and more up-market crowd. Popularity of dancing spots and watering holes changes rapidly; the place that 'everybody' was going to last month may be eclipsed by some new place this month, or the crowd may simply walk around and drift from one place to another.

Though Friday night is the big night for going out, most of the places mentioned have entertainment on both Friday and Saturday nights, some from Wednesday or Thursday to Saturday nights. Typically they stay open till around midnight most nights, staying open later, till around 2 am, on Friday nights. On Saturday nights they shut with a bang at midnight so as not to be revelling on Sunday.

The *Banana Court Bar* on the main street in Avarua is the best-known drinking hole and dance hall in the Cook Islands, indeed it's one of the best known in the whole South Pacific. The *Vaka Lounge* in the same building is also popular. *Ronnie's*, also on the main drag, is another popular drinking spot, especially on Friday nights, with drinking outdoors on the large garden patio. Right behind Ronnie's, there's dancing in the *Reefcomber Cabaret*.

Trader Jack's, on the waterfront near the traffic circle, is a restaurant/bar very popular with the up-market set, with a live band for dancing on weekends. Nearby, *Metua's Cafe* in Browne's Arcade is another popular restaurant/bar, with a live band for dancing on the patio out under the stars. The *Empire Theatre* across the road has a teenage disco on Friday nights, after the movies are over. Also nearby, *TJ's Nightclub*, a disco with super-loud music and flashing lights, is popular with the under-25 age group.

The *Staircase* restaurant/bar, upstairs in the rear of the Top Shape Health & Fitness Centre building, is a smaller, quieter family bar, featuring Mann Short singing and playing the guitar on Monday to Friday evenings. Another small, intimate bar, the *Hideaway Bar*, is in the Cook's Corner arcade in the centre of Avarua. Friday nights there's a band for dancing on the patio behind the bar and Wednesday nights feature a karaoke.

Tere's Bar opposite the Avatiu Harbour is another popular spot, with tables outdoors or under cover, and a live band for dancing from Wednesday to Saturday nights.

Around the Island At the *Edgewater Resort*, the *Reef Restaurant & Bar* has nightly entertainment of one kind or another. Nearby, the *Tumunu* restaurant/bar is cosy and there's a weekly darts competition.

The *Right-on-the-Beach Bar* which is at the Manuia Beach Hotel is attractively tropical, with a thatched roof and sandy floor. The poolside bar at the *Rarotongan Hotel* is another pleasant tropical-style place.

At Muri Beach, the *Pacific Resort* has the attractive beachfront *Barefoot Bar* with a lovely view of the lagoon and tables both indoors and out on the patio. Nearby, upstairs at the Sailing Club, the *Sails Restaurant* also has a pleasant bar.

All of these places are rather up-market but there are a couple of places around the island that are cheaper and attract more of a local crowd.

The *RSA & Citizens Club* opposite the airport is a casual bar and social club with pool tables, darts, and a live band for dancing on weekends. Locals come here to play pool and darts, and visitors are always welcome. They boast that their beer prices are some of the cheapest on the island.

The only other place to go out dancing local-style on weekends, apart from in Avarua, is the *Beach Cargo*, occupying a former packing shed in Titikaveka on the south side of the island. On weekend nights there's a live band for dancing, and a lot of drinking going on; it attracts a lively crowd of all ages. You probably won't see another tourist there, but you're welcome to go and join in the fun.

Cinema

The Empire Theatre in Avarua shows films every night except Sunday, usually with double features. Cost is NZ$4 (children NZ$2.50).

Video

There are innumerable video-hire shops around Rarotonga. You can hire a video machine, and even the TV to go with it, from Video Block (☎ 23-366) in Matavera. Cost is NZ$15 per day for the video machine alone, NZ$10 per day for the colour TV alone, or NZ$20 per day for both together. Delivery is available for a small extra fee.

Other Entertainment

Let's not forget Piri Puruto III (☎ 20-309) who zips up coconut trees, demonstrates traditional firemaking and gives a generally entertaining show at various locations around the island. Cost is NZ$12 (children NZ$6) for a one-hour performance. He also takes tourists fishing on the reef or in the lagoon (NZ$26 for 2½ hours) and stages a weekly 'Piri's Fan Club Picnic' on Sunday with a delicious traditional umukai, a feast cooked in an underground oven. The cost of NZ$30 (children NZ$15) includes his usual one-hour performance. Transport can be arranged.

THINGS TO BUY

Arts & Crafts

There are numerous shops around Avarua selling island handicrafts. Island Crafts has an excellent selection of very good items, including an impressive collection of masks from around the Cook Islands and the Pacific, with plenty of dramatic ones from Papua New Guinea. Both the prices and the quality here are some of the highest on the island.

Other places selling island arts & crafts include the Punanga Nui open-air market near Avatiu Harbour, the Women's Handcraft Centre there, the Beachcomber Gallery in Avarua and the Cook Islands Cultural Village in Arorangi. Tivaevaes are sold at several of these places, plus at the Are Tiki shop on the main road just east of Avarua.

Pearls & Jewellery

Pearls are a speciality of the Cook Islands. Manihiki in particular, in the northern group, is an important producer of black pearls, but pearls in other colours, including golden ones and white ones, are also produced in the Cooks and sold on Rarotonga. Being on Rarotonga gives you the chance to see a fine selection of pearls and buy them at much better prices than you'll find elsewhere in the world.

Several shops in Avarua sell pearls – loose pearls, pearl jewellery, pearls still embedded in their shells, mother-of-pearl shells and many other innovative creations. Check out The Pearl Shop in the Cook's Corner arcade, The Pearl Hut near the Banana Court Bar, the Beachcomber Gallery and June's Pearls.

Shell jewellery is also popular in the Cooks. You'll find it at many of the arts & crafts places mentioned in this section.

Shells & Shell Products

Products made using local shells – necklaces, handbags, fans, wind chimes, statues, jewellery boxes and many other items – are sold at a number of places in Avarua including Island Crafts, the Women's Handcraft Centre and at a number of stalls in the Punanga Nui open-air market near Avatiu Harbour.

Shells & Craft, a small shop by the main road at Muri Beach, is the pet project of a retired shell collector, Mr Terry Lambert. It has a remarkable array of shells for sale, with everything from tiny, intricate shells to amazingly large ones. Most of the giant-size ones come from the northern group islands, where the lagoons are large and the water is warm.

Perfumes, Soaps & Coconut Oil

Locally made perfumes, made from local flowers including frangipani, starfruit, jasmine and gardenia, and locally made soaps made from pure coconut oil and scented with the same flowers, are sold direct from the manufacturers at The Perfume Factory in Avarua and at Perfumes of Rarotonga, with a small shop beside the Banana Court in Avarua and another shop on the main road in Matavera village.

Pure coconut oil, good for skin and hair, is sold at many places around Avarua, including Island Crafts, the CITC Pharmacy, the Punanga Nui open-air market and both the perfume shops. You can buy it plain or scented with various local flowers and herbs. Mauke Miracle Oil contains a special medicinal herb *(pi)* which gives protection from the sun and is good for healing cuts.

Pareu

The most typical clothing on Rarotonga is, of course, the pareu, worn by men, women and children. A pareu is simply a length of fabric, which you wrap around yourself. It can be tied in a variety of ways – a book has even been published showing some of the many ways of tying pareu. Called by a number of names, the pareu serves as the general all-purpose garment of the Pacific islands.

Rarotonga has several distinctive styles of pareu. Most popular are tie-dyed pareu, often with overlays of breadfruit leaves and other designs. Printed pareu are also popular. You can find pareu on sale for around NZ$15 at many places around Rarotonga. At least a dozen shops in Avarua sell them, including the large CITC department store, the crafts shops, the clothing shops and the Punanga Nui open-air market. Circle around the island on the coast road and you'll see many other places selling pareu.

Other Clothing

T-shirts and singlets (tank tops) emblazoned with logos, including the words Rarotonga, Cook Islands or South Pacific are sold in many shops around Avarua and in the Punanga Nui open-air market. The Linmar's shop, the T-Shirt Factory and the Punanga Nui open-air market all have wide selections and good prices. There's a lot of competition so shop around before you buy.

There are a number of boutiques, such as Joyce Peyroux and June's, selling locally manufactured clothing, including distinctive Cook Islands muu-muus and Mother Hubbard-based dresses. Prices tend to be quite high – NZ$100 for a dress is not uncommon. Much of the clothing is exported to New Zealand.

Duty-Free

There are a number of duty-free shops around Avarua and though prices aren't bad, Rarotonga is definitely not Hong Kong or Singapore for shopping. Don't make duty-free shopping a major reason for coming to Rarotonga.

GETTING THERE & AWAY

See the earlier Getting There & Away chapter for information on getting to Rarotonga from overseas and the Getting Around chapter for inter-island transport within the Cooks.

Airline Offices

On Rarotonga, all the airlines have offices at the International Airport. They include:

Air New Zealand ☎ 26-300, fax 23-300
Air Rarotonga ☎ 22-888, fax 20-979
Polynesian Airlines ☎ 20-845, fax 23-288

Shipping Offices

The *Avatapu* (☎ & fax 22-369, PO Box 131) and the *Marthalina* (☎ 27-651, fax 21-138, PO Box 378) are the two ships carrying passengers around the Cook Islands. Both have offices beside the wharf at Avatiu Harbour. Also at Avatiu Harbour, the Waterfront Commission office (☎ 21-921, fax 21-191, PO Box 84) has general information about all shipping matters.

GETTING AROUND

To/From the Airport

Most hotels, motels and hostels send vans to the airport to meet incoming international flights; independent taxis are also there to meet incoming flights. If you've pre-booked your accommodation, you'll probably be met by a van from your hotel. If you opt for a taxi you'll be very efficiently organised into parties going in various directions, funnelled into waiting taxi mini-buses and shot off – all for a fare of NZ$8 per person.

If on the other hand you're a real shoestringer and think NZ$8 per person is pretty outrageous for travelling, say, five km to Arorangi, you can get together a group and check the taxis, or even just stand on the main road in front of the airport and wait for the public bus (NZ$2 to anywhere on the island's coast road). Unfortunately, some flights come in at ungodly hours when the public bus doesn't operate.

Bus

There's a round-the-island bus service which runs right round the coast road in both directions. The bus is a good way of getting around and an easy way to do a complete round-the-island circle and get an initial feel for the place. It takes 50 minutes to make a complete round-the-island circle and you can flag the bus down anywhere along its route.

The bus departs on the hour and on the half-hour from the bus stop at Cook's Corner in Avarua. Buses going clockwise round the island depart from Cook's Corner every hour on the hour from 7 am to 4 pm weekdays, 8 am to 1 pm Saturday. Buses going round the island in an anti-clockwise direction depart from Cook's Corner every hour on the half-hour, from 8.30 am to 4.30 pm, Monday to Friday only. There are no buses on Sunday. The service seems to run pretty much on time so you can work out relevant arrival times around the island. The fare is NZ$2 for one ride, NZ$3 for a return trip (two rides) or NZ$15 for a 10-ride ticket. There's also a NZ$5 all-day bus pass good for a whole day from 7 am to 4.30 pm.

The same buses operate at night, but on a more limited schedule. Most go around the island in a clockwise direction. Departure times from Cook's Corner are at 6, 7, 9 and 10 pm Monday to Saturday, with additional late-night buses departing at midnight on Friday and Saturday nights and an even later bus, departing at 1.30 am, on Friday night. Cost is NZ$2 per ride; the NZ$3 return tickets and the NZ$5 passes are good only for the daytime buses.

Bus timetables are available from the bus driver, or at the bus office in the Cook's Corner complex, or in the *What's On* tourist booklet available free from the tourist office.

Taxi

Taxis are radio-controlled so you can phone for them. They're unmetered but fares are usually around NZ$2 as a base fare and then NZ$1 a km. A lot of the taxis are small Japanese minivans and they'll often pick up a couple more passengers going your way and offer you a lower fare.

Taxi services include BK Taxis based in Ruatonga (☎ 20-019), Kapi Taxis in Ruatonga (☎ 23-510), Silver Cabs in Pue (☎ 27-021), NTP Taxis in Kavera (☎ 21-773), Ngatangiia Taxis in Ngatangiia (☎ 22-238) and Muri Beach Taxis in Muri (☎ 21-625).

Car Rental

Before you can rent a car or motorcycle you must obtain a local driving licence from the police station in Avarua. It's a straightforward operation taking only a few minutes and costing NZ$10. Even an international driving permit is not good enough for the Cooks and if your home licence does not include the type of vehicle you'll be driving on Rarotonga – motorcycles, for example – you'll have to pay another NZ$2 and take a practical driving test which seems to consist of riding down the road from the police station, round the traffic circle outside the Banana Court and back again, without falling off. You can get your licence any day between 8 am and 4 pm. You must present your home driving licence, or if you don't have one, your passport as identification when you apply for your licence.

You don't need to hire anything very big on Rarotonga – the farthest place you can possibly drive to is half an hour away. It's worth phoning around to check the prices, as every company seems to have some sort of special deal going. Be sure to ask if insurance is included in the stated cost.

At one extreme there are the big international rental car companies, Budget and Avis, with the widest selection of cars. Avis has Jeeps and small cars at NZ$50 per day for one day, NZ$45 per day for three days or NZ$40 per day if you keep it for a week. Medium-size cars cost NZ$5 more; eight-seater mini-buses cost NZ$10 more. If you pick the car up after 1 pm on Friday and return it by 9 am Monday, you're charged for only two days.

Budget Rent-A-Car and Polynesian Bike Hire are the same company. Budget offers small cars at NZ$55 per day for one or two days, NZ$50 per day for three to five days NZ$45 per day for six to seven days. Medium-size cars are NZ$5 to NZ$15 more, Jeeps and station wagons are NZ$20 more and nine-seater mini-buses are NZ$30 more.

Locally owned TPA Rentals has cheaper cars, medium size, at NZ$35 per day or NZ$30 per day on a weekly rate. Several other locally owned companies hire cars at prices somewhere between TPA and the 'big boys'. Rarotonga Rentals, for example, hires cars and Jeeps at NZ$55 per day for one day, NZ$40 per day for three days, and MG sports cars at NZ$70 per day for one day, NZ$50 per day for three days.

The main Rarotonga rental car companies are:

Avis Rental Cars
    Avarua (☎ 22-833, fax 21-702); Arorangi (☎ 21-901); Airport (☎ 21-039)
Budget Rent-A-Car
    Avarua (☎ 20-895, fax 20-888); Edgewater Resort (☎ 21-026); Rarotongan Resort Hotel (☎ 20-838); Airport (☎ 21-036)
Hogan's Service Centre
    Arorangi (☎ 22-632)
Rental Cars
    Avarua (☎ 24-441, 24-444, fax 24-446)
Tipani Rentals
    Avarua (☎ 21-617, fax 25-611); Arorangi, opposite Edgewater Resort (☎ 22-328)
TPA Rental Cars
    Arorangi (☎ 20-611)

There are few surprises for drivers on Raro. The driving is reasonably sane (except late on Friday and Saturday, the two nights when there's heavy drinking) and there's no reason to go fast as there's not far to go wherever you're going. The speed limit is 40 km/h (25 mph) in town, 50 km/h (30 mph) out of town. You drive on the left – like in New Zealand, Australia, Japan and much of the Pacific and South-East Asia.

Be cautious and pay attention to all pedestrians on or near the roadway. Unlike in many parts of the world, where pedestrians keep their wits about them and take precautions not to get hit, on Rarotonga it's often the other way around: pedestrians casually wander onto and across the roadway and it's the *driver* who must watch out. In particular, watch out for children, but also be aware of adults, families, bicyclists, slow motorcycle riders, tractors, dogs, pigs and even crabs – not to mention potholes, which seem to appear overnight. This is an especially good reason *never* to drive fast.

If you're on two wheels watch out for loose stones on some stretches of road.

There are two rental car rules: don't leave windows open, not because of the risk of theft but because of the chances of an unexpected tropical downpour leaving the car awash; and don't park under coconut palms, because a falling coconut can positively flatten a tiny Japanese car.

Motorcycle Rental

Small motorcycles are the principal mode of transport on Rarotonga and there are lots of motorcycles to hire, mostly 50cc to 100cc models. Many places rent them; ring round to find the best deal. Lowest rates are about NZ$15 per day, NZ$90 per week. Many hotels also rent motorcycles but their rates are often higher, around NZ$20 per day. Ask at the place you're staying, and compare prices. Most places offer discounts for weekly rentals.

Agencies hiring motorcycles include:

Mel's Tie Dyes
  Muri (☎ 22-207)
NTP Rentals
  Kavera (☎ 21-773)
Odds & Ends
  Avarua (☎ 20-942)
Polynesian Bike Hire
  Avarua (☎ 20-895); Edgewater Resort (☎ 21-029); Rarotongan Resort Hotel (☎ 20-838; after hours ☎ 25-260, 23-888)
Tipani Rentals
  Avarua (☎ 21-617, fax 25-611); Arorangi, opposite Edgewater Resort (☎ 22-328)

See the previous Car Rental section for advice on obtaining a Cook Islands driving licence, which you must have before you can hire a motorcycle, and for advice on driving on Rarotonga.

Bicycle Rental

Bicycles are just as readily available and generally cost about NZ$6 to NZ$10 a day for mountain bikes. The island is compact enough and the traffic is light enough to make riding a pleasure, particularly on the inland roads. Many hotels have pushbikes for hire. Several agencies include:

Mel's Tie Dyes
  Muri (☎ 22-207)
Ngatangiia Taxis
  Ngatangiia (☎ 22-238)
Polynesian Bike Hire
  Avarua (☎ 20-895); Edgewater Resort (☎ 21-029); Rarotongan Resort Hotel (☎ 20-838; after hours ☎ 25-260, 23-888)
Tipani Rentals
  Avarua (☎ 21-617, fax 25-611); Arorangi, opposite Edgewater Resort (☎ 22-328)

Aitutaki & Manuae

Aitutaki

Population: 2357
Area: 18.1 sq km

Aitutaki is another Cook Islands' entrant in the 'most beautiful island in the Pacific' competition. It's the second largest island in the Cooks in terms of population although in area it only ranks sixth. It's also the second most popular island in terms of tourist visits. The hook-shaped island nestles in a huge triangular lagoon, 12 km across its base and 15 km from top to bottom. The outer reef of the lagoon is dotted with beautiful motus (small islands) and they're one of the island's major attractions.

Aitutaki is also historically interesting, with a number of impressive pre-European maraes which can still be visited today. Aitutaki is also historically significant because it was the first foothold in the Cooks for the London Missionary Society. Only after converting Aitutaki's population did they move on to Rarotonga.

Aitutaki has one of the best 'island nights' in the Cook Islands; try to arrange to be on the island on a Friday night to catch this authentic local occasion.

History

Various legends tell of early Polynesian settlers arriving at Aitutaki by canoe. The first settler was Ru, who according to various traditions came from either the legendary Polynesian ancestral homeland of Avaiki, or from Tubuaki, which may be the present-day island of Tubuai in the Austral Islands, now part of French Polynesia. Wherever Ru's homeland was, it had become overcrowded so Ru, his four wives, his four brothers and their wives, and a crew of 20 royal maidens sailed off in search of new land. Eventually they landed on Aitutaki at the motu Akitua, and decided to make this their new home.

Ru went to the highest point on the island, the top of Mt Maungapu, and surveyed the island. He divided the land into 20 sections, one for each of the 20 royal maidens, but completely forgot about his brothers! One brother had been killed as the huge canoe was hauled onto land, rolling it over logs. The three remaining brothers left the island in anger – they had come all that way to find a new land to settle, and yet Ru allotted no land for them. They continued over the ocean and eventually wound up in New Zealand.

The original name of Aitutaki was Ararau Enua O Ru Ki Te Moana, meaning 'Ru in search of land over the sea'. Later this long name was shortened to a more manageable mouthful: Araura. Still later the name was changed again to its present one of Aitutaki – *a'i tutaki* means 'to keep the fire going' – but the old names are still used in legend and chant. Akitua, the motu now occupied by the Aitutaki Lagoon Hotel, was the party's landing place and was originally named Uri Tua O Ru Ki Te Moana, or 'Ru turning his back to the sea'.

Various canoes came after Ru's party, from Tonga, Samoa and islands in French Polynesia, landing on different parts of the island. Each new people had to be accepted by one of the 20 maidens or their descendants in order to have a space on the island to settle. One explorer from a far-off land, guided to Aitutaki by Are Mango, the god of sharks, came ashore on the south part of the island and built the marae Tokongarangi to honour that god.

The island's European discoverer was Captain William Bligh on board the *Bounty* on 11 April 1789. The famous mutiny took place just 17 days later as the ship was en route to Tonga. Two years later in May 1791, Captain Edward Edwards came by in HMS *Pandora* searching for those mutineers, and

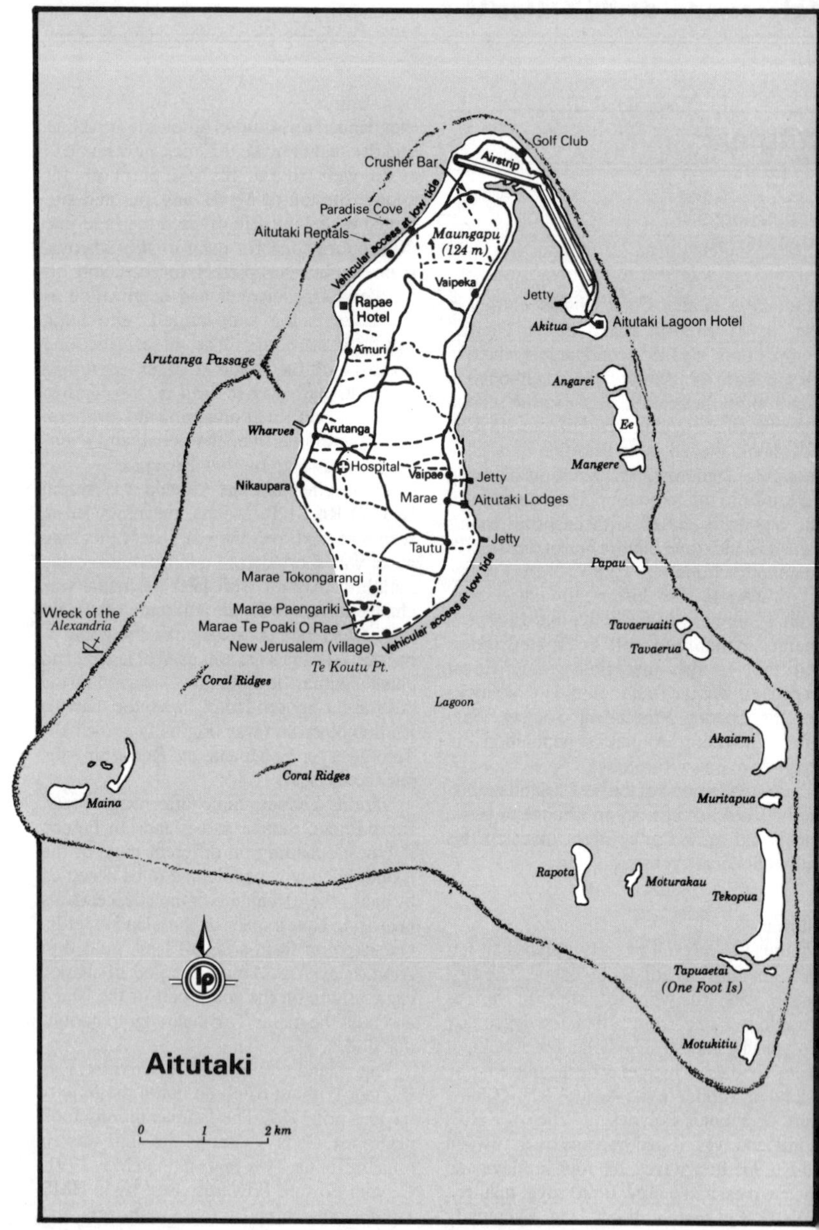
Golf Club
Airstrip
Crusher Bar
Paradise Cove
Aitutaki Rentals
Vehicular access at low tide
Maungapu
(124 m)
Vaipeka
Jetty
Akitua
Aitutaki Lagoon Hotel
Rapae
Hotel
Amuri
Arutanga Passage
Angarei
Ee
Wharves
Arutanga
Hospital
Mangere
Vaipae
Jetty
Nikaupara
Marae
Aitutaki Lodges
Tautu
Jetty
Papau
Marae Tokongarangi
Wreck of the
Alexandria
Marae Paengariki
Marae Te Poaki O Rae
New Jerusalem (village)
Vehicular access at low tide
Tavaeruaiti
Tavaerua
Te Koutu Pt.
Coral Ridges
Lagoon
Akaiami
Coral Ridges
Maina
Muritapua
Rapota
Moturakau
Tekopua
Tapuaetai
(One Foot Is)
Motukitiu
Aitutaki
0
1
2 km

in 1792 Bligh paid his second visit to the island.

In 1814 Captain Goodenough turned up with his ship *Cumberland* after his visit to Rarotonga came to its ill-starred conclusion. He left behind three Rarotongans whom he had taken with him on his sudden departure. In 1821 the missionary John Williams visited Aitutaki briefly and left behind Papeiha and Vahapata, converts from the island of Raiatea near Tahiti, to begin the work of Christianising the Cooks. Williams returned two years later to find Papeiha had made remarkable progress so he was moved on to greater challenges on Rarotonga.

Later European visitors included Charles Darwin on the famous voyage of the *Beagle* in 1835. The first European missionary took up residence in 1839, and the 1850s saw Aitutaki become a favourite port of call for the whaling ships scouring the Pacific at that time. During WW II Aitutaki went through great upheaval when a large American contingent moved in to build the island's two long runways, which until the mid-70s were larger than Rarotonga's airport runway.

Aitutaki suffered the impact of a major hurricane in 1977. At the Rapae Hotel, water washed right through the restaurant and kitchen area, and the family unit up the hill was turned into an emergency dining room. The CICC church in town, which is well back from the waterfront, also suffered extensive damage.

Orientation

You can do a complete circular tour of the island in just a few hours. The road runs close to the coast most of the way, and you pass through several pleasant villages. There's plenty to see – crabs duck into holes as you come by, ripe fruit lies under trees where it falls, exuberant children laugh and sing by every harbour jetty, the water glitters turquoise bright on sunny days. Look for the huge banyan tree arching over the main road just north of the Aitutaki Lodges turn-off in the village of Tautu.

Arutanga, about halfway down the west coast, is the island's main settlement. Other villages, or districts, on the island include Amuri, Nikaupara, New Jerusalem, Tautu, Vaipae and Vaipeka. The numerous small motus around the edge of the lagoon are unpopulated.

On the south coast of the island, New Jerusalem is a religious village built in the early 1990s. Its residents are all members of one faith, known as the Free Church; the village is constructed entirely of native materials, in the style of an old traditional Cook Islands village.

Information

The Survey Department on Rarotonga has an excellent large-scale topographical map of

Dogs & Pigs

There are no dogs at all on Aitutaki and nobody is allowed to bring dogs to the island. There haven't been any for quite a few years and there are numerous stories as to what happened to them. Probably the best is that the Aitutakians, like the Tahitians, savoured dog-meat and eventually ate them all. Another is that the dogs were thought to be carriers of leprosy, which at one time was rampant on the island. Still another story is that a dog mauled an ariki's (high chief's) child and he then banned all dogs. Whatever the reason, it's a relief not to be tripping over them all the time. And Aitutaki does have some healthy looking stray cats!

There are also plenty of pigs – that most popular of Pacific domestic animals. South Sea pigs have learnt to make coconuts a major part of their diet although well-kept pigs also have papaya and taro mash! They're tasty pigs. There are even some pigs, kept on one of the motus, which have learnt to dig up and break open the *pahua* clam shells which are an Aitutakian delicacy! ■

Aitutaki, widely available on both Rarotonga and Aitutaki, showing all the roads and trails and the coral formations in the lagoon. *What's On in the Cook Islands* and *Jason's*, the two free tourist publications available at the Tourist Authortiy Office, hotels and other places on Rarotonga, contain maps of both Rarotonga and Aitutaki, with items of interest to visitors (hotels, restaurants, sights etc) clearly marked.

The post office is at the Cook Islands Administration Building at the intersection of the two main roads in Arutanga: the coast road and the road leading down to the wharf. Aitutaki issues its own special postage stamps which are not available on Rarotonga. The post office is open Monday to Friday from 8 am to 4 pm.

The Telecom office is at the post office and you can buy phone cards here to use in the card phone outside the building.

Also at the Administration Building is the Treasury, where foreign currency can be exchanged Monday to Friday from 8 am to 3 pm. If you need a cash advance on a credit card, you can get it from the Aitutaki Lagoon Hotel or the Rapae Hotel, but only if you're one of their guests.

The Air Rarotonga office (☎ 31-888) is on the main road in Arutanga. It is also the representative for Air New Zealand, Hawaiian Airlines and Polynesian Airlines. Office hours are Monday to Friday from 7.30 am to 4 pm, Saturday closing at 1 pm.

Ask at your hotel if you should boil your water before drinking it. At some places, the water comes from underground and should be boiled first. At others, you may take your drinking water from a special rainwater tank.

A round of golf at the nine-hole golf course by the airport costs NZ$5.

Arutanga

Arutanga is a pleasant, sleepy little place redolent of the South Seas. There are a number of typical island trade stores and the weathered, old CICC church picturesquely situated by the playing fields next to the harbour. Built in 1828 the church is the oldest in the Cooks, and also one of the most beautiful, with red, yellow, green and white carved wood all around the ceiling, more dark woodcarving over the doorways, simple stained-glass windows, and an anchor placed on the ceiling with the inscription Ebera 6:19 (Hebrews 6:19). A colourful mural over the altar shows angels announcing 'Tapu, Tapu, Tapu' ('Holy, Holy, Holy'). This church also has some of the best acoustics in the Cooks, wonderful for enjoying the spirited hymn singing. In the churchyard there's a double-sided monument to the London Missionary Society's pioneering Reverend John Williams and to Papeiha, the Polynesian convert, who Williams left here in 1821.

The harbour is a quiet affair although there are often a few visiting yachts moored offshore. Larger ships have to be unloaded by lighters, outside the lagoon. You can get an excellent view of the island's whole western coastline from out on the tip of the jetty. A huge banana packing plant to handle the

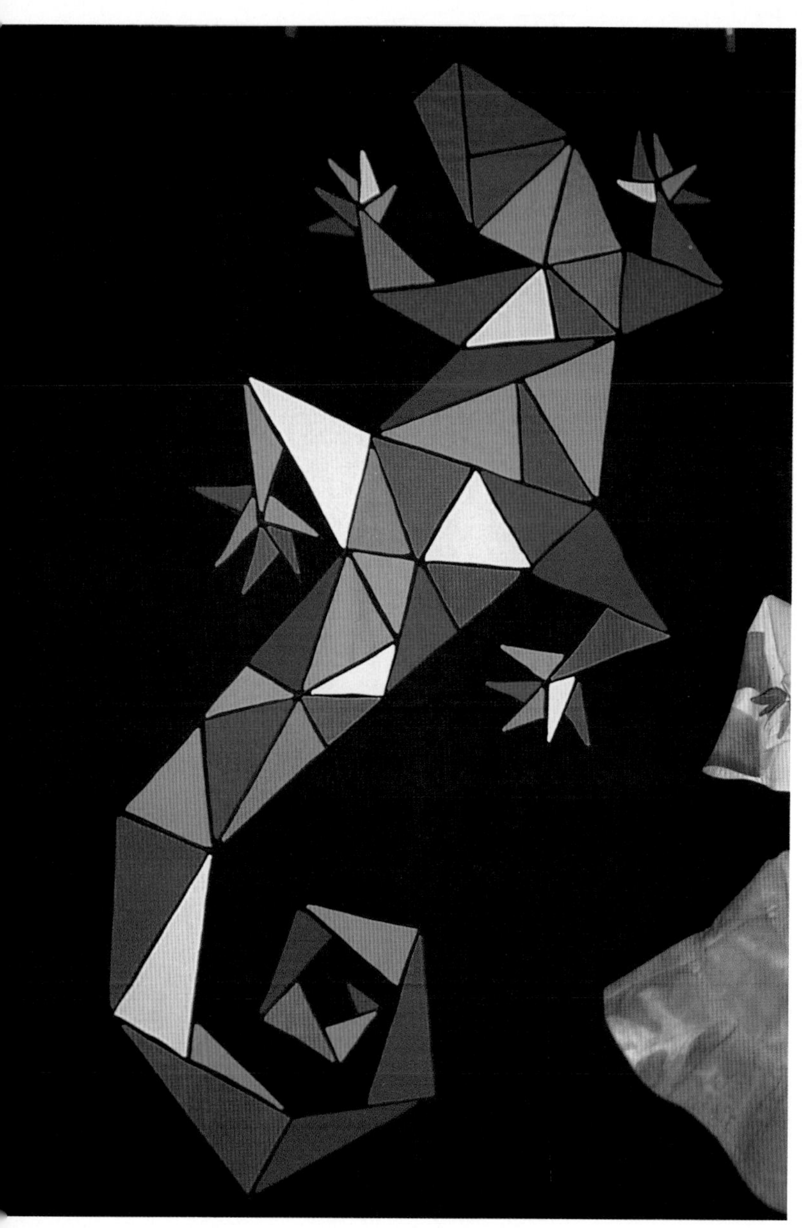

/aevae, a famous handicraft of the Cook Islands (NK)

Top: Woman in market selling tie-dyed clothing, Avarua (TC)
Left: Market stall, Avarua (TC)
Right: The principal transport vehicle on Rarotonga (TC)

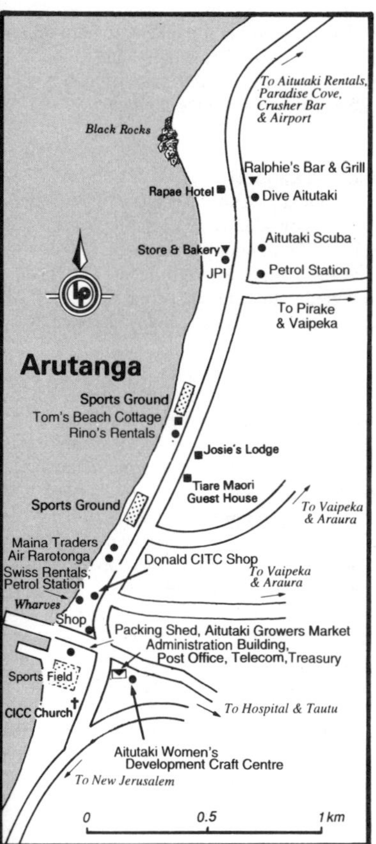

island's major export crop stands beside the harbour; one part of it is occupied by the Aitutaki Growers Market, where local farmers and fishermen come to sell their products.

Marae

The Aitutaki marae are notable for the large size of the stones. The main road goes right through a big marae at the turn-off to the Aitutaki Lodges; the stones are along both sides of the road.

On the inland road between Nikaupara and Tautu, signs saying 'Marae' and 'Marae/Jerusalem' direct you to some of the most magnificent marae on the island. Tokongarangi, near a watermelon patch just off this road to your right, is a marae built in honour of Are Mango, the god of sharks. The story goes that Ikaroa, a seafarer coming to Aitutaki from the far-off island of Raiatea in French Polynesia, travelled with a carving of Are Mango on the prow of his canoe. As he headed across the sea towards Aitutaki, the carved god shifted directions. He kept sailing in the direction the god faced and eventually arrived at Aitutaki. He landed on the south part of the island and built this marae to honour the god who protected him on his journey. Later in history, the fierce Rarotongan warrior Tairi Terangi was defeated on this marae.

Farther south along this same road is Taravao – a sign nailed up on a tree announces the spot. From this crossroads, there are two very large marae, one on either side of the road. The one on your left (east), Te Poaki O Rae ('The Stone of Rae'), covers

Tairi Terangi Meets His End at Tokongarangi

In pre-European times a huge and powerful warrior, Tairi Terangi, came from Rarotonga to try to overpower Aitutaki. He started at the north of Aitutaki and worked his way south down the island, defeating or killing everyone and everything in his path. As he forged southwards, the people became increasingly terrified, and the taungas (high priests) tried to divine, with a fortune-telling power they had using coconut shells, what the outcome would be. In place after place, the shells prophesied the victory of Tairi Terangi – all the way to the south of the island, to the marae Tokongarangi. When the ta'ungas cast the shells on this marae, they predicted that Tairi Terangi would be defeated.

Since Tokongarangi is practically at the southern tip of Aitutaki, if Tairi Terangi had prevailed here, it would have meant the defeat of the entire island. But when he arrived on the marae, a much smaller man, Pukenga, inspired with the divine power and assistance of Are Mango, god of sharks and god of this marae, killed him, releasing the whole island from the reign of terror. ■

about 1.6 hectares (four acres). It has several groupings of stones but the tallest one, at 2.8 metres, is attributed to Rae, who brought it from a more ancient marae elsewhere on the island. The line of stones on your right as you enter the marae area were where watchmen used to stand to guard the marae.

On the west side of the Taravao crossroads sign, another large marae arrests your attention as you come over the hill, with its large expanse and big black volcanic stones. Called Paengariki, only part of the marae is visible today; more stones, covering an area as large or larger than the visible marae area, are hidden in the dense bush on the south side of the visible marae area. Each of the large black volcanic basalt stones has its own name. This marae is attributed to Kakeroa, who is said to have sailed to Aitutaki from Avaiki and married Ruano'o, a woman from Ru's canoe, though one genealogy places him only around 11 generations ago. Kakeroa is also credited with one of the stone groupings at the Te Poaki O Rae marae nearby.

Mt Maungapu

Maungapu is the highest point on the island at just 124 metres (372 feet). It's an easy 30-minute hike to the top, from where there's a superb view of the island and the entire lagoon.

The route to the top takes off from opposite the Paradise Cove motel and is marked by a sign on the road. It starts off gently and gets steeper as you near the top.

Aitutaki Lagoon

The lagoon of Aitutaki is one of the wonders of the Cook Islands. It is large, colourful and full of life, although fortunately not sharks. The snorkelling is magnificent. The lagoon is dotted with sand bars, coral ridges and 21 motus (small islands), many of them with their own stories.

Maina Maina ('Little Girl'), at the southwest corner of the lagoon, offers some of the lagoon's best snorkelling on the coral formations near its shore and around the large powder-white sandbars just to the north and east. It is also the nesting place of the Red-Tailed Tropic Bird, which used to inspire Cook Islanders from as far away as Atiu to come seeking its red tail feathers for use in their spectacular headdresses. If you're here at the right time of year you may get to see them nesting on the island; their nesting season ends around December when they fly off to other lands.

Just north of Maina, out on the reef, is the shipwreck of the *Alexandria*, which crashed on the reef during the 1930s as it was carry-

Aitutaki Gets a Mountain

Apparently Aitutaki was once just a low atoll. The inhabitants decided they needed a mountain for their island, so they went off across the sea in search of one. Coming to Rarotonga, they spotted Raemaru, the mountain behind the village of Arorangi, and thought that it would be perfect. However, it was rather large for Aitutaki, so they decided they'd take just the top off and bring that home.

Late at night, they sneaked up the sides of Raemaru and encircled it, thrust their spears in until they had severed the top from the bottom, and took off with it. They held it aloft with their spears as they set off for Aitutaki in their canoes, spread out in the sea all around the mountain.

When morning came, the Arorangi villagers looked up and noticed something was wrong. They set off in hot pursuit of the Aitutakians to get their mountain back. But the fierce Aitutakian warriors beat the Rarotongans back, using only their single free hands while still holding the mountain aloft between them with their spears in their other hands. They succeeded in bringing the mountain top to Aitutaki, and placed it in the north part of the island. Raemaru today has a distinctly cut-off, flat-topped appearance. ■

ing a load of Model T Fords from the United States to New Zealand. Fortunately, there was no loss of life. You won't see any old Model Ts around the wreck, but the skeleton of the ship is still there.

Rapota Rapota, a volcanic islet farther east, was once a leper colony.

Akaiami Akaiami is the motu where the old flying boats used to land to refuel. You can still see their wharf on the lagoon side of the motu. There are some thatch houses not far from the wharf, used for short camping trips to the island.

Eastern Motus From Akaiami southwards, the eastern motus are interesting to explore, but the snorkelling is not so good because there is little coral. If you visit them during the December to April wet season be sure to bring mosquito repellent.

Tapuaetai Perhaps the most famous motu, and certainly the one that most tourists visit, is Tapuaetai, or One Foot Island, with its lovely white stretch of beach. The brilliant pale-turquoise colour of the water off this beach is truly amazing. The pure white sand of the lagoon is very shallow in the channel between One Foot Island and its neighbour Tekopua, causing the water to gleam. Since there is no coral the snorkelling is not so good but the clear water compensates.

Beaches & Snorkelling

Beaches on most parts of the main island are beautiful but not that good for swimming because the water is so shallow. From beside the Rapae Hotel you can walk all the way out

The Coral Route

Aitutaki had a pioneering role in Pacific aviation as a stopping point in Tasman Empire Air Line's 'Coral Route'. Back in the 1950s TEAL, the predecessor to Air New Zealand, flew across the Pacific on an Auckland – Suva (Fiji) – Apia (Western Samoa) – Aitutaki – Papeete (Tahiti) route. The first leg to Suva was flown by DC-6s but the rest of the way was by four-engined Solent flying boats.

The stop at Aitutaki was purely to refuel, indeed this was carried out at the uninhabited motu of Akaiami. It took over two hours so passengers had a chance to take a swim in the lagoon. Flying in those days was hardly a one-stop operation: one day took you from Suva to Apia and the next day required a pre-dawn departure from Apia in order to make Papeete before nightfall. The flying boats were unpressurised so they did not fly above 3000 metres and they sometimes had to descend to less than 500 metres.

The old Solents carried their 60-odd passengers in seven separate cabins and in some degree of luxury. Food was actually cooked on the aircraft, in contrast to today's reheated airline meals. At that time the fortnightly flight into Papeete was the only direct air link between Tahiti and the rest of the world, and the aircraft's arrival was a major event.

Usually the trips were uneventful but on one occasion a malfunction at Aitutaki required off-loading the passengers while the aircraft limped on to Tahiti on three engines. It was a week before it arrived back to collect the passengers – who by that time had begun to really enjoy their enforced stay on hotel-less Aitutaki. On another occasion, the aircraft was forced to return to Aitutaki when the Tahiti lagoon turned out to be full of logs. The trip to Tahiti was attempted twice more before the lagoon was clear enough for a landing. One of the TEAL flying boats is now on display in the MOTAT transport museum in Auckland, New Zealand.

Solents were also used by British Airways (BOAC in those days) on routes from England through to India and Australia. A couple were still in use by Ansett Airlines in Australia for Sydney-Lord Howe Island flights right into the early 1970s, but flying-boat travel was really ended by WW II. Prior to the war, most long-range commercial flights were made by flying boats because suitable airports for long-range land planes did not exist. After the war not only had large, long-range aircraft been greatly improved but there were airport runways capable of handling them all over the world. The flying-boat days were over. ■

One Foot Island (Tapuaetai)

One Foot Island (Tapuaetai), out of all the 21 motus, wasn't always the major tourist attraction that it is today.

In 1978, a photographer working for Air New Zealand came to Aitutaki to take publicity photos and a photo of this islet's beautiful beach was used for a big promotional poster. Travel writers who came to the island sought out this idyllic stretch of beach and its fame soon spread.

Technically, the name Tapuaetai means not 'one foot' but 'one footprint'. There are several versions of how the motu got its name. One legend tells how a father and son, fleeing warriors from the main island, sought refuge on Tapuaetai. Upon reaching the motu's shore, the father picked his son up and hid him in a tree. When the warriors arrived they killed the father but having seen only one set of footprints leading away from his canoe did not realise his son was there. The son returned to Aitutaki and told the story of how the single set of footprints had saved his life.

In another legend, a seafarer from Tonga was crossing the seas with his sister. She died but he wanted to bury her on land, not throw her to the sharks, so he kept her body in the canoe until he sighted land. He came into Aitutaki's lagoon near Tapuaetai and landed there, hoping to bury his sister on the motu. As he alighted from the canoe, however, some fierce Aitutakians emerged from the bush and he jumped back into the canoe and sailed away, still bearing his sister and leaving only a single footprint in the sand. ■

to the outer reef on a natural coral causeway which starts only 50 or so metres from the shore – at low tide it's not more than knee-deep all the way. There are interesting coral rockpools just inside the outer reef and there are places you can snorkel there. A little to the north of where this causeway gets to the outer reef you can fish in the Tonga Ruta passage. The branches of the passage are very narrow – some as narrow as 30 cm – but they are over 15 metres deep and full of fish. This is one of the main passages through which the lagoon drains.

If you continue round the corner beyond the black rocks on the beach on the north side of the Rapae Hotel there's a slightly better beach, with water about 1.5 metres deep and some interesting snorkelling. Beware of stonefish in this area, however.

The snorkelling is actually pretty good along this same stretch of coast all the way up to the airport, even though the water is not deep, because the reef here is close in, with the coral formations supporting an abundance of life. Snorkelling is also good in the channel separating Akitua motu (where the Aitutaki Lagoon Hotel is) from the main island, especially on the outer side of the channel, towards the reef, and on the lagoon side, around the far tip of the motu. Lots of local children come to this channel to swim.

Anywhere there's a jetty – beside the wharf in Arutanga, or around the jetties on the east side of the island – there's water deep enough to swim in, and you're likely to find lots of friendly local children doing just that.

The best swimming, snorkelling and beaches are found out on the lagoon motus.

Lagoon Cruises

Several operators offer trips on the lagoon and to the motus around it. Ask around, and in your hotel, about who is doing the cruises at the time you arrive. Also ask exactly what is included in a cruise. Some go to only one island, some go to many; most are full-day cruises and include transport to and from your accommodation, free snorkelling gear and a barbecued fresh-fish lunch on the motu. Prices are about NZ$30 to NZ$40 for a full day with lunch. All of them operate every day except Sunday, when the whole island takes a day off.

Ru's Cruise (☎ 31-164) conducts full-day cruises to Maina Island for NZ$30 per person, and three-island cruises to Akaiami, Motu Rakau and One Foot Island for NZ$35 per person. Paradise Cove Tours (☎ 31-218, 31-069) does the same, at NZ$35 and NZ$40, or a two-island cruise to both Maina and One Foot Islands for NZ$35 with no lunch or NZ$45 with lunch. Bishop's

Lagoon Cruises, also called Lagoon Adventures (☎ 31-009, fax 31-493) does full-day cruises to One Foot Island for NZ$40. Vikings Watersports & Adventures (☎ 31-180, fax 31-407) does cruises to One Foot Island for NZ$40 per person, to Maina Island for NZ$45 per person, and multiple-island or brunch cruises for around NZ$45 per person.

Other operators offering lagoon cruises include Aitutaki Lodges (☎ 31-334, fax 31-333) and Ian Guinea (☎ 31-040).

All of these operators use speed boats of one kind or another. If you're in the mood for something quieter, check out David Tengaru (☎ 31-023) who does a variety of lagoon cruises on a seven-metre (21 foot) outrigger canoe equipped with a sail, which holds just two passengers plus the captain. Cost is NZ$35 per person for a full-day trip but you can also do shorter trips – like a two-hour sunset sail – for around NZ$10 per person.

Or you can go water skiing in the lagoon with Aitutaki Sea Charters (☎ 31-281); cost is NZ$60 per person for a two-hour trip.

Scuba Diving

Scuba diving outside the lagoon is another attraction. Diving on Aitutaki is relaxed, visibility is good, and it's suitable for everyone from novices to experts. Features include drop-offs, multi-levels, wall dives, deep dives, cave dives, shipwreck dives and more. The drop-off at the edge of the reef is as much as 200 metres in places and divers have seen everything up to, and including, whale sharks, humpback whales and an operating submarine!

Neil Mitchell at Aitutaki Scuba (☎ 31-103, fax 31-310) is the longest-established professional diving operator on the island, offering diving trips for NZ$65 if you use their gear, NZ$55 if you use your own. You must be a certified diver to go on these dives, but you can also pay just NZ$15 and go along to snorkel. Aitutaki Scuba also offers courses leading to full diving certification; cost is NZ$450 for a minimum four-day course.

Dive Aitutaki (☎ & fax 31-326) is a newer company with similar dives and prices. They also offer PADI 'Discover Scuba Diving' resort courses for non-certified divers as an introduction to diving for NZ$75, plus night dives and a variety of PADI dive courses, including open-water diving, advanced open-water, rescue, and dive master courses.

Big-Game Fishing

You can go big-game fishing outside the reef with a variety of operators. Aitutaki Sea Charters (☎ 31-281), Clive Baxter (☎ 31-025) and Ian Guinea (☎ 31-040) all offer four to five-hour game fishing trips for around NZ$110 per person, including all gear. Marlin, tuna, wahoo and mahi mahi are all found outside the reef.

Places to Stay – bottom end

Paradise Cove (☎ 31-218, fax 31-456), on the north-west side of the island, is on a beautiful stretch of beach with fine white sand and good snorkelling possibilities. It offers two types of accommodation. Facilities include a large house with shared kitchen, bathroom and lounge areas, and five twin or double bedrooms priced at NZ$20/30 for singles/doubles. Plus there are six basic free-standing bungalows right on the beach, each sleeping two people, with singles/doubles at NZ$30/40. Each has its own fridge, but bathroom and kitchen facilities are shared. Though rustic, the bungalows are very charming, with thatched roofs and all-natural materials – it's the only place we saw in the Cook Islands where you can sleep in an old-fashioned *kikau* hut (traditional thatch-roofed hut).

Aitutaki has three other guest houses – *Tom's Beach Cottage, Josie's Lodge* and the *Tiare Maori Guest House* – all in Amuri on the main road between the Rapae Hotel and the centre of Arutanga. All are priced the same, with singles/doubles/triples at NZ$28/38/48. All offer similar facilities and standards, with several simple bedrooms and shared kitchens, bathrooms and sitting areas.

Right on a beautiful stretch of beach and also convenient to town, *Tom's Beach Cottage* (☎ 31-051, fax 31-409) is friendly and relaxed, and you can have barbecues, lounge around or even sleep on the beach if you like.

A little closer to town, *Josie's Lodge* (☎ 31-111) and the *Tiare Maori Guest House* (☎ 31-119) are practically next door to one another and they're very similar to each other. *Josie's* has six regular bedrooms plus one larger family room sleeping four people for NZ$52. The *Tiare Maori* has seven bedrooms.

You can do your own cooking at all the guest houses – it's free at all except the *Tiare Maori*, where there's an extra charge of NZ$2 per day if you want to use the stove. All three give you the option of ordering meals for an extra charge of around NZ$5 for breakfast or lunch, NZ$10 to NZ$15 for dinner.

Planned for around the time of this book's publication, *Nelly's Airport Beach Cottages* is scheduled to open on the lagoon near the airport and be another budget alternative, with private cabins.

Places to Stay – middle

The popular and pleasantly situated *Rapae Hotel* (☎ 31-320, fax 31-321) is set in lush gardens right beside the beach, about two km north of the centre of Arutanga. It has 13 rooms, 12 of them studio doubles in duplex units – they're simple but comfortable with bathroom, tea/coffee making equipment and a big shady verandah. Singles/doubles are NZ$85/95. There's also a larger family unit for NZ$110 per night, occupying the same space as a regular duplex, with separate bedroom and sitting room, and beds for six people. The Rapae has a pleasant open-air lagoon-view restaurant, the best Island Night on Aitutaki every Friday, and offers full-day lagoon cruises for NZ$40, bicycle hire for NZ$10 per day, motor scooter hire for NZ$30 per day or car hire for NZ$75 per day.

Other middle-range accommodation on the island is on a smaller scale. *Tom's Beach Cottage* (see the previous 'places to stay-bottom end' section) has one private self-contained honeymoon unit by the beach for NZ$89 per night. Also on the beach, but closer in to Arutanga, *Rino's Rentals* (☎ 31-197) has four self-contained studio units, each sleeping two to four people, at NZ$80 per night.

Places to Stay – top end

Aitutaki Lodges (☎ 31-334, fax 31-333) on the east coast of the island has six A-frame chalets, each with a kitchenette, one queen-size bed and one single bed, and a large verandah with a splendid view of the lagoon and the motus stretching away in the distance. The view is unsurpassed on the island; the only drawbacks are that the beach here is volcanic rather than white sand, and you're about 3.5 km from town (a half-hour's walk); staff will hire you a motorcycle at NZ$30 per day. You can cook for yourself or arrange for cooked meals; it has an open-air bar and dining room under a thatched roof. Room cost is NZ$145 for one or two people, NZ$29 per extra adult.

At the far end of the airstrip, the *Aitutaki Lagoon Hotel* (☎ 31-200, fax 31-202) is on Akitua motu, across a narrow channel from the main island and joined to the main island by a narrow footbridge. It has all the mod cons including a restaurant, bar and swimming pool and many activities are on offer. The resort has nine beachfront bungalows and 15 garden bungalows, each with a double and a single bed, a sink and a fridge. Nearly everybody staying here will be on some sort of all-inclusive package deal booked through travel agencies, which may make it cheaper, but the walk-in rates are NZ$145 in the garden bungalows or NZ$190 in the beachfront bungalows. The major drawback is the resort's considerable isolation from the rest of the island. The locals often call it the Akitua Resort, after the motu.

Places to Stay – renting a house

Rino's Rentals (☎ 31-197) on the main road in Arutanga has a three-bedroom house complete with everything you need, for NZ$200 per week.

Places to Eat

The restaurant at the *Rapae Hotel* is a beautiful, relaxed open-air restaurant overlooking the lagoon and white beach. It has good food – their home-cured ham sandwiches are delicious and they have hot lunch and dinner main dishes for around NZ$12 to NZ$15, sandwiches, soups, starters and desserts for around NZ$6. On Friday night their excellent Island Night buffet (NZ$25) begins at around 7.30 pm and provides a varied spread of island specialities from octopus to roast pork, fried fish to taro, curried goat to clams. A floor show and dance follows and being there for the buffet gets you a ringside seat. On Sunday night beginning around 8 pm there's a barbecue for NZ$20. Book in advance for these popular functions.

Opposite the Rapae, *Ralphie's Bar & Grill* serves lunch and dinner Monday to Saturday, dinner only on Sunday. The menu has everything from fine dining to takeaways – there are seafood, steaks and pastas with prices about the same as the Rapae as well as inexpensive fare such as burgers and chips.

On the north side of the island, the *Crusher Bar* is a true island-style place, with an open-air thatched dining room, lots of island decor, and live music and dancing every night. Weeknights there's a choice of grilled steak or fish of the day with salad bar for NZ$9.50; Sunday there's a roast pork dinner for NZ$15 (drinks and desserts extra). There's lots of tropical greenery which unfortunately is a favourite hangout for mosquitoes – be sure to wear plenty of repellent. Reservations are essential (☎ 31-283) and transport can be arranged. It's open from 6 pm every night except Friday.

The bar/restaurant at the *Aitutaki Lagoon Hotel* serves all meals and has a changing dinner menu served from 7.30 to 10 pm, with soups, starters and desserts for NZ$5.50, main courses for around NZ$18 to NZ$25. Saturday night is Island Night, beginning at 7.30 pm with a buffet, floorshow and dancing afterwards (NZ$25). On Sunday evenings there's a Mongolian barbecue (NZ$23).

Self-Catering The stores have the usual Cook Islands' selection of tins and the usual limited selection of fresh fruits and vegetables. The choice is more restricted than on Rarotonga and the prices are higher. It's worth bringing some supplies with you, particularly if you plan to cook for yourself.

The shop opposite Aitutaki Scuba, near the Rapae Hotel, has excellent fresh-baked bread. Aitutaki's large lagoon supplies the best variety of fresh fish in the islands but you've got to catch them yourself or know somebody who has been fishing! If you go on a lagoon cruise you're likely to come back with some.

Otherwise, check early in the morning (around 7 or 8 am) at the Aitutaki Growers Market by the wharf in Arutanga. There's usually some variety of locally grown produce and freshly caught fish. The sign says the Growers Market is open Monday to Friday from 7 am to 4 pm but most of the buying and selling is done in the morning.

Entertainment

Island Night at the *Rapae Hotel* on Friday night is a social event only outdone by the Sunday church service. There's a buffet served from around 7.30 pm which costs NZ$25 and eating here, or simply being a Rapae Hotel guest, also gets you a ringside seat, but if you don't want to eat there's no cover charge or entry cost.

The band starts playing around 8 pm and the dancing gets under way around 9 pm. It's an hour of raucous fun. Large matrons return from the bar through the dancers, and show very clearly that they can still swing a hip as well as any upstart teenager! The finale involves pulling papa'a out of the audience and getting them to show what they've learnt. By this time most people have had enough to drink for embarrassment to be minimal. The band continues on until around 1 am with an increasingly unsteady but highly entertaining crowd.

Ralphie's Bar & Grill opposite the Rapae also has Friday night entertainment, with a floor show immediately following the floor show at the Rapae and then a dance following that. Those who want to see both floor shows rush from the Rapae to Ralphie's to catch the next one, and the crowd then drifts back and forth between the two dances.

The *Aitutaki Lagoon Hotel* has its Island Night on Saturday, beginning with a buffet at 7.30 pm with a floor show and dancing afterwards. Cost for the buffet is NZ$25, but again, if you wish to come for the entertainment only, starting at around 9 pm, there's no charge.

The *Crusher Bar* on the north part of the island features dinner, live music and dancing every night except Friday. Transport can be arranged.

Things to Buy

The Aitutaki Women's Development Craft Centre (☎ 31-353) in central Arutanga, up behind the Administration Centre, sells a variety of Cook Islands handicrafts, including fancy white rito church hats (NZ$50), pandanus hats (NZ$22) and purses (NZ$14 to NZ$20), shell-and-rito fans (NZ$25), pareu (NZ$13 to NZ$17), wooden drums and home-made ukeleles (NZ$40), kikau brooms (NZ$5) and shell jewellery. There's also a good assortment of home-made coconut oil, scented with herbs and flowers, at prices much cheaper than on Rarotonga. The centre is open Monday to Friday from 7 am to 3 pm.

Getting There & Away

Air Aitutaki's large airstrip was built by US forces during WW II. It's the only airport in the Cooks with a two-way runway and it could handle much larger aircraft than those currently used. You could fly Boeing 737s into Aitutaki.

Aitutaki was the first outer island in the Cooks to have regular air links with Rarotonga. Air Rarotonga operates three or four flights a day to Aitutaki, plus a day tour, except on Sunday when there are no flights at all. Fares are NZ$142 each way on most flights. The last flight of the day from Rarotonga to Aitutaki and the first flight of the day from Aitutaki to Rarotonga are cheaper (NZ$99), but only if you book and purchase your ticket locally, in cash.

All the Rarotonga travel agents offer package deals for transport and accommodation on Aitutaki. Day tours are another option; see Day Tours in this section.

Sea See the Getting Around chapter earlier in this book for details and a fare schedule of passenger ship services between Rarotonga and Aitutaki. Often a stop on Aitutaki is included in trips between Rarotonga and the northern group islands.

Aitutaki is a popular yachting destination, but the narrow reef passage is too hazardous for large ships to enter so cargo is taken by lighters outside the reef.

Day Tours Air Rarotonga offers day trips from Rarotonga to Aitutaki, departing from Rarotonga Airport at 8 am and returning there by 7.30 pm. Trips include a tour of the island, a lagoon cruise with snorkelling gear provided, lunch on one of the motu beaches, and plenty of time for swimming, snorkelling and soaking up the sun. Cost is NZ$289 (children age two to 15 NZ$145, under two – free). Bookings can be made directly with Air Rarotonga (☎ 22-888, fax 20-979) or through Rarotonga travel agents.

Getting Around

To/From the Airport An Air Rarotonga minibus connects with all arriving and departing flights; cost is NZ$5 between town and the airport. Some hotels provide airport transport for their guests.

Taxi There is taxi service on the island but you have to ring to get one, or make arrangements in advance. Ask the place you're staying at to arrange it for you.

Car, Motorcycle & Bicycle Rental Motorcycles and bicycles can be hired from a number of places on the island. Ask at your hotel to see if they rent them; several hotels do.

In Arutanga, Swiss Rentals (☎ 31-223, 31-372) operates from the petrol station near the wharf. They hire 18-speed mountain bikes (NZ$10 per day), motorbikes (NZ$25 per day) and cars (NZ$65 to NZ$85 per day). Discounts are offered if you hire for three or four days, and if you keep it for a week you get seven days for the price of six.

Aitutaki Rentals (☎ 31-127), on the main road north of Arutanga, also hires bicycles (NZ$10 per day), motorcycles (NZ$25 per day) and cars (NZ$70 per day).

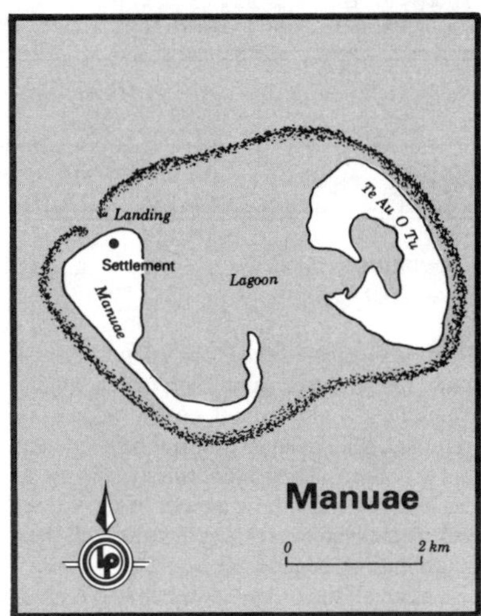

Manuae

Population: unpopulated
Area: 6.2 sq km

The two tiny islets of Manuae and Te Au O Tu are effectively unpopulated – occasionally copra-cutting parties visit from Aitutaki. The Cook Islands Government has suggested that in view of the unspoilt nature of the lagoon, the islands should be declared an international marine park.

The two islets are actually the only parts of a huge volcanic cone which break the surface. The cone is 56 km from east to west, 24 km north to south. The other highpoint on the rim of this vast cone is the Astronomer Bank, 13 km west of Manuae. It comes to within 300 metres of the ocean's surface. Manuae is 101 km from Aitutaki and coconuts were often collected from the atoll by Aitutakians.

History

Cook was the European discoverer of the atoll. He sighted it in 1773 during his second voyage, and in 1777 on his third voyage he paused to investigate but did not land. The islands were named the Hervey Islands by Captain Cook, a name which for a time was applied to the whole southern group, but fortunately that name is rarely used.

In 1823 the missionary John Williams, visited the island and there were about 60 inhabitants. There were only a dozen or so in the late 1820s and the missionaries took them to Aitutaki. Later a series of Europeans made temporary homes. The best known was the prolific William Marsters who in 1863 was moved to Palmerston with his three wives. Today, that island's entire population is descended from him.

Atiu & Takutea

Atiu

Population: 1006
Area: 26.9 sq km

The third largest of the Cook Islands, Atiu is noted for its raised coral reef, or makatea, a phenomenon also found on the islands of Mangaia, Mauke and Mitiaro. The island has had a colourful and bloodthirsty history as the Atiuans were the warriors of the Cooks and specialised in creating havoc on all their neighbouring islands.

Unlike all the other Cook Islands, including Mangaia with its similar geography, the villages on Atiu are not on the coast. The five villages are all close together in the centre of a hill region – Areora, Ngatiarua, Teenui, Mapumai and Tengatangi. Prior to Christianisation, the people lived spread out around the lowlands, where the taro is grown. When the missionaries persuaded the people to come upland and move the original settlements together, they effectively created a single village – the island's Administration Centre and CICC church form the centre, and the 'villages' radiate out from this centre on five roads, like the five arms of a starfish.

Atiu is surprisingly interesting for the visitor – there are some fine beaches, magnificent scenery, excellent walks, ancient marae and the makatea is riddled with limestone caves, some of them used as ancient burial caves. You can also see coffee production, visit the fibre arts studio and there's a fine place to stay. Most visitors stay for only a couple of days, and that really isn't long enough. Atiu is not, however, a place for easy lazing around – you have to get out and do things; burn some energy. This was one of our favourite places in the Cooks and the island really deserves more visitors!

History

Atiu was once known as Enua-manu which can be translated as 'land of birds' or 'land of insects'. Numerous legends tell of early settlers arriving by canoe and of visits by legendary Polynesian navigators. What is more certain is that some time before the first European arrival three ariki controlled the island and began to extend their power over the neighbouring islands of Mauke and Mitiaro.

The European discovery of Atiu is credited to Captain Cook on 3 April 1777. The previous day the Atiuans had made friendly visits to his ships, the *Resolution* and *Discovery*. The Atiuans were uninterested in any items they were offered for trade but they did want a dog. They had heard of but not seen such an animal and Cook would have been happy to oblige them for, 'We had a Dog and

Atiu Cross Section

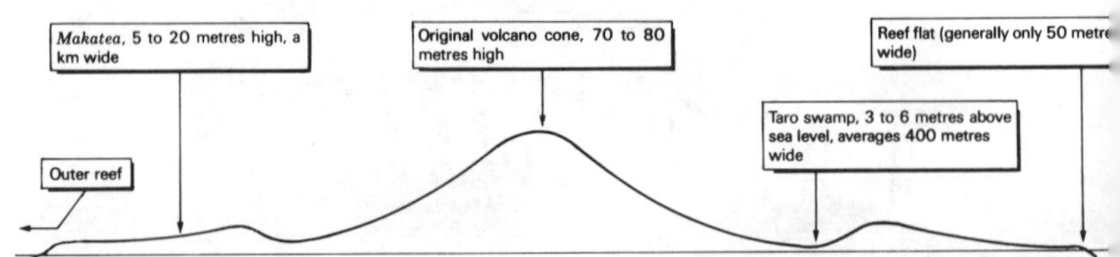

Atiu Crest of Identity

a bitch on board belonging to one of the Gentlemen, that were a great nusence in the Ship', but the 'gentleman' was reluctant to part with them. Fortunately the Tahitian, Omai, who Cook had taken back to England on his previous voyage, offered one of his dogs.

The next day the captain sent three of his boats ashore to try to procure supplies. His men spent a long day being feted (and pick-pocketed) by the Atiuans – they watched wrestling matches and dancing displays – but came back effectively empty handed. At one point, when a large oven was being prepared, Omai was so frightened it was intended for himself and his companions that he came straight out and asked the Atiuans if they were preparing to eat them. The Atiuans expressed shock at the mere thought of such an idea but subsequent tales of the Atiuans' eating habits amongst the people of Mauke and Mitiaro makes you wonder about their ingenuousness.

With his men safely back on board, Cook 'resolved to try no more and thought my self well off that it ended as it did'. He sailed away and managed to find the necessary provisions, principally for the cattle he had on board, on the neighbouring island of Takutea, where he left 'a hatchet and some nails to the full Value of what we took from the island'.

Forty years were to pass before the next European contact when in late 1822 or early 1823 two Polynesian 'teachers' were sent from Bora Bora near Tahiti. They were singularly unsuccessful, although when the Reverend John Williams turned up a few months later on 19 July 1823 searching for Rarotonga, he quickly persuaded the Atiuans to take the first steps of burning their 'idols', destroying their marae and starting work on a church.

About eight or nine months prior to Williams' arrival, an Atiuan named Uia had made a prophecy that soon some people would arrive on Atiu in a huge canoe with no outrigger, their bodies, heads and feet covered, with a mighty God in heaven called Jehovah, and that the Atiuan gods would be burnt with fire. The chiefs were indignant and ordered that Uia be caught and punished, but he escaped the chiefs' wrath and was never heard of again. On board the mission ship was an ariki from Aitutaki, who told Rongomatane, the leading Atiuan chief, that Aitutaki had already converted to Christianity and many of the gods there had already been burnt; this also influenced him greatly.

The day after Williams' arrival, Rongomatane took the mission party to his own marae and challenged them to eat the sugar cane from a sacred grove. When Williams, Papeiha and the rest of the group ate the cane and did not drop dead on the spot Rongomatane became an instant convert, ordered all the idols on the island burnt and told his people to come and listen to the missionaries' teachings.

Rongomatane told Williams that he had two other islands close by – Akatokamanava (Mauke) and Nukuroa (Mitiaro) – and that he would like the people on those islands to receive the gospel as well. He accompanied Williams' ship to these two islands, converting the inhabitants with amazing speed. This conversion of Mauke and Mitiaro had a rather macabre sidelight. Some time before Williams' visit a dispute had evolved between Atiu and Mauke. Rongomatane had rushed off to Mauke bent on revenge and virtually wiped out the islands' inhabitants. Having killed, cooked and eaten their fill, the Atiuans took back canoe-loads of cooked Maukeans for the rest of the Atiuans to sample.

This was not the first time Rongomatane had descended upon Mauke and the Atiuans had also worked off their appetites on the unfortunate inhabitants of Mitiaro. It's hardly surprising that shortly after, when Williams and his new Christian convert, only recently a bloodthirsty cannibal chief, turned up on Mauke the poor inhabitants of the island embraced Christianity with such alacrity and fervour!

After Williams' profitable visit to Atiu, Mauke and Mitiaro, he still had not found Rarotonga, the island he was looking for in the first place. Rongomatane had never been to Rarotonga, but he knew where it was and easily directed Williams towards it. Taking the ship to Oravaru beach on Atiu's western shore, they lined up the stern of the ship with the big rock in the lagoon, Williams took a compass reading and sailed off in a bee-line to find Rarotonga, arriving on 26 October 1823.

The missionaries subsequently made occasional visits to Atiu from Tahiti but in 1836 the Tahitian convert Papeiha was sent back from Rarotonga and started the serious work of Christianising the island.

Gospel Day is still celebrated on Atiu on 19 July every year, often with *nuku* plays acting out the drama of how the gospel came to Atiu.

Geology

Atiu's geology is fascinating. It's thought that Atiu rose out of the sea as a volcano cone around 11 million years ago. The cone was worn down to a shoal, then upheaval (or a drop in the sea level) raised the shoal to form a flat-topped island. Further eons produced a wide coral reef around the island but then, about 100,000 years ago, the island rose another 20 or so metres out of the sea. The coral reef then became a coastal plain, stretching back about a km from the new coastline to the older central hills. In the past 100,000 years a new coral reef has grown up around most of the island, but this is only 100 or so metres wide.

The island today is rather like a very low-brimmed hat with a flat outer rim. This outer rim, or makatea, is principally rough and rugged, fossilised coral densely covered in tropical greenery including shade trees, coconut trees, vines, ferns and mosses. The makatea starts off around five metres in height at the coast and gradually slopes up to around 20 metres at its inner edge. Then instead of sloping up immediately into the central hills – the old volcanic core – there's a circular band of swamp. It seems that water running off the hills permeates the edge of the makatea and has eroded it away to form this damp swamp area. It's extensively used for taro cultivation but it's also a breeding ground for mosquitoes! Inland from the swamp is the inner plateau, the most fertile area of the island where coffee and other crops are grown.

Economy

A number of crops are grown for local consumption but the island's only major export crop is its coffee. Taro is also an important crop on the island.

Information

The Administration Centre and the CICC church form the centre of the island. Foreign currency can be exchanged at the Administration Centre. If you need a cash advance on a credit card (Visa, MasterCard or Bankcard) you can get it from *To Tatou Toa – Our Shop* in Areora village. There are banks on the island but they are only for local savings accounts.

The post office used to be at the Administration Centre but it's moved to the Telecom office in Mapumai village. There's a card phone in front of the Administration Centre which you can use anytime; otherwise long distance phone calls can be made from

Telecom, Monday to Friday from 8 am to 4 pm.

Electricity on Atiu operates every day from 5 am to midnight.

What to Bring Two important items to bring with you to Atiu are a torch (flashlight) and mosquito repellent. The Atiu Motel lends you a torch for cave exploring but you'll want a backup in case of emergencies when underground. And the mosquitoes in the swamp region are voracious and exceedingly numerous, especially during the rainy season from around mid-December to mid-April.

Leave your fancy restaurant clothes behind on Raro. You'll want to look reasonably decent in town but if you'll be poking around in caves or on the makatea you'll need things like old T-shirts, torn shorts and worn-out running shoes. Be prepared to get muddy, sweaty and tired! The big exception is if you plan to go to a dance or to church. Fancy dress is not needed, but you should be able to meet the demands of local modesty and women must wear a dress or skirt, sleeves and a hat to church.

Standards of modesty on Atiu, as on all the outer islands, are more conservative than on Rarotonga and locals become upset about women wearing shorts in town, men going without a shirt, and *anyone* wearing very short shorts or swimming gear in town. The first time that guests of the Atiu Motel went to town wearing their swimming gear, motel owner Roger Malcolm received a visit from the Island Council complaining that his guests had been walking around the island in their underwear!

Books If you want more information on Atiu there are a couple of interesting books to look for. *Atiu through European Eyes* (Institute of Pacific Studies, University of the South Pacific, 1982, paperback) is fascinating. It's subtitled 'A Selection of Historical Documents 1777-1967' and is a collection of references to Atiu from books and reports, reproduced in facsimile form. There are three sections: 'explorers' is principally from the logbook for Cook's visit in 1777; 'missionaries and traders' has accounts of Atiu by those early visitors; and the third section includes more modern academic reports on Atiu's archaeology, its fascinating geology and various customs and social systems.

Also published by USP's Institute of Pacific Studies *Atiu, an Island Community* (1984, paperback) is a modern study of Atiu's current conditions and customs, written by Atiuans. There's an impressive bibliography of 82 books in which Atiu makes an appearance.

The small paperback *Atiu Nui Maruarua*, also published by USP's Institute of Pacific

Atiu Mosquitoes

A few years ago there was an especially bad outbreak of mosquitoes on Atiu, following a period of rain. Everybody walked around in the streets carrying paint cans full of smouldering coconut bark, creating a smokescreen around themselves to keep the mosquitoes away!

Wherever they are, voracious, tall tales concerning mosquitoes are soon concocted. The Atiuans relate that during this time a local doctor had some pigs which he kept down in the makatea, as is the usual custom. One pig died and its body looked horrible and emaciated. Could it be some kind of a serious pig illness that might spread to other pigs on the island? The doctor decided to perform an autopsy on the pig to find out for sure what had killed it. He found that the pig had died because 80% of its blood had been sucked out by mosquitoes!

Despite their ferocious reputation, however, mosquitoes are only a problem on Atiu during the rainy season from around mid-December to mid-April. The rest of the time they're not too bad. After visiting Atiu one time during mosquito season, we were pleasantly surprised on our next visit to find they were no problem at all! It's still a good idea to bring repellent with you at all times of year, though, just to be on the safe side, especially if you'll be tramping around near swamps, on the makatea or in caves. ■

Studies (1984), is a bilingual collection of legends about Atiu told in Maori (Atiuan) and English. All the books published by USP are available at the USP's Rarotonga Centre in Avarua.

The parts about Atiu and Atiuans in chapter four of Ronald Syme's book *The Lagoon is Lonely Now* (Millwood Press, Wellington, 1978, hardback) are particularly insightful and amusing.

1 Post Office, Telecom
2 School
3 Bakery
4 School
5 Power House
6 Atiu Fibre Arts Studio
7 Atiu Nui Maruarua Hall
8 CICC Church
9 Marae Te Apiripiri
10 Administration Centre, Marae Te Au Tapu, Hospital
11 To Tatou Toa - Our Shop
12 Bakery
13 Tivaivai Cafe
14 Atiu Island Coffee Factory
15 Atiu Motel

Caves

The makatea is riddled with limestone caves, complete with stalactites and stalagmites. You'll stumble across many small ones in any ramble through the makatea so take a torch (flashlight). Take your bearings too as it's very easy to get totally confused underground and when you finally find your way out it may be by a different exit.

Tours of the various caves on Atiu typically take about two to three hours and cost around NZ$15 plus NZ$5 for each additional person. It's necessary to go with a guide, partly because the caves can be difficult to find but also because the caves are on owned land and permission must be obtained before you enter. Many of the caves were used for burials although when and why, nobody knows. If you visit one of these caves do not move or take any of the bones. At the very least there will be a curse on you if you do! Roger Malcolm at the Atiu Motel can help you to arrange a guide.

The Te Ana O Raka burial cave is one cave you can visit by yourself. You can approach it either by taking the road down from the central plateau or by taking the road which runs inland from about three quarters of the way down the airstrip. The cave is just off the road and very easy to find. There are, however, numerous entrances and exits to this extensive cave and it is very easy to get confused.

In the south-east of the island is Anatakitaki or 'cave of the kopeka'. The cave is reached by a longish walk across the makatea from the plateau road. Kopekas are tiny birds, very much like swifts, which nest in huge numbers inside the cave. When they come out to hunt insects they are never seen to land, only in the cave do they rest. Inside the pitch dark cave they make a continuous chattering, clicking noise which they use to find their way around, like bats. Try to dissuade your guide from catching the birds, a trick they perform by throwing a shirt or jacket over the sleeping birds on the roof of the cavern.

Some of the chambers in this extensive cavern are very large. Although this is the main kopeka cave they do nest in smaller numbers in at least one other cave. There's a legend that relates how a Polynesian hero, Rangi, was led to this cave which concealed his missing wife, by a kingfisher bird.

In the south-west the Rima Rau burial cave is a smaller cave reached by a vertical pothole. There are many bones to be seen in this cave and nearby there's a very deep sink hole with a deep, cold pool at the bottom.

Lake Tiroto is noted for its eels which are a popular island delicacy. On the western side of the lake is a cave which leads right through the makatea to the sea. You can wade through it for a considerable distance if the water in the lake is low enough. Vaine Moeroa (known as 'VM') goes eeling in the cave about every three weeks or so, and will take visitors along; Roger Malcolm of the Atiu Motel can put you in touch with him. Or you

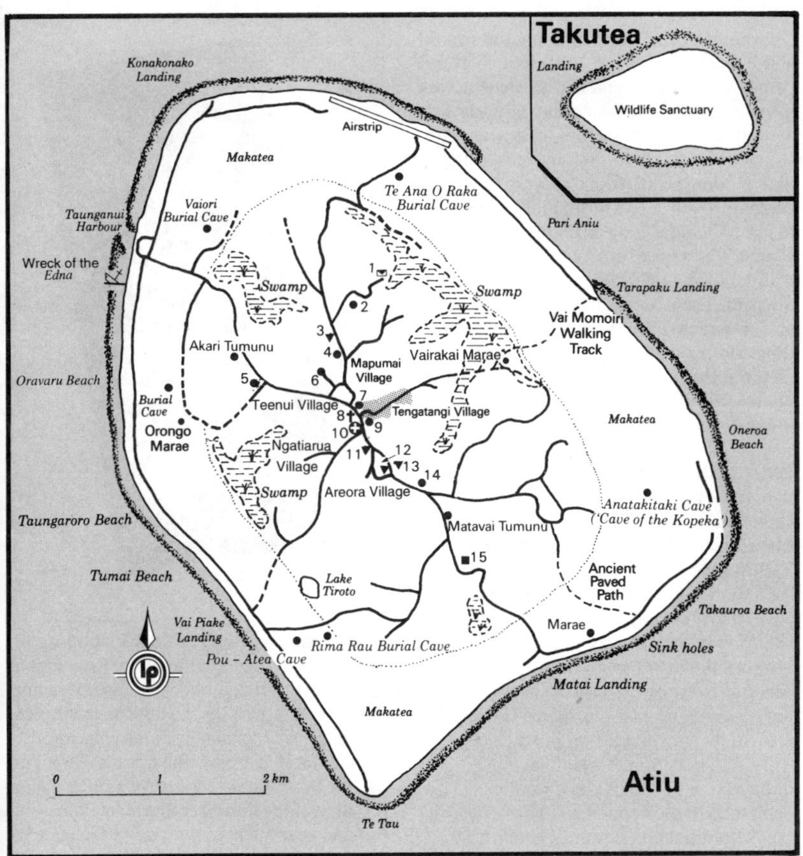

can go by yourself. Be prepared to get very muddy, however. And watch out for eels.

Warning Take great care when you are walking across the makatea – the coral is extremely sharp. It's often like walking across razor blades and if you slipped and fell you'd be slieed to pieces. Wear good shoes too; if you stubbed your toe while wearing thongs you'd probably cut it right off.

Vai Momoiri Track & Vairakai Marae

From Tarapaku Landing on the north-east coast a walking track leads inland all the way to the central villages. It's best to arrange transport round to the landing so you can walk the whole way inland. At first the track winds across a beautiful stretch of makatea with thick vegetation, colourful flowers and impressive outcrops. Much of the track is paved with stone slabs placed there in ancient times; a Cook Islands historian says it was about a thousand years ago. Numerous small caves are found very close to the path. At one point you can see the Vai Momoiri, a deep canyon off the track to the left, filled with brown water. A short stretch of tunnel connects this water to a second, similar sink hole.

Eventually the path heads into the swamp and it's easy to get lost as there are several paths. At one time you had to wade across the swamp but it's easier going nowadays as a road across the swamp has been constructed. The track follows irrigation ditches and at one point turns sharply across a cement culvert. Look to your left at this point to the 37-metre-long wall of the Vairakai Marae. It's somewhat overgrown but stands parallel to and only a metre or so away from the path. There are 47 large limestone slabs, six of which have been cut with curious projections on their top edge. Shortly after this impressive wall the path climbs steeply up to the plateau and enters Tengatangi village.

Other Marae

Atiu has a number of interesting marae remains. One of the best known is the Orongo Marae near Oravaru Beach. An international Earthwatch party came in 1985 to clean up the marae, which was practically an excavation project since it had become so overgrown that it was almost lost in the jungle; unfortunately the site has now become overgrown once again. You must have a guide to visit this marae because it's difficult to find and it's on private land.

Te Apiripiri Marae where Papeiha is said to have first preached the gospel in 1823 is behind the tennis courts and house opposite the Administration Centre. There's little left of the marae apart from some stalactites or stalagmites lying on the ground but there's a memorial stone to mark the spot. Te Au Tapu, a marae still used for investiture ceremonies, is between the Administration Centre and the palace of Ngamaru Ariki.

Coffee Plantations

Until the early 1990s when Aitutaki joined Atiu in commercial coffee production, Atiu was the only place in the Cooks to grow coffee commercially – but it has been a precarious activity.

Coffee was introduced to Atiu by early 19th century traders and missionaries. By the beginning of the 20th century coffee played an important economic role, with almost 50 tons of coffee exported in 1906. Production and export declined after that, however, for the next 40 years. By the 1940s it was produced only for local home consumption.

Atiu's coffee production was revitalised in the 1950s when a few growers once again began working the old coffee plantations and brought in some new Kenyan coffee strains. The government also became interested, establishing nurseries and two small farms. About 16 hectares (40 acres) of coffee were brought into cultivation, and green coffee beans were exported. Once again, however, production went into decline and by 1980 the industry had dwindled to the point where coffee was again picked only for local consumption.

This was the state of the industry when German-born Juergen Manske-Eimke moved from Nigeria to Atiu in 1983 and changed his occupation from economist to coffee grower. In 1984 he imported modern machinery and equipment from Germany and the USA, set up a coffee factory, and the

Atiu Coffee Growers Association was formed.

The Atiu coffee business is now rebounding and Juergen hopes that the 7½ tons of coffee the island currently produces will expand to twice that level. At present there are once again about 16 hectares of coffee being grown but that could potentially be expanded to around 50 hectares (125 acres), which could yield up to 37 tons of green coffee or 33 tons of roasted coffee annually. Now that coffee grown on Aitutaki is being processed on Atiu, Juergen estimates that by around 1995 the combined yield should be over 10 tons per year. The supermarkets and fancier restaurants of Rarotonga alone use about 2½ tons of coffee a year and Atiuan coffee is now being exported to New Zealand, Tahiti and the USA.

The coffee is usually picked from February to May, although there are variations in many years. Because of the small scale of production and relatively low labour costs Atiuan coffee is 100% sun-dried and hand selected. Coffee growing on Atiu has its problems – wild pigs, too much sunshine and the perennial Cook Islands land-ownership questions all cause hassles. It's good coffee though, and you can buy a half-kg package from the Tivaivai Cafe on Atiu for NZ$12 (cheaper than in Rarotongan shops) or by mail order.

Juergen gives tours of the coffee plantations, pulping factory and the factory where it's hulled, roasted and packed. Tours cost NZ$10 (additional people NZ$5). The tour ends with a cup (or two) of Atiuan coffee at the Tivaivai Cafe operated by his wife Andrea, who also runs the Atiu Fibre Arts Studio. Tours can be booked at the Tivaivai Cafe (☎ 33-027) or directly (☎ 33-031, fax 33-032; PO Box 13, Teenui, Atiu, Cook Islands).

Atiu Fibre Arts Studio

The Atiu Fibre Arts Studio specialises in tivaevaes, the colourful patterned bedspreads which are among the most famous handicrafts of the Cook Islands. Tivaevaes are normally made only for home use; this studio is the only place in the Cook Islands that they are produced for commercial sale. Cost for a machine-sewn double to queen-size tivaevae is about NZ$500 to NZ$1100; a hand-sewn one, requiring countless hours to make, costs NZ$1300 and up. You can buy one on the spot or custom order it in the pattern and colours you want. Tivaevaes are available in traditional or contemporary patterns, and are made using traditional or contemporary methods.

The studio also produces a variety of other textile arts, mostly using appliqué techniques similar to those used in making tivaevaes. All products of the studio are exhibited in the Tivaivai Cafe on the main road in Areora village. Also on display at the cafe are artwork, jewellery, pandanus mats, purses and other items, all of exceptional quality. Work from the Atiu Fibre Arts Studio is also on display at the Beachcomber Gallery in Avarua, Rarotonga.

Andrea Eimke, operator of the studio and originally from Germany, can tell you everything you want to know about the local arts and crafts. You can usually find her at her studio in Teenui village Monday to Friday; drop by the Tivaivai Cafe for a map with directions to the studio. Andrea is interested

Tivaivai 'Sweet Scent of Paradise' – Design by Andrea Eimke

in promoting cultural exchange, inviting artists and craftspeople to come and share their skills with the studio and learn Atiuan crafts. For visiting artists she can arrange accommodation, craftsmaking facilities and anything else that might be needed. Contact Andrea Eimke, PO Box 13, Teenui, Atiu, Cook Islands (☎ 33-031, 33-027, fax 33-032).

Beaches & Coast

Atiu is not a great place for swimming – the surrounding lagoon is rarely more than 50 metres wide and the water is generally too shallow for more than wading and gentle splashing around, unless you swim at Taunganui Harbour, as many of the locals do. There are, however, countless beautiful, sandy strips all along the coast. You can easily find one to yourself and when you tire of sunbathing just slip into the water for a cooling dip. Some of them are easily reached but to get to others a little pushing through the bush is required, although the coastal road is rarely more than 100 metres from the coast.

On the west coast Oravaru Beach is thought to be where Cook's party made their historic landing. There's a large rock in the water just off the beach, which the chief Rongomatane used in directing John Williams to Rarotonga. Farther south is the longer sweep of Taungaroro Beach. It is backed by high cliffs and slopes fairly steeply into the water. South again is Tumai Beach and there are plenty of others. The water at Taunganui Harbour is clear and deep enough for good swimming and snorkelling.

The south-east coast takes the brunt of the prevailing northerly winds and the sea, washing fiercely over the reef, is often unsafe for swimming. There are, however, a series of picturesque little beaches including Matai Landing and Oneroa. Oneroa is the best beach for finding beautiful shells; a surprising number of old shoes are also washed up!

South of Oneroa is the turn-off to Takauroa Beach, by a stretch of old pig fence. If you walk back along the rugged cliff face about 100 metres there are some sink holes deep enough for good snorkelling. They are only safe at low tide or when the sea is calm.

On the north-east coast there's a km-long stretch where there is no fringing reef and the sea beats directly on the cliffs. At the end of the road there's a rarely used emergency boat landing, Tarapaku, and there's also a pleasant stretch of beach. There are more beaches south to Oneroa.

The most popular beaches on the island are Matai Landing and Taungaroro, because of their beauty and their ease of access.

Other Things to See & Do

There are a couple of dusty display cases with some **Atiuan artefacts** in the library of Atiu College. The **CICC church** in the centre of the village has walls over a metre thick and is in the traditional island style.

Atiu has a surprising number of **tennis courts** – a few years ago the five villages got into a tennis court building competition, each attempting to build a better one than the next! There are now nine tennis courts on the island.

Organised Tours

You can arrange for a two to three-hour Cultural Tour visiting the marae, historical spots and other points of interest on the island. Cost is flexible, depending on the number of people going and the mode of transport. Roger Malcolm at the Atiu Motel will arrange for a guide.

See the Caves section earlier in this chapter for details on tours of other caves on the island.

Places to Stay

The *Atiu Motel* (☎ 33-777, fax 33-775) is the only organised accommodation on the island. It is situated about a km out of Areora village on the road that leads down to the beach. Roger and Kura Malcolm have four units at NZ$80/90/100 for singles/doubles/triples. They are delightful, individual A-frame chalets that make maximum use of the local materials. The main beams are sections of coconut palm trunks retaining the outer bark. Coconut palm wood is used extensively inside (it's a beautiful wood) and other local woods are also used.

The rooms have a single and double bed and a mezzanine area where another person or two could sleep. There's also one larger family unit sleeping up to six people. All have a verandah in front, and a kitchen area where you can fix your own food – each unit comes with a fridge and cupboard full of food and at the end of your stay you're simply billed for what you've used. Island meals can also be arranged, and there's an outdoor barbecue where guests often hold get-togethers.

The motel has a lawn tennis court with lawn bowls every Saturday afternoon. Beside this is a large open-air thatch pavilion and bar where dances are held every Saturday night.

Bookings for the motel can be made at the Air Rarotonga office on Rarotonga (☎ 22-888, fax 20-979) and at the Rarotonga travel agents.

Places to Eat

The *Tivaivai Cafe* on the main road in Areora village is operated by Andrea Eimke, who also operates the Atiu Fibre Arts Studio and whose husband Juergen operates the Atiu Island Coffee factory. Atiu coffee is served at the cafe, of course, along with cakes, snacks and fresh juices. The cafe also serves as a gallery where tivaevaes, wall hangings, clothing and other arts & crafts from the Atiu Fibre Arts Studio are on display. The cafe is open weekdays from 9.30 am to 4 pm and Saturday from 10 am to 2 pm.

There are several trade stores on Atiu, two bread bakers and three places that make doughnuts. The amount of bread produced is quite amazing, as on all the islands. Doughnuts are supplied on a loop made from a strip of leaf and you can hang it from the handlebar of your motorcycle and ride off. *Maroro* (flying fish) are an Atiuan delicacy; they're caught in butterfly nets on the 10th, 11th and 12th nights after the new moon during the spawning season, from June to December.

Tutaka & Tivaevae

Twice a year, a committee goes around to inspect all the houses on Atiu for their condition, cleanliness, etc. This *tutaka* is done in many of the Cook Islands, but on Atiu it's made into a big occasion, with the local ladies bringing out all their best handicrafts to proudly put on display in their homes. The major tutaka of the year is just before Christmas; there's another one in the last week of June. It's easy to spot the inspection committee going around, since they're all in uniform, and if you ask permission you can join them. The tutaka inspection is held on a Wednesday and Thursday, and that same Friday there's a big ball, with prizes handed out for the village that wins the competition.

Exhibitions of tivaevaes, the colourful patterned bedspreads and cushions which are one of the most distinctive local handicrafts, take place during the last week of May and the last week of November in the CICC Sunday school hall. Or you can see them on display at the Tivaivai Cafe anytime. ■

Entertainment

Dances are held in the thatched open-air pavilion bar at the Atiu Motel every Saturday night, beginning around 9 pm. They feature a rousing local band and occasional floor shows. Being the only regularly scheduled entertainment on the island, the dances attract visitors and locals alike.

Dances are also held on occasional Friday nights at the Atiu Nui Maruarua Hall which

No Dancing in Hurricane Season

Up until 1990, dances on Atiu had an interesting twist between 1 January and 31 March, a holdover from the 'blue laws' days. The original London Missionary Society missionaries who founded the CICC church managed to convince the people of Atiu that if they held dances during the hurricane season, it could cause a hurricane to strike the island! Until 1990, the CICC was still opposed to dances being held at that time. The Roman Catholics, however, had no such compunctions so dances usually managed to go on regardless. ■

Bush Beer Schools

Don't miss the opportunity to visit a tumunu while you're on Atiu. It's a direct descendant of the old kava ceremony of pre-missionary times. Kava was a drink prepared from the root of the pepper plant *piper methysticum*. It was not alcoholic but it certainly had an effect on its drinkers – ranging from a mildly fuzzy head to total unconsciousness. Drinking kava was always a communal activity with some ceremony involved; you could not be a solitary kava drinker. In Fiji, kava is still popular today but in the Cook Islands the missionaries managed to all but totally stamp it out. During that missionary period, however, when drinking was banned, the tumunu came into existence and men would retreat to the bush to drink home-brewed 'orange beer'. The 'tumunu' is the hollowed out coconut palm stump which was traditionally used as a container for brewing the beer.

Tumunu are still held regularly at various places on the island, although the container is likely to be plastic these days and the beer will be made from imported hops, much like any Western home brew, rather than from oranges as in the old days. Technically, however, the bush beer schools are still illegal. If you stay at the Atiu Motel, Roger will arrange an invitation for a visit to the local tumunu. Traditionally the tumunu is for men only, and women rarely participate, but for tourists the rules relax somewhat and any visitor, male or female, is welcome.

There's still quite a tradition to the tumunu gathering. The barman sits behind the tumunu and ladles the beer out in a coconut-shell cup. Each drinker swallows his cup in a single gulp and returns the empty cup to the barman who fills it for the next in line. You can pass if you want to but by the end of the evening everybody is decidedly unsteady on their feet. Including, sometimes, the barman who is supposed to stay sober and keep everyone in line! At some point in the evening the barman calls the school to order by tapping on the side of the tumunu with the empty cup and then says a short prayer. Guitars and ukeleles are usually around to provide music and accompaniment to song. As a visitor to the tumunu you should bring a kg of sugar or the equivalent in cash as a donation towards the next brew. ■

is opposite the CICC church. People of all ages appear and it's always good fun.

For more sedate entertainment, lawn bowls are held on the tennis court at the Atiu Motel on Saturday afternoons.

Getting There & Away

Air Air Rarotonga flies between Rarotonga and Atiu every day except Sunday. The 40-minute flight costs NZ$127 (double for return), cheaper (NZ$180 return) on the Super Saver fare. Flights also operate from Atiu to Mitiaro and from Mitiaro on to Mauke, but the last time we checked, direct flights between Atiu and Mauke had been suspended. Since flights from Atiu to Mitiaro and from Mitiaro on to Mauke take only 10 minutes each, many travellers take the chance to visit all three islands. Airfare is cheaper – NZ$99 per sector – if you visit more than one island.

Rarotonga travel agents organise package tours either to Atiu alone or as part of an Island Combination tour to Atiu, Mitiaro and Mauke. See the Getting Around chapter for details.

Atiu's airport is on the north-east corner of the island. It was built in '83 because the old airstrip, itself built only in '77, was too small. The new strip's coral surface is also better. Roger Malcolm from the Atiu Motel meets incoming guests and drops off outgoing ones.

Sea Inter-island passenger freighter ships sail to Atiu; see the Getting Around chapter for details. Cost will depend on whether you want to visit Atiu only, or combine it with other islands. The all-weather harbour at Taunganui was built in 1974 but it's still too small to take ships so they have to be unloaded onto a barge while they're standing offshore.

Prior to 1974, when the present harbour was built, getting ashore on Atiu could be a pretty fraught business. In fact some say the Atiuans, once the terror of Mauke and Mitiaro, could have been the terror of many more places were it not for their lack of harbour facilities. As it was the Atiuans could never build really big ocean-going canoes.

Instead they used smaller canoes and once offshore lashed two together to make a larger and more stable vessel.

Day Tours Day trips from Rarotonga to Atiu and Mauke are planned by Air Rarotonga; travel agents and Air Rarotonga will have details. On Atiu the day trips will include visits to one of Atiu's more spectacular caves, with a hike through the makatea along the way; a tour of the Atiu Island Coffee plantation and factory; a drive through several of the villages, with stops at the Te Apiripiri and Te Au Tapu maraes; a tea break at the Tivaivai Cafe, where you can see the

The Wreck of the *Edna*

There isn't much left of it but you can still see the wreck of the *Edna* just south of Taunganui Harbour. Originally stranded out on the reef, the bow of the wreck was washed up onto land during a hurricane and last time we were on Atiu we found it wedged into a crevasse near the harbour. The stern of the ship is underwater just off the reef, and can be seen by snorkelling or diving.

The *Edna*, a 45-metre (135 foot) sailing cargo ship, was a Dutch ship built in 1916 as a riveted iron fishing lugger. Her American captain, Nancy Griffith, had first brought her from Hawaii to the Cook Islands in 1987, sailing between Honolulu and the northern group islands. But the ship met her end on Atiu on 28 November 1990, at about 1.30 am.

Earlier on the day of the 27th, the *Edna* had arrived in Atiu to unload cargo. The deck cargo was all unloaded, but a large load of cement was in the hold. Since it was too late to get it all unloaded before nightfall, Nancy decided to anchor for the night and unload it the next day.

Since Atiu's harbour is too small for ships to enter, the ship had to be anchored offshore. However, since the drop-off is so steep on Atiu, it is not possible to anchor very far offshore. Nancy and her crew anchored the *Edna* just off the reef and settled down to spend the night on the ship.

The weather was very quiet that day, and in the evening it was unusually, deadly quiet. A hurricane was passing by near Palmerston, to the north-west, but since it was so far away, Nancy was not worried about it. Later when she saw satellite photos of the weather pattern that day she realised that what probably happened was that a small 'cell' – a sort of spinoff from a hurricane – must have hit Atiu that night.

That evening, the weather was eerily still. It was a pitch dark, overcast night with no moon and perfectly silent. Suddenly a blast of wind and rain slammed into the island, coming from the west. The *Edna* was pushed toward shore and although Nancy and the crew were all on board and immediately leaped into action to save the boat, the centre of the boat had become lodged on a shoal of coral before anything could be done. Even with the anchor cut and the engine going full steam, there was no way to get the vessel free of the coral. The wind spun the ship around sideways, parallel to the reef. Then, just as suddenly as it had come, the wind disappeared and the night was still again. The next day dawned clear, bright and calm, with no trace of what had occurred the night before – except that the *Edna* was stranded on the reef.

Nancy, the crew and many volunteers salvaged everything they could from the vessel, making a human chain from the shipwreck across the reef and up onto land. Later that day, huge waves from the hurricane reached the island. The weight of the cement cargo in the hold bore the ship down onto the coral with great weight, and the high waves striking the vessel side-on rocked it scraping back and forth over the sharp coral. Eventually the iron bottom wore through, water flooded the hold, and the boat broke in half, with the bow remaining on the reef and the stern sunk underwater. The cement was carried away in the current and disappeared.

Eventually storms and hurricanes broke up the bow on the reef, sweeping away much of it and pushing part of it farther up onto land, where it can still be seen today.

After the wreck, Nancy stayed on Atiu for about two weeks, salvaging what could be salvaged, regrouping and trying to figure out what to do next. The island still had a need for cargo shipping services. Roger Malcolm organised a group of shareholders to join in buying another cargo ship to serve Nga Pu Toru (Atiu, Mitiaro and Mauke), electing Nancy to find a suitable vessel. She went to Japan, found the *Avatapu* and brought it to the Cooks, where it is based at Avatiu Harbour in Avarua. ■

tivaevaes, arts & crafts exhibits, and buy some Cook Islands handicrafts; a visit to the Atiu Motel; a view over Lake Tiroto, and of the entrance to Rima Rau Cave; and a drive along the coast road with visits to Taungaroro Beach, Oravaru Beach and Taunganui Harbour, with a stop at the wreck of the *Edna*.

Getting Around

Atiu is great for walking but you need a motorcycle to get around. The Atiu Motel rents motorcycles for NZ$25 per day.

Takutea

Population: unpopulated
Area: 1.2 sq km

Clearly visible from Atiu, this small sand cay is only six metres above sea level at its highest point. The island has also been called Enua-iti which simply means 'small land'. Cook visited Takutea in 1777, shortly after he left Atiu, and paused to search for food for the livestock on his ship.

Takutea is only 16 km north-west of Atiu and copra collecting parties used to come from that island. Today it is unpopulated and rarely visited. Many seabirds including frigates and tropic birds nest on the island.

Rakoa (White-Tailed Tropicbird) *Phaethon lepturus* (JK)

Mauke, Mitiaro & Palmerston

Mauke

Population: 639
Area: 18.4 sq km

Mauke is the easternmost of the Cook Islands. It's one of the more easily visited islands since there is a regular flight schedule and it can easily be combined with a visit to nearby Atiu and Mitiaro. Mauke, Mitiaro and Atiu are often referred to by the collective name Nga Pu Toru, 'The Three Roots'.

History

Mauke takes its name from its legendary founder Uke but there are several versions of what the name means. The most obvious is simply 'land of Uke' but another relates that it means 'clean Uke'. This legend tells of Tangiia, one of the two famous mariners who settled Rarotonga (the Ngatangiia district of Rarotonga still bears his name today), coming to ask Uke's aid in going to war against the Samoans. Uke replied, 'my hands are clean' – he did not want war. It is said that Uke came to Mauke in search of a peaceful place to live, and he wanted to continue to live in peace.

Prior to this, Mauke was known as Akatokamanava, which means 'my heart is at rest, at peace'. These were the first words uttered by Uke when he arrived from the legendary homeland Avaiki, landing at Arapaea on the eastern coast in the huge canoe *Paipaimoana*, carrying a large group of settlers. Mauke is still referred to as Akatokamanava in song, dance, legend and in formal address.

Uke arrived on Mauke with a wife he had brought from the Vanuatuan island of Erromango – the same island where the missionary John Williams would later be killed and eaten. They had six children, four boys and two girls. The two girls were renowned for their exceptional beauty, and when the two famous Rarotongan settlers, Tangiia and Karika, came seeking these girls for marriage, they went to live on Rarotonga. Uke's sons also went to other islands, and thus Uke became a common ancestor for all the islands of the southern group

Prior to the arrival of Christianity, Mauke was totally dominated by the island of Atiu. The Atiuans would descend on murderous, cannibal raids. Akaina, an Atiuan chieftain, settled on Mauke and spirited away the wife of an island chief. Swearing revenge the jilted chief killed Akaina and most of his compatriots but one escaped and, in a small canoe, made the perilous crossing to Atiu. Incensed by this affront to Atiuan power Rongomatane, the great chief of Atiu, set out for Mauke at the head of a fleet of 80 war canoes. The terrified Maukeans took refuge in caves but many of them were hauled out, beaten to death with clubs, cooked and eaten. Satisfied that justice had been done Rongomatane installed an Atiuan named Tararo as chief and sailed back to Atiu.

The surviving islanders regrouped, however, and under Maiti attacked the Atiuans. Unfortunately for the Maukeans Tararo survived and once again an emissary sailed off to alert Rongomatane. And once again the Atiuan war canoes sallied forth to Mauke. This time the Atiuans showed at least some restraint and spared a number of the women and children, taking them back to Atiu as slaves, the cooked flesh of their husbands and fathers accompanying them in the canoes.

The European discovery of Mauke is credited to the pioneering missionary John Williams who arrived on Mauke on 23 June 1823. And who accompanied Mr Williams? Why none other than that unpleasant previous visitor, Rongomatane! It's hardly surprising that the Maukeans were converted to Christianity with an ease and speed that astonished the missionaries. Despite Christian influence Mauke still remained subject to Atiu with ariki appointed from Atiu.

Author and island personality Julian Dashwood (known as 'Rakau', the Maori word for 'wood', on the island) lived for years on Mauke where he ran the island store. See the introductory Books section in the Facts for the Visitor chapter for more information. His second book, *Today is Forever*, is largely about Mauke.

Geology

Like Atiu, Mangaia and Mitiaro this island is a raised atoll with a surrounding makatea. Inland from this fossil coral reef there is a band of swampland surrounding the fertile central land. Mauke is like Mitiaro – the central area of the island is flat, rising virtually no higher than the makatea. In contrast to Atiu and Mangaia where the central area is hilly, Mauke rises barely 30 metres above sea level at its highest point. Like Atiu and Mangaia there are numerous limestone caves

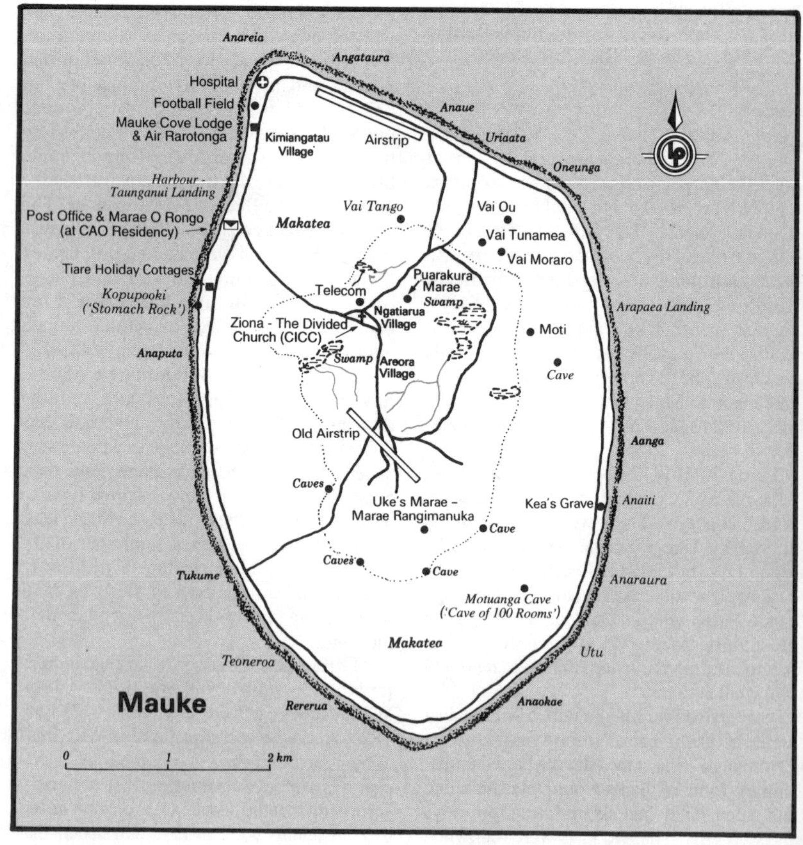

in the makatea, which is densely forested with lush jungle-like growth.

Economy & Crafts

Mauke's economic development has been erratic. The economy is primarily agricultural, with a variety of fruits and vegetables grown, mostly for local consumption. One important island export is *maire*, a type of leaf traditionally used for making eis in Hawaii, where they are called *leis*; a shipment of maire eis leaves Mauke bound for Hawaii each week. A handful of cattle are raised on the island.

Mauke is noted for its pandanus mats, purses and hats and for *kete* baskets. Bowls shaped like the leaves of the breadfruit tree and carved from *miro* wood are another traditional Maukean craft. Tivaevaes are also made on Mauke, but only for home use.

> **The People of Mauke**
>
> On one of their murderous forays to Mauke, the Atiuans tempted the unfortunate inhabitants out of their cave hideaways by claiming they were on a friendly visit and inviting them (the Maukeans) to a feast that they (the Atiuans) were setting up. This was not totally untrue, as the unfortunate people of Mauke found, but they did not anticipate their role at the feast. They were henceforth labelled 'Mauke kaa-kaa' ('Mauke the easily fooled').
>
> Some say that when deciding which women to eat, the Atiuans always ate the ugliest and spared the most beautiful, which accounts for the extraordinary beauty of Maukean women today! ■

Information

The electricity schedule on Mauke is the same as on Mitiaro and Atiu: the power comes on from 5 am to midnight.

The island's post office is in the Administration Building beside the harbour at Taunganui. The Telecom office in Ngatiarua village in the centre of the island is open for long distance phone calls Monday to Friday from 7.30 am to 4 pm, and there's a card phone outside that you can use anytime.

The Divided Church

Mauke has two villages in the centre, Areora and Ngatiarua, and one on the coast, Kimiangatau. The coastal village was built in 1904 because some of the Maukeans had decided to become Roman Catholics and could no longer tolerate living with those who still followed the London Missionary Society.

Religious disputes were nothing new to the Maukeans as the 1882 CICC church illustrates. At that time there were still just two villages and they got together to build the church. When the outside was complete, however, the two sides could not agree on how the inside should be fitted out. Eventually the argument became so acrimonious that the only solution was to build a wall down the middle and let each village have its own church within the church.

A new pastor eventually managed to convince his congregations that this was hardly the spirit of neighbourly Christianity and the wall was removed, but the two sides of the church are still decorated in different styles and each village has its own entrance. Inside, the two villages each sit on their own side of the aisle and they take turns singing the hymns! The pulpit, with old Chilean dollars set into the railing, is centrally placed but there's a dividing line down the middle and the minister is expected to straddle the line at all times. The interior of the church is painted in soft pastel colours.

Today, Mauke's population is about 50% CICC, 50% Roman Catholic, with a few families of Mormons, Seventh Day Adventists and Baha'is.

Caves

Like Atiu and Mangaia, Mauke has makatea riddled with limestone caves, many filled with cool water, wonderful for a swim on a hot day. Walking through the makatea to the caves is like walking through a lush jungle, with coconut palms and shade trees, pandanus, mosses, ferns and tropical greenery in wild profusion. The shade is welcome on a hot day.

The easiest cave to reach, and also one of the larger ones on the island for swimming, is Vai Tango, just a short walk from Ngatiarua village. You'll probably need someone to show you how to get there the first time, but that's no problem as everybody knows where it is. It's often full of children on Saturday and after school, but at other times you may get it all to yourself.

Other interesting caves in the north part of the island, just a short walk off the main road, are Vai Ou, Vai Tunamea and Vai Moraro. Vai Ou is in a beautiful, lushly tropical grotto, with an ancient coral pathway leading to it. Vai Moraro is also known as the 'Crawling Cave' – you have to crawl down through a slit in the rockface to get in. It opens up into a big cave inside, but the pools are small, although deep, and they taste like salt water. Be especially careful walking around in this one, as the rocks are wet and very slippery. Just a little farther on is Vai Tunamea.

Motuanga Cave or the 'Cave of 100 Rooms', each with its own pool, is the best-known cave on the island. The cave is entered on land and extends out toward the sea and under the reef. In some of the last rooms you can reach, the waves can be heard crashing above you.

There is nobody around today who has reached all of Motuanga's 100 rooms; they say that nowadays you can only get into 12 of them. But there is a legend of one man, Timeni Oariki, who did swim through all of them, finally emerging out into the sea where he was eaten by sharks. So he never got to tell anybody about it!

Marae

Mauke, like all the other Cook Islands, has many marae, or ancient religious meeting grounds. The three most important are those associated with the three ariki.

The best preserved, and still used for ceremonial functions, is the Puarakura Marae, in the village of Ngatiarua. There's a triangular area enclosed within a rectangle within another larger rectangle, with seats for the ariki, the mataiapo and the rangatira. All the stones are whitewashed, just for decoration.

Out past the old airstrip is Marae Rangimanuka, the marae of Uke, Mauke's famous ancestor and namesake. It's hidden

Kovitoa Ariki & Marae O Rongo

Kovitoa Ariki had two sons, Koumu and Kaivaiva, and when his wife died he remarried to a woman who had five small children. Because he wanted to be sure that his own two sons, who were away on Atiu at the time, would inherit his title, he concocted a plan to get rid of the five small children of his wife.

He took the children out to his plantation on successive occasions, and each time sent them off on various errands, keeping one with him to help him. When the rest of the children returned, they found their father had prepared meat in an umu (underground oven) and their little brother or sister was gone. Each time, Kovitoa told the children that he had killed a pig in the bush and that their brother or sister had gone home. When the child was not at home upon their return, he said it must be those Atiu people who had spirited him away.

Finally, when there were only two children left, the older one was getting very suspicious. When Kovitoa sent him away, he hid in the bush, and saw his brother killed. He ran back to the village and told the people what Kovitoa had done. Not long after that, when Kovitoa was sleeping, someone bashed his head with a coconut grater, and he was roasted and eaten on his own marae, Marae O Rongo.

As the people were washing Kovitoa's body down at the present-day harbour, with the roasting oven blazing away, one of Kovitoa's two sons arrived in a canoe from Atiu. He ended up avenging the death of his father by killing his assassin in his sleep with the same coconut grater that had been used on his father, and he took over his father's ariki title. ■

in an overgrown area but it's not difficult to get to with a guide who knows the way.

Near the harbour, behind the CAO Residency, the Marae O Rongo was once a huge marae but all you see today is one large stone and a coral platform under a very big tree. According to tradition, this is the only marae on Mauke where anyone was killed and eaten.

Beaches

A road runs right around the coast of Mauke, a total distance of 18 km. The fringing reef platform is narrow but Teoneroa beach is fairly good as is the beach at Arapaea Landing on the east side of the island. The beaches on the south side of the island like Anaokae are pleasantly secluded. Other beaches, like Anaraura and Teoneroa, have picnic areas with thatched shelters providing welcome shade on a hot day. Oneunga, on the east side, is also a nice little beach for a picnic. All around the island, the waves have beaten the shoreline cliffs into an overhanging formation.

Heading south from the Tiare Holiday Cottages, the very first turn-off towards the sea leads you to Kopupooki ('Stomach Rock') beach. The name comes from a cave situated to your left as you face out to sea – go just past the last outcrop of rock that you see from the beach and you come to this lovely cave full of fish that is good for swimming and snorkelling. Except for the harbour this is about the only place deep enough for a good swim, since the reef all around the island is quite shallow. You can only reach it at low tide; at other times, the pounding waves make it too dangerous. There are many more little caves and beaches around the island.

Places to Stay & Eat

The *Tiare Holiday Cottages* (☎ 35-083, 35-102, fax 35-683) is right on the coast, near to

Kea's Grave

One of Mauke's beaches, Anaiti, has a special history. Up on the cliff to the right of the beach as you face the sea is a mound of grey coral stones. This is the grave of Kea.

Kea's husband, Paikea, was out fishing one day in his canoe when Kea, up on the cliff, saw a huge storm coming across the sea. She shouted to her husband to come back to land, but he didn't hear her. The storm caught him at sea and blew him farther and farther away from the island. Kea believed her husband was dead, and she cried and cried on that cliff overlooking the sea until she died of grief, and the people buried her there.

In the early 1970s, after a severe storm, Kea's bones became exposed, the surrounding sand having been washed away. The people covered her bones again with big coral stones which are still there today.

Paikea had not died at sea, however. He was blown very far by the storm, but he finally did reach land – the island of Mangaia. The people there did not want him to stay and were on the point of killing him when a woman who was half-Maukean took him under her protection. With her help, he escaped from Mangaia and sailed to Rarotonga. On Rarotonga, Paikea stayed in Ngatangiia, and finally left on the Takitumu canoe when it sailed with the fleet to New Zealand around 1350 AD.

The people of Mauke did not know the ultimate fate of Paikea until the 1940s. During WW II some New Zealand Maoris were visiting Mauke, and shared with them their legends and histories. One told of Paikea, who had come from a far-off land after being blown by a storm from his home island. The Maukeans wero electrified – it fitted exactly with their legend of Paikea, the husband of Kea, who had been blown away in a storm and never seen again!

In the mid-1980s, New Zealand descendants of Paikea came to the Cooks to trace their family history. They went first to Rarotonga and were told, 'No, he's not from here, he came here from Mangaia'. In Mangaia the historians said, 'He came here from Mauke'. And so they finally traced their ancestor back to his homeland. The Paikeas are now a big family in New Zealand – apparently Paikea went on to have many children and grandchildren in the new land. ■

the village and to Kopupooki, one of Mauke's nicer beaches. It has three simple cottages, each with cement walls, a thatch roof and its own fridge. You can do your own cooking in the separate kitchen/dining area, or have meals prepared for you. Showers are in a separate area nearby. Cost is NZ$30/35 for singles/doubles in these units. There's also one self-contained family unit, sleeping up to four people, for NZ$50 a night. Discounts are offered for stays of one week or longer, or if you help out around the place. The friendly owners, Tautara & Kura Purea, will meet you with eis at the airport, take you around to see the island, take you to the Divided Church on Sunday if you want to go, and to any special occasions on the island. Motorcycles and bicycles are available for hire.

The *Mauke Cove Lodge* (☎ 35-888, 35-664, fax 35-094) operated by Kura & Archie Guinea is a large two-bedroom, two-bathroom house at the north edge of Kimiangatau village. Singles/doubles are NZ$28/44, plus NZ$16 for each additional adult; the house can sleep up to six people.

Things to Buy

Carved wooden drums and wooden bowls shaped like breadfruit leaves are made by a mens' carving collective opposite the rugby field in the centre of the island. You are welcome to stop by, look at the carvings, meet the woodcarvers and buy anything that might strike your fancy.

Getting There & Away

Air Air Rarotonga flies five times a week between Rarotonga and Mauke. Cost is NZ$142 (double for return) for the 50-minute flight, cheaper (NZ$198 return) on a Super Saver fare. Many travellers combine a visit to Mauke with a visit to Atiu and Mitiaro, since the three islands are close to one another and stopping at more than one island brings the fare down to just NZ$99 per sector on a multi-island pass. The Rarotonga travel agents can organise a variety of one-island or multi-island package tours including airfare and accommodation. See the Getting Around chapter for details.

Mauke now has an airstrip on the island's north coast, replacing the older one in the centre of the island.

Sea See the Getting Around chapter for details on passenger freighter ship services among the Cook Islands. A visit to Mauke can often be combined with visits to some of the other southern islands.

Day Tours Air Rarotonga is planning to begin day tours to include the islands of Mauke and Atiu all in one go. Check with the Rarotonga travel agents or Air Rarotonga for details.

Getting Around

The Tiare Holiday Cottages hires motorcycles (NZ$20 per day) and bicycles (NZ$7.50 per day) to guests and non-guests alike. Both hotels provide free airport transfers.

Mitiaro

Population: 247
Area: 22.3 sq km

Mitiaro is not one of the Cooks' most physically beautiful islands, but there are a few very enjoyable things you can do there to pass a pleasant few days. The people on the island are usually happy to see a new face; when you stop to talk to them they are very friendly. They all live in one small village on the west side of the island.

To see the sights of Mitiaro, especially the caves and the marae, you'll need a local person to guide you. This can easily be arranged at the place you stay.

Mitiaro's eels and dried bananas are renowned delicacies.

History

Like Mauke the island of Mitiaro was subject to repeated raids from Atiu, but unlike the Maukeans the Mitiaroans did not hide in caves. They stoutly defended their fortress, Te Pare, but were, nevertheless, eventually overcome by the Atiuans. The small and declining population that lives on Mitiaro today is thought to be almost entirely descended from raiding Atiuan warriors. The Reverend John Williams arrived on Mitiaro on 29 July 1823 accompanied by Rongomatane as he had been on Mauke and the island was soon Christianised, but Atiuan raids continued, even after the arrival of Christianity, into the 1840s.

Before Christianity came to Mitiaro, the people lived in inland villages – Taurangi, Atai, Auta, Mangarei and Takaue. As on Rarotonga, when the missionaries came, they moved the people out to live on the coast, where they built a village centred around the church. Today the old village sites are the plantation areas where the food is grown.

Geology

Mitiaro is another of the southern islands with a raised coral limestone outer plain, or makatea. Like Mauke, but to an even greater

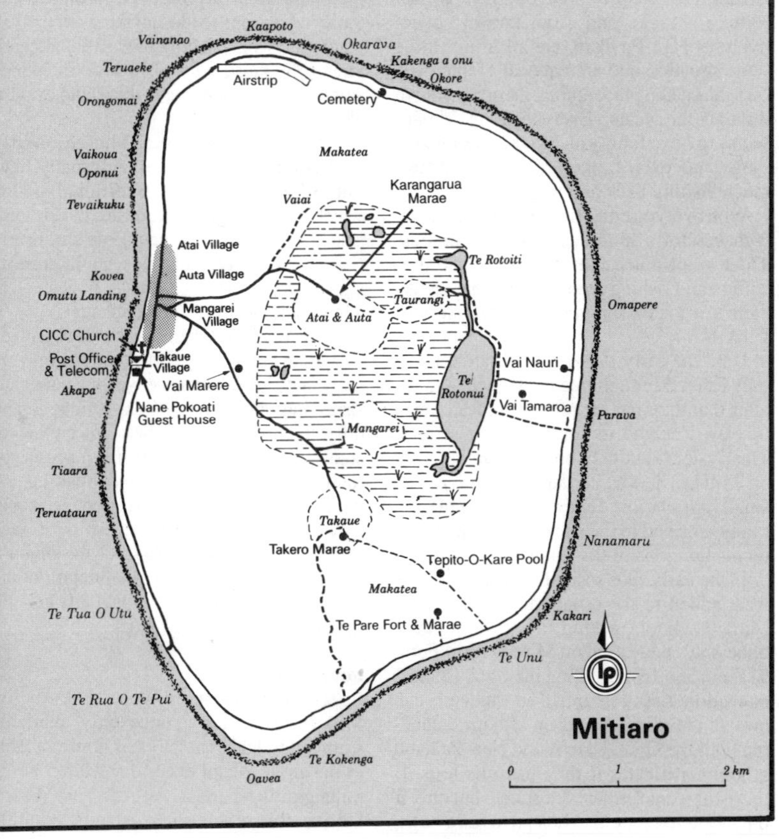

degree, the interior of the island is very flat – the makatea rises to a maximum of nine metres above sea level, the interior foodlands to about 12 metres. Much of the interior of Mitiaro is swampland, just one metre above sea level. Two parts of this swamp are deep enough to be labelled as lakes: Rotonui ('big lake') and Rotoiti ('small lake').

People, Economy & Culture

All the inhabitants of Mitiaro are related to one another in some way. The local ladies sometimes bemoan the situation, saying, 'We'll *never* find a husband on this island! All the men here are our cousins!' In fact Mitiaro, Mauke and Atiu, known collectively as Nga Pu Toru, are all in much the same situation and a great deal of intermarriage has taken place among them right down through the years. Everybody on Mitiaro seems to have family on Mauke, Atiu, Rarotonga and even farther afield, and there's much visiting back and forth.

With everyone on Mitiaro being a relative, it makes for a high degree of cooperation. There's not much money around, but agriculture and fishing produce abundant yields; there's a lot of sharing and everyone gets what they need.

Until the early 1990s, the Mitiaro schools only catered for children up to about age 12; after that they had to go to Atiu, Rarotonga or New Zealand to continue their studies. This system routinely broke up the families on Mitiaro; it was certainly a cause of the small population figure because children rarely returned to the narrow social and economic horizons of the island.

In the early '90s secondary school classes were added to the programme at the small Mitiaro school, making it possible to continue one's education on Mitiaro up to Form 5 (about age 16), fulfilling the Cook Islands' education requirement. The students can now sit their final exams on Mitiaro, achieving both the Cook Islands and New Zealand school certificates if they pass the tests. If they still want further education – but only if they want it – they can then go to Rarotonga, New Zealand or farther afield to continue their studies.

Not being forced to leave the island to attend school has resulted in more young people staying on the island. There are very few unemployed young people on the island. Plantation work or fishing is about all Mitiaro has to offer, though, and the work is in family-related businesses. This is great for feeding the family but not so hot for getting cash money, as all the fish and plantation produce is used here on the island and most of it gets traded back and forth among families. On the one hand, there's plenty of work for the young people to do and everyone on the island has plenty to eat; on the other hand, those who want to do anything other than plantation work, fishing or traditional handicrafts, or those who want to earn money somehow, must still leave the island eventually.

Although most people on Mitiaro now live in Western-style houses, they usually have outbuildings made of traditional thatch which may serve as cookhouses, fishermen's shacks etc. A very few people do still live in traditional thatch huts; it's an interesting sight to see an electricity meter hooked up to a hut made of sticks and pandanus!

Many traditional handicrafts are still made on Mitiaro, and many traditional customs are still practiced. Women weave long pandanus strips into floor mats, fans, handbags and other craftwork. Big bowls are carved of solid wood and canoes are still made in the traditional way. Fishing and planting are done according to the phases of the moon. Boys grow up learning the habits of each type of fish – at what phase of the moon it will be found, where, at what depth, doing what and so on. The traditional arts are still taught to both boys and girls.

Information

Progress has arrived very recently on Mitiaro. Electricity, once only available from individual generators, is now available to the entire island every day from 5 am to midnight, the same as on Atiu and Mauke. Unlike the other outer islands, though,

Mitiaro has the distinction of having street lights!

Mitiaro also now has a modern telephone system. Direct local, inter-island and international telephone calls can be made and received. The post office and Telecom office are in one building, so you can send and receive mail or telephone calls, telex and fax messages all in the same place. It's open Monday to Friday from 8 am to 4 pm.

If you need to change money, change it before you come to Mitiaro.

The island road was completely overhauled in 1989 and now extends right around the island.

What to Bring Be well prepared to ward off mosquitoes when you come to Mitiaro. The mosquitoes here seem fiercer than in other places; a significant portion of the island is covered by either lake or soggy swampland, providing an ideal breeding ground for the nasty critters, and maybe having a population of only 247 people on the island makes them that much more determined to bite what few people are around! While in Rarotonga's rainy season we usually did fine with just a mosquito coil, the mosquitoes of Mitiaro just laughed when we lit a coil and called their friends and relations to come and join them for a meal. Bring plenty of repellent.

If you'll be doing any walking on the island, you'll need that repellent, and if you'll be doing any walking across the makatea, be sure to bring some sturdy shoes. Old ones are best because they'll definitely receive a beating in the razor-sharp makatea. Don't try to walk across the makatea in sandals (jandals) or thongs as you could easily cut yourself very badly.

You may want to bring some food supplies with you, as food in the small village shops is considerably more expensive than on Rarotonga.

Since the power goes off at midnight, be sure to bring a torch (flashlight).

Bring your sunglasses as the white surface of the roads on Mitiaro is extremely reflective and bright all around the island.

Plantations

In the old days people made their villages where they grew their food. Even after moving the houses to the seaside village in the 1800s, they have continued using the same traditional plantation areas. Nowadays there are roads across the makatea to the plantations and one can drive there, although many people still make the long walk on foot. The new visitor may wonder why they don't simply grow their produce closer to the village but there's a good reason for it: the old agricultural areas with their surrounding peat deposits are the most fertile spots on the island, as well as being at the highest elevation.

The CICC Church

The inhabitants of Mitiaro are all concentrated in one village on the west coast. The village is an amalgamation of the villages moved to the coast when the missionaries arrived. The white-painted CICC church (the third church that the London Missionary Society built in the Cooks), with its blue trim, parquet ceiling decorated with black and white stars, and stained-glass windows is a fine sight and the singing on Sunday is superb. There's also a small Catholic church.

Marae & Fort

There are marae in the inland areas where the villages used to be although many are now overgrown. In 1988 an international team of archaeologists led by Dr Hiro Kurashina of Japan located and excavated the Takero marae, in the old Takaue village area. The huge stone seat of the ariki – he must have been a very big fellow! – had been broken in two and they found the other half and put the seat back together. The side that was lost had turned white while the other side was brown, so today the seat is two different colours. There are several old graves near the marae.

The same team returned in 1989 and excavated another marae, Karangarua, in the old Atai village area. It's a huge marae, large enough for hundreds of people to gather, with seats for the ariki and other important people. You're welcome to visit it but you'll need a guide to find it.

In the south-east part of the island are the stone remains of the ancient Te Pare fort, built as a defence against Atiuan raids. An underground shelter was large enough for the people to congregate in during times of danger, while above was a lookout tower from which approaching canoes could be watched for. Footsteps could be easily heard on the loose stone pathway to the fort. The important marae in the fort complex ensured there was spiritual as well as physical protection. Despite all of this, the fierce Atiuan warriors eventually did overpower the island. The present three ariki of Mitiaro – Ma'eu O Te-Rangi Ariki, Tiki Tetava Ariki and To'u Ariki – are descended from the foremost Mitiaro warriors, who were appointed by the Atiuan conquerors to represent the people.

To visit the Te Pare fort and marae, you must first ask permission of Tiki Tetava Ariki, the ariki to whom the marae belongs. His speaker will take you to the fort; the long walk across the makatea is well worthwhile.

Cemetery

Many old cemeteries are dotted around the island, indicating that in the past the population may have been much more widely spread than it is today. The cemetery on the north side of the island is the most interesting one. It has a few modern-style cement tombs, but also many older graves simply marked by an upright slab of coral. At almost every grave, both the old and the modern ones, some possessions of the deceased person are left at the headstone. Most of the graves have a plate, bowl, cup, glass, bottle and/or silverware sitting by the headstone – some carefully placed, just as if someone was going to sit down to a meal, others more haphazardly piled up. They are placed there so that if the spirit of the deceased comes, they can eat a meal on their own dinnerware!

Immediately after a death, the family brings food out to the grave and leaves it until it is gone. This may continue for a month or two, until it is felt that the spirit has departed, but the plates and cutlery are left permanently. There is a very strong belief that the spirit continues to live on after death, and every effort is made to ensure that the spirit will not become angry with the living. At older graves, you'll see tin or enamel bowls and cups while newer graves have modern plates and cutlery. At one grave we saw a whole box full of what appeared to be medicine bottles, some still containing the medicine; another grave has a baby bottle and a tiny pair of baby shoes.

Lakes

It's hard to tell where the surrounding swamp ends and the lakes begin. Except in one spot, where a road now makes it possible to drive right up to the shore of Lake Rotonui, the lakes are hard to approach and although the water is clear the lake bottoms are horribly muddy. If you approach the lakes by any other means than that one road, the ground becomes increasingly soggy and wallows more and more unsteadily under your feet the closer you get to the lake. Where the road arrives at Lake Rotonui, though, the ground is firm, there's a boat landing and a pleasant picnic spot.

You can also approach the lakes from the Taurangi plantation area, which is quite easy since there is no makatea to cross – only a wide strip of very black mud. If you have a motorbike you can take it all the way to the end of the Taurangi area pathway. From there it's only a 15-minute walk to the lake but the mud you have to cross may deter you.

The local men often fish in the lakes for the prolific small fish and the famous eels. The eels are caught at night by blinding them with a light and then hitting them with a bush knife. They can also be caught by baited hooks, like fishing, or by hooking them around the body and hoisting them out of the water. There are plenty of eels in the lakes; 10 or more eels can easily be caught in a couple of hours.

Peat

There are many areas of natural peat on the island, principally around the lakes, adjacent

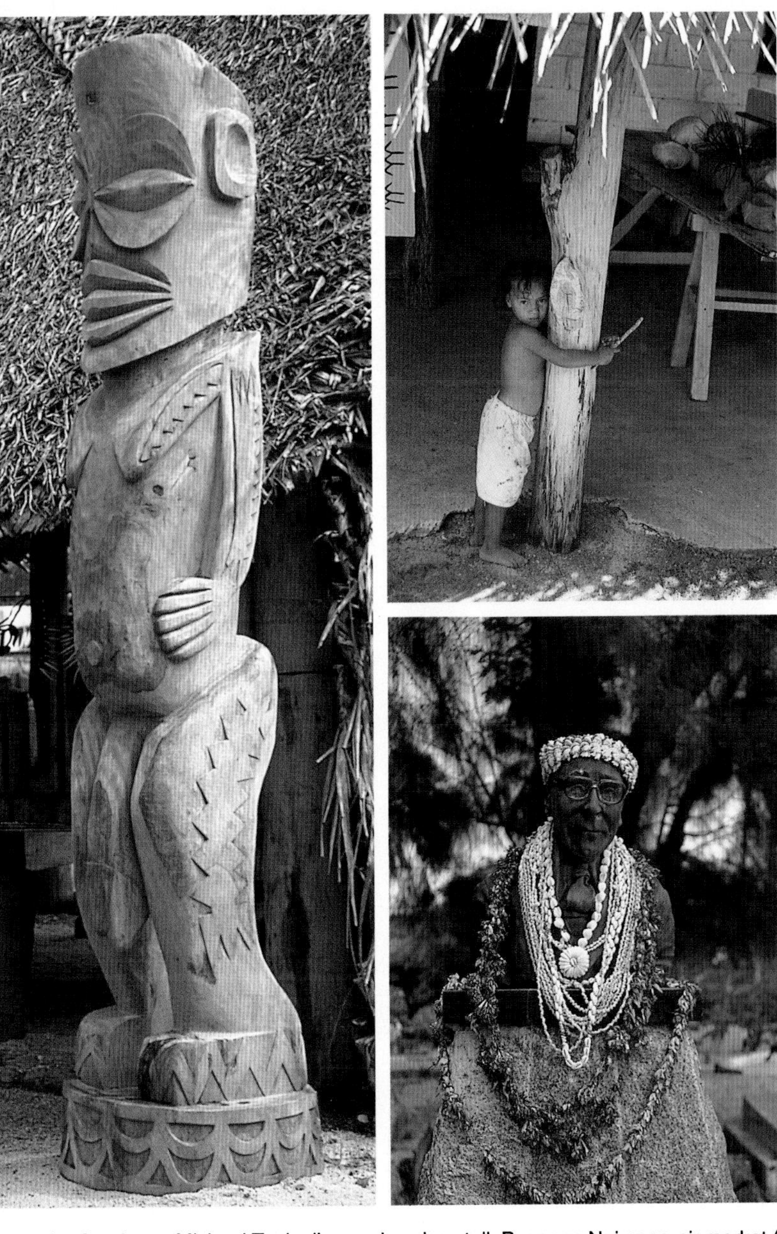

Left: Carving at Michael Tavioni's woodcarving stall, Punanga Nui open-air market (NK)
p Right: Little girl at small roadside market (TC)
m Right: Sir Albert Henry's grave, CICC churchyard, Avarua (NK)

Top: CICC church, Mitiaro (NK)
Bottom: Mitiaro women having a good time (NK)

to the foodlands and in the swamp. A particularly rich strip is located by the Parava boat landing on Lake Rotonui, where the road meets the lake. A 1988 study concluded that the peat could not be efficiently used for energy but farmers do use it to enrich the soil.

When you walk near the lake, or on the roads through the swamp towards the plantation lands, there is a pleasant peat smell in the air. Crossing the peat to the lake is quite an adventure as it can wobble like jelly beneath your feet. In places, logs have been placed to spread the weight.

Terevai
The women of Mitiaro have a delightful custom known as the *terevai*. A group of women get together and go to one of the island's pools, often to Vai Nauri or Vai Tamaroa. Along the way, they sing the old bawdy songs of the ancestors – many of which are action songs, with graphic movements accompanying the lyrics. The mood gets exuberantly racy and by the time the women have trekked out to the pool, everyone is in high spirits. At the pool a prayer, a hymn and a chant precede a synchronised leap into the water. ■

Beaches, Caves & Pools

Mitiaro has some fine little beaches and the reef at low tide is excellent for walking on all around the island. In common with the other islands with makatea it also has a number of beautiful caves, with pools of fresh water that make great swimming holes. The makatea looks parched and dry; you would never guess that out there somewhere are cool, clear pools, hidden under the ground. The water in the pools, as well as in the lakes and the swamp, rises and falls with the tides. There's no trace of saltwater in the pools but they must somehow be connected to the sea.

Just a 10-minute walk from the village on the Takaue road, Vai Marere is the only sulphur pool in the Cook Islands. All you see from the road is a big hole in the ground but it opens up into a large cave with stalactites. The water is darker than in other pools, possibly due to the sulphur content. It's refreshingly cool and makes your skin and hair feel wonderfully soft.

Vai Tamaroa and Vai Nauri are on the eastern side of the island. Vai Tamaroa is about a 15-minute walk across sharp makatea from the coast road; the start of the track is marked by a sign commemorating a Boys Brigade project in 1985. You'll still need a local to take you there, though, since the trail across the makatea is faint. A road to Vai Nauri has now been cut, so you can drive right up to it.

Vai Nauri is a large, brilliantly clear pool in a big cave. You can reach the water either by climbing down one side and wading in, or by going around to the other side and leaping off the three-metre cliff, like the locals do. It's beautiful to sit peacefully in the cool cavern and listen to the water dripping down from the stalactites on the ceiling, falling down like rain.

Vai Tamaroa is another large pool, but open to the sky. All around it are cliffs about 10 metres high, and the locals love to jump down into the water, climbing back up the cliffs again for another leap. The women hold their *terevai* gatherings at both Vai Tamaroa and Vai Nauri.

Vaiai or the Sandalwood Cave, named for the sandalwood that grows there, is in the north of the island and also has a good freshwater swimming hole. People rarely go there nowadays, though, because the track to reach it is difficult to find since it was destroyed by a cyclone a few years ago. You'll need a good guide to reach Vaiai.

Tepito-O-Kare, in the south-east part of the island, is too small for swimming but it has fresh water good for drinking. Fishermen used to stop by here to quench their thirst as they walked back inland from Te Unu after fishing trips.

Places to Stay & Eat

For several years there's been only one organised accommodation on Mitiaro: the *Nane Pokoati Guest House* (☎ 36-107, fax 36-683) operated by Nane Pokoati, who runs the house like a big family home (which it is) and who is justly famous for her friendliness and warmth as well as for her cooking.

Unfortunately Nane is closing the guest house for one year, from April '94 to April '95, though it will still be open on a strictly limited basis to local Cook Islanders, to government or other island workers, or to those who have been there before. If you don't fall into one of these categories, you can still ring Nane to ask if there's anyplace else to stay on the island; as we were going to press she was talking to people in the village and trying to come up with an alternative. The Rarotonga travel agents should also be able to advise you of accommodation possibilities. As on other Cook Islands, if there is no place for you to stay, you won't be allowed to fly to the island.

Limited food supplies are available at the small village food shops but prices are higher than on Rarotonga; you may want to bring some supplies with you. Mitiaro's dried bananas wrapped in banana leaves *(pieres)* are a local delicacy. The local eels are also delicious and there's a good variety of fish and fresh produce. Passionfruit and mangoes simply fall on the ground under the trees and there are coconuts everywhere.

Pieres – Dried Bananas Wrapped in Banana Leaves

Things to Buy

It isn't commercially organised but you could probably arrange to buy some local products during your visit. Mitiaro women still make a variety of woven pandanus products for everyday use – floor mats, smaller mats, fans, handbags, baskets etc. Pandanus no longer grows on Rarotonga and has been virtually eliminated on Atiu too, while pandanus trees still grow profusely all over Mitiaro. A visit to Mitiaro could be a good chance to find something made of pandanus. Carved wooden bowls are another possibility.

Getting There & Away

Air Air Rarotonga flies to Mitiaro four times a week. Cost is NZ$142 (double for return) for the 50-minute flight, cheaper (NZ$19 return) on the Super Saver fare.

Many travellers combine a visit to Mitiaro with visits to Mauke and/or Atiu – each i only a 10-minute flight from Mitiaro, and i you visit more than one island, the cost pe sector is reduced to NZ$99. The Rarotong travel agents can also fit Mitiaro in on multi-island package tour with airfare accommodation and hotel transfers al included. See the Getting Around chapter fo details.

Sea See the Getting Around chapter fo details on passenger freighter ship service among the Cook Islands. Passenger freighte stops at Mitiaro are often made in conjunc tion with visits to Atiu and Mauke, both o which are very close to Mitiaro.

Palmerston

Population: 49
Area: 2.0 sq km

Palmerston is something of a Cook Islan oddity: it's only a little north of Aitutal otherwise the northernmost of the southe group islands, but it's also far to the west the other southern islands. Furthermore, i

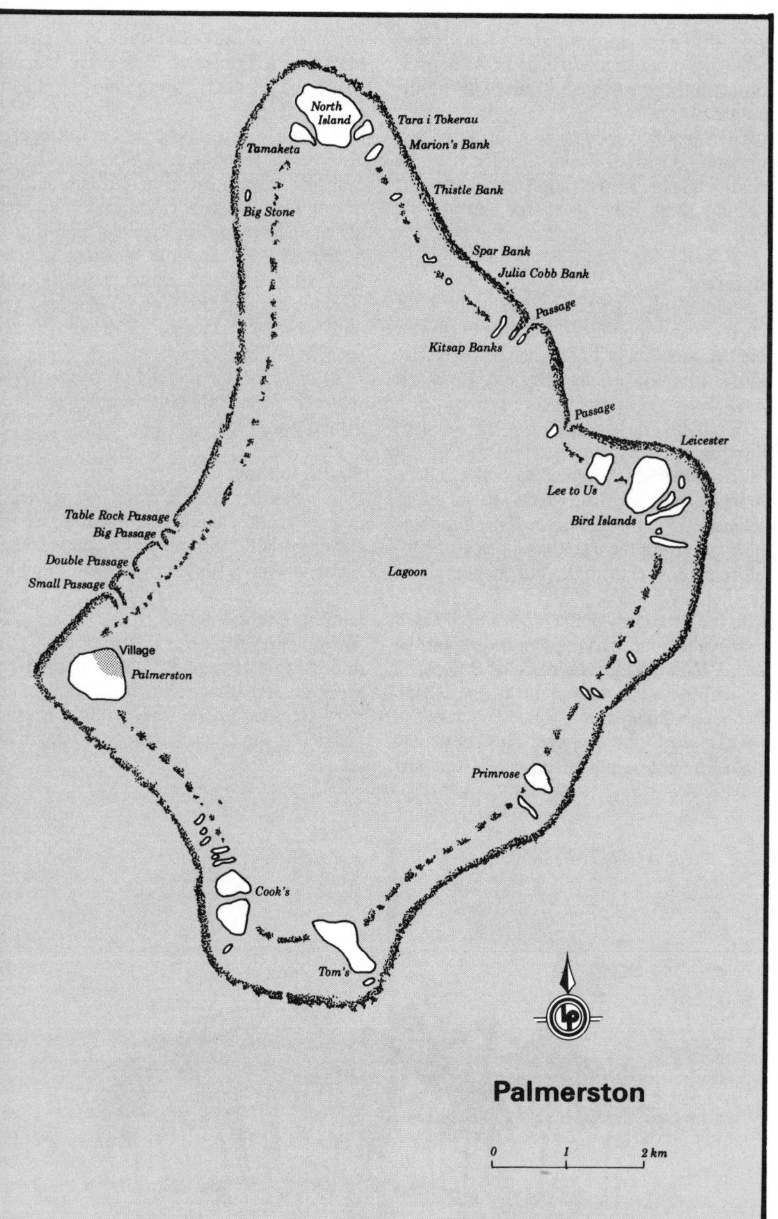
North Island
Tara i Tokerau
Tamaketa
Marion's Bank
Thistle Bank
Big Stone
Spar Bank
Julia Cobb Bank
Passage
Kitsap Banks
Passage
Leicester
Lee to Us
Bird Islands
Table Rock Passage
Big Passage
Double Passage
Small Passage
Lagoon
Village
Palmerston
Primrose
Cook's
Tom's
Palmerston
0
1
2 km

an atoll like the northern group islands and unlike the other southern islands. As a result it sometimes gets treated as part of the northern group.

The lagoon is 11 km wide at its widest point and 35 small islands dot the reef. At low tide the lagoon is completely closed off. Visiting ships have to anchor outside the reef.

History

Captain Cook sighted the island in 1774 when it was unpopulated. He did not stop on that occasion but in 1777 when he passed by on his third voyage his ships did pause and boats were sent ashore to seek provisions.

A passing missionary ship en route to Tahiti stopped at Palmerston in 1797 and in 1811 another ship stopped to collect bêche de mer and shark fins, which are valued as delicacies by the Chinese. The Tahitians talked of using the island as a place of banishment for criminals but it remained uninhabited.

In 1850 the crew of the *Merchant of Tahiti* discovered four starving Europeans on the island. When they took them to Rarotonga the ship's captain laid claim to the island, then passed the claim to a Scottish trader in Tahiti named John Branden. This gentleman placed a representative on the island and some time later discovered William Marsters, a European, living on Manuae island and persuaded him to move to Palmerston in 1863.

William Marsters became a living legend. The present inhabitants of the island are all Marsters, descended from William and his three Polynesian wives. They not only populated Palmerston: to this day you'll find people with the surname Marsters all over the Cooks and it's a common name on cemetery headstones. Old William Marsters died on 22 May 1899 at the age of 78 and is buried near his original homestead.

At one time the population of the island was as high as 150 but it's a quiet and little visited place today.

Places to Stay

Palmerston has no organised accommodation for visitors, but if you do come, see the Reverend Bill Marsters and he can arrange accommodation for you with local families.

Getting There & Away

There are no flights to Palmerston, but the inter-island passenger freighter shipping services do sometimes stop here, though not very frequently. See the Getting Around chapter for details on shipping services in the Cooks.

Mangaia

Population: 1214
Area: 51.8 sq km

The second largest of the Cook Islands, Mangaia is not much smaller than Rarotonga, although its population is much less and has declined sharply in recent years. The island is a geological oddity very similar to Atiu. Like Atiu the central hills are surrounded by an outer rim of raised coral reef known as the makatea. The lagoon inside the fringing coral reef is very narrow and shallow.

Although Mangaia's geography is basically similar to Atiu's it is much more dramatic. The makatea rises rapidly from the coast and in most places it drops as a sheer wall to the inner region. There are places where you can climb to the top of the cliff for impressive, uninterrupted views. The inner cliff of the makatea is such a major barrier that some of the cuttings through it are quite spectacular, one of the ones through to Ivirua in particular.

All the streams and rivers running down from the central hills run into a dead end at the inner cliff of the makatea, filtering through the makatea and emerging as small freshwater springs at or near the seashore. After heavy rains, streaks of Mangaia's red soil can be seen stretching from the makatea out into the sea from these water runoffs.

Scrub, ferns, vines, coconut palms and other trees grow on the makatea. Taro swamps are found around the inner edge of the makatea where water collects between the hills and the coral flatlands. The central hills are the most fertile part of the island and they're planted with various crops. Much of the hilly central area, though, has been ravaged by fire and does not have the lush foliage you might expect – a fire in June '92 which burned around 50 hectares was followed by a large-scale fire in January '93 which burned around 600 hectares. Baby Caribbean pine trees have been planted to refoliate the island but so far the hills still look quite bare.

Pineapple, which a few years ago was the island's principal export crop, is still grown but not on the grand scale it once was. After one year in the early '90s when hundreds of boxes of pineapples rotted on the wharf waiting for shipment, most farmers now raise pineapple only on a small scale for home and Cook Islands' consumption. Mangaia pineapples are still justly famous, though – big, sweet and juicy. Mangaia taro is also said to be some of the finest in the Cook Islands.

Before a World Health Organisation dam and water reservoir was built in 1986, the Mangaia villages all had water problems. You'll still see water tanks beside many houses, storing the rainwater from the roofs.

Mangaia Cross Section

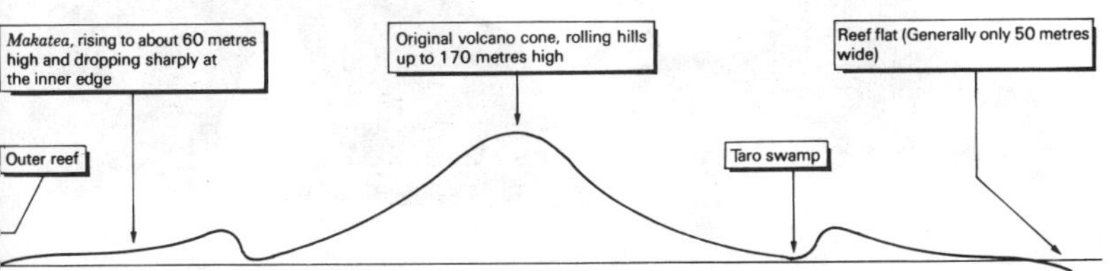

History

The Mangaians have an unusual legend of their early history. Most Polynesian islands have some sort of legend about a great ancestor arriving on a fantastic canoe. Not the Mangaians: nobody sailed from anywhere to settle Mangaia. Rangi, Mokoaro and Akatauira, the three sons of the god Rongo, father of Mangaia, simply lifted the island up from the deep, becoming its first settlers and the ancestors of the Nga Ariki tribe.

P H Buck, in his 1934 book *Mangaian Society*, suggests that the reason for Mangaia's unusual creation myth is that when Tangiia arrived on Rarotonga from Tahiti around the year 1250 AD, he brought along a group of people with no rank and no chance of rising in status on Rarotonga. He says that a couple of centuries later, around 1450 or 1475 AD, some of these people, under the leadership of Rangi, left Rarotonga and migrated to Mangaia to get a fresh start, inventing a creation myth to disguise their origin. On the other hand the early missionary William Wyatt Gill, writing in 1876, said the Mangaian people originated from Samoa.

The island's current name is comparatively recent. The traditional name of the island was A'ua'u ('terraced'), short for A'ua'u Nui O Rongo Ki Te Au Marama ('big terraced land of Rongo in the world of daylight'). The spiritual name of the island was Akatautika ('well-poised').

The current name of the island is short for Mangaia Nui Neneva ('Mangaia monstrously great'), a name bestowed by Tamaeu, an Aitutakian, who arrived on Mangaia in 1775, two years before Captain Cook made the first European discovery of the island. Mangaia means 'peace' or 'temporal power'. The name apparently relates to the interminable battles between the island's various groups and the peace which was finally established when one leader eventually achieved *mangaia*, or power, over the whole island – after 42 separate battles which had various victors.

Captain Cook claimed the European discovery of Mangaia during his second Pacific

Mangaian People

voyage. He arrived on 29 March 1777 but since the reception was not the friendliest and it was not possible to find a place to land, the *Resolution* and *Discovery* sailed on to a more friendly greeting at Atiu.

The reception was even less inviting when John Williams turned up on Mangaia in 1823. The pioneering missionary had left Aitutaki to search for Rarotonga, which he eventually found by way of Atiu. Coming first upon Mangaia he attempted to set Polynesian missionary 'teachers' ashore but the Mangaians attacked them, so he quickly dropped the idea and sailed off again. On 15 June 1824, however, Tiere and David, two Polynesian missionaries from Tahaa, the island sharing the same lagoon with Raiatea in present-day French Polynesia, were landed on the island and, as elsewhere, the conversion to Christianity was soon underway. Missionary work on Mangaia was directed from the Tahitian mission until 1839, when it was switched to the supervision of the Rarotongan mission headquarters.

Traditionally, the Mangaians had a reputation for being a dour, ethnocentric lot, an attribute which perhaps helped to keep the aggressive Atiuans at bay. The warriors of Atiu wreaked havoc on Mauke and Mitiaro but never had much success against Mangaia.

More recently Mangaia has suffered from a dramatic population decline. Since the mid-70s the population of the island, stable for some time at around 2000, has fallen by a third. The Mangaians have positively and consistently refused to have anything to do with the central Land Court's attempts to administer land disputes.

Orientation

Oneroa, Tamarua and Ivirua, the three main villages, are all on the coast, with Oneroa on the west side of the island, Ivirua on the east side and Tamarua on the south. Oneroa, the main village, has three parts: Tava'enga and Kaumata are on the coast, with Temakatea up above, reached through a road cut through the makatea cliff. The airstrip is on the north side of the island.

Information

Mangaia is a long way from Rarotonga, development-wise. Electricity only arrived in late '85; it operates daily from 5 am to midnight.

The Telecom office, in the upper part of Oneroa village not far from the hospital, is open Monday to Friday from 7.30 am to 4 pm. Here you can make long distance telephone calls, send and receive faxes, and there's a card phone outside the door that you can use anytime.

Churches & Marae

There are typical, old CICC churches in Oneroa, Ivirua and Tamarua. Look for the sennet rope binding on the roof beams in the Tamarua and Oneroa churches. In front of the Oneroa church is an interesting monument detailing the ministers, both papa'a and Maori, of the church and also the Mangaian ministers who have worked as missionaries abroad.

Mangaia has numerous pre-missionary maraes but you'd need a local expert to find them. Tuara George (see the Caves section) can take you to see the maraes if you like – there are 24 around the island – but he says it wouldn't be worth it, since most of them are way out in the bush and all of the island's maraes are overgrown and disused. Maraes on Mangaia are not looked after or kept clean because, unlike on Rarotonga, on Mangaia they are no longer used.

Rangimotia & Island Walks

Rangimotia (169 metres) is the highest point on the island. It's not a straightforward peak, more of a high plateau. You know when you're at the top but you have to explore in several directions to see all the coast. From the Oneroa side of the island there's an old dirt road, suitable for 4WDs, motorcycles or mountain bikes, right to the top. At the top the track forks and you can follow either fork back down to the coast. The roads follow the ridges of Mangaia's rolling hills and even

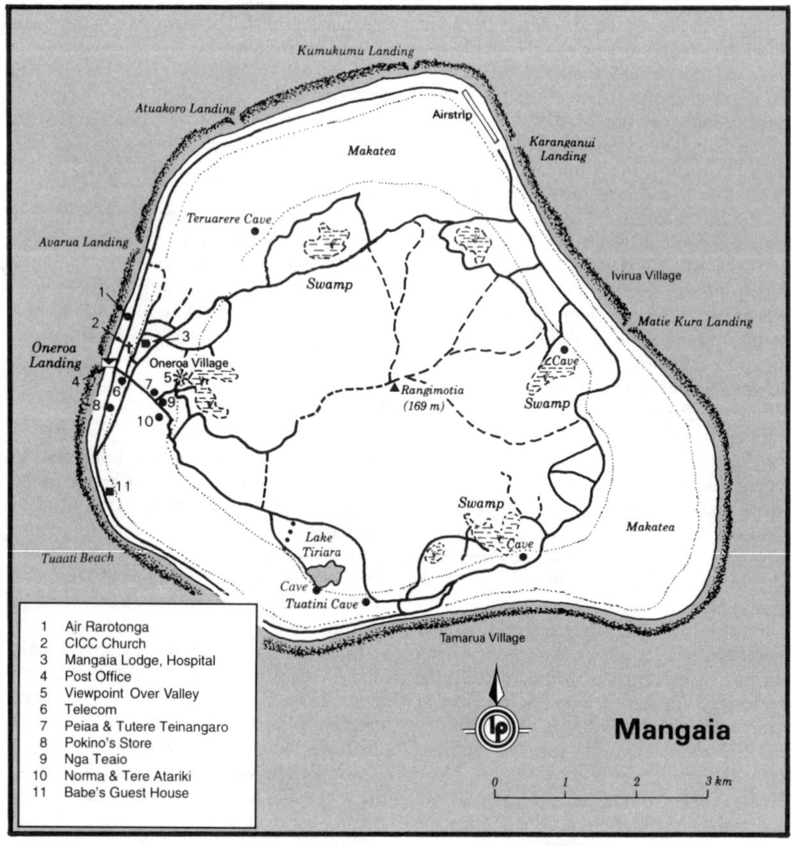

when the roads are indistinct it's easy to find your way.

If you've taken the fork heading towards Ivirua, you can turn south from Ivirua and head to Tamarua, the third village on the island. The dirt road runs just inland from the makatea for most of the distance. Along this stretch the makatea is not edged with much of a cliff but shortly after the trail climbs back onto the raised coral there is an impressive drop and at a point shortly before Tamarua you can turn off the road for a view over an area of taro swamp. From Tamarua the road runs close to the coast with numerous paths down to the reef. Or you can take the shorter direct route back to Oneroa.

This a pleasant but quite long day's walk. It's probably more than 25 km in total. There's no chance of going thirsty or hungry along the way as long as you have your Swiss Army Knife handy – coconuts, papaya, mango, passionfruit, bananas and pineapples can be found along the way.

Several of the cuttings through the makatea cliffs are quite beautiful places for short walks, with narrow roads winding between the high grey makatea cliffs, lush with vegetation. The cutting from Ivirua village heading inland to the taro swamp behind the village is probably the most beautiful on the island; the one heading south from the Temakatea part of Oneroa village to Tuaati Beach is also very beautiful.

Caves

The makatea is riddled with caves but the largest and most spectacular is Teruarere. Tuara George (☎ 34-105) is the guide for this cave. He charges NZ$15 per person for a two to three-hour tour of the cave, passing by a number of ancient human skeletons inside the cave. Teruarere was used as a burial cave in the distant past but was rediscovered in the 1930s by Tuara's grandfather, Tuaratua, and Robert Dean Frisbie – see the introductory Books section of the Facts for the Visitor chapter. Teruarere means 'jump' (possibly because people used to jump down into the cave opening).

You do have to climb down into the opening. There's a tree whose branches emerge at ground level and at the other end of this opening chasm there's a fine view out from the makatea cliff. As you enter, the high, narrow cliffs seem to close overhead. At first there are several small openings high above you and a tree root winds down through one to floor level. Then you have to slither through a low, muddy opening and the cave becomes much more enclosed. Be sure to bring a torch (flashlight) and insect repellent as there are many mosquitoes near the cave entrance. The cave is not difficult to explore but do wear your old clothes as you'll get quite dirty and muddy,

This is a very dramatic cave and most of the time it is very high although fairly narrow. It holds many crystalline, glistening-white stalactites and stalagmites but the most interesting feature, apart from the human skeletons, is simply how far it continues. There are no major side chambers but the main cavern continues on and on. Tuara George's father, George Tuara, reckons that the cave continues at least two km. Although he has been going into the cave for nearly 50 years he has never reached the end, and it's said that no-one else has ever reached the end, either.

There are many other caves all over the island and several legendary ones no-one has yet discovered. One is said to contain the bones of ancient Mangaians of gigantic size. Another, the legendary cave of Piriteumeume, is said to be filled with the skeletons of countless Mangaian warriors, each with his weapons laid beside him.

Beaches & Lake

There are countless little beaches and bays around the coastline although nowhere is there the kind of white, sandy beach with good swimming that you can find on some of the other Cook Islands. The reef is very shallow and generally close to the coast. About the only place you can go swimming with water deep enough to go over your head is at the wharf at Avarua Landing near Oneroa. Many locals swim at the wharf, afterwards going across the makatea about 100 metres to the left (south) to where a small freshwater spring gushes up from the makatea beside the seaside, with refreshing cool water and tiny fish. The spring is too small for swimming but you can sit in the water to wash off the sea salt.

On the south-west side of the island, Tuaati Beach is a tiny unmarked beach too shallow for swimming, but you can splash around and it's an attractive little beach. There's also a sandy beach at Karanganui Landing on the north-east side of the island, where again you can get wet but it's too shallow for swimming.

Lake Tiriara is the only lake on the island but it's difficult to distinguish it from the surrounding swamp, where high reeds grow. You may need to ask a local to point the lake out to you. From the road, you can follow a trail until you bump into the high makatea cliff near the lake, turn to your left, and walk until you reach the lake – a very muddy walk as you near the lake. A canoe is usually moored at this point, which you can paddle over the lake and into a cave at the far end of the lake.

Mangaian Hut

Places to Stay

Most of the island's visitor accommodation is in Oneroa, the island's principal village. Oneroa consists of a road along the coast, a road up from the coast through a cutting in the makatea and a couple of roads along the coastal edge of the makatea. Most of the accommodation is in Temakatea, the upper part of the village. Since there are no restaurants on the island, all the places to stay make some provision for their guests to eat, either cooking meals for you or allowing you to do your own cooking.

The *Mangaia Lodge* (☎ 34-097, 34-042) near the hospital in Temakatea has three very large bedrooms in a sprawling old colonial-style home. The nightly cost of NZ$30 per person includes breakfast, dinner, and free tea and coffee. The lodge is operated by the Island Council; they may be leasing it long-term to a team of ostrich farmers from Australia, so check before you arrive. If the lodge does become unavailable, its manager, Mrs Ngatamaine Ruatoi (☎ 34-042) says she will try to assist visitors in finding alternative places to stay.

Meanwhile, several families in Temakatea are opening their homes to visitors in anticipation of the lodge's closing. All are found along the upper part of the road heading up from the makatea cutting and all are operated by friendly locals who would go out of their way to make sure their guests enjoy the island.

Peiaa & Tutere Teinangaro (☎ 34-168) have three bedrooms available in the family home. The nightly cost of NZ$25 per person includes breakfast and dinner. They will take you on boat trips around the island, and hire you a motorcycle for NZ$20 per day including petrol; a pick-up truck is also available for hire.

Norma & Tere Atariki (☎ 34-206) have a small house which you can either rent all for yourself or share with the family, whichever you prefer, and you can do your own cooking or have meals provided. Cost is flexible depending on the arrangements.

Nearby, *Nga Teaio* (☎ 34-164) has a house available for NZ$20 per day or NZ$100 per week. Here you have the whole house to yourself – one very large room with a verandah all around, it can sleep up to seven people – and you do your own cooking.

Also in the Temakatea section of Oneroa, near the hospital and overlooking the sea, *Liz & Tuaine Papatua* (☎ 34-164) have a one-bedroom house for rent, sleeping four people, for a daily rate of NZ$35 per person with meals included, or NZ$25 per person if you do your own cooking.

Down in the Kaumata section of Oneroa, beside the sea and not far from Tuaati beach, *Babe's Guest House* (☎ 34-092, fax 34-078) is a modern three-bedroom house which can sleep up to six people. The nightly cost of NZ$48 per person includes three meals a day. There's a bar here open on Friday and Saturday nights for a dance which is the only regularly held dance on the island – great if you like music and socialising, not so great if you want a silent night! Come during the week if you want a quiet time.

There isn't much accommodation available outside Oneroa. Jan & Tu Kristensson on Rarotonga (☎ 22-236) are planning to open the *Are Moana* south-east of Ivirua around the time of this book's publication, up on a cliff with an ocean view and several free-standing, self-contained one-bedroom units, each with one double bed and one single bed. Cost will be about NZ$80 to NZ$100 per unit.

Places to Eat

If you're staying long you might want to bring some of your own food with you. There are several trade stores around but their selection is rather limited – fresh vegetables are in particularly short supply, which seems odd when the island is so fertile. Pokino's Store in Oneroa is probably the best-stocked shop on the island but even its selection is limited. There's a weekly Friday morning market beside the post office in Oneroa where you can get whatever fruits and vegetables might be around. In Oneroa there's a bakery on the back road behind the hospital, and a couple of places that make doughnuts.

Entertainment

The only regularly scheduled entertainment on the island is the dance on Friday and Saturday nights at Babe's Guest House in Oneroa.

Things to Buy

A variety of traditional arts & crafts are practiced on Mangaia and although there is no shop on the island which sells them, the people who make them welcome interested visitors stopping by to have a look. All of the following craftspeople live in Oneroa.

Mangaian ceremonial adzes are a well-known Pacific artefact in world museums. Mayor Tuaiva Mautairi (☎ 34-001) makes both the pedestal and hafted types in various sizes, all in the authentic style with intricate carving, basalt heads and sennet binding. He also makes *pates* (a Mangaian style of decoratively carved wooden drums), wooden fruit bowls and various other wood carvings, and taro pounders of cokite stone.

George Tuara (☎ 34-105) also makes ceremonial adzes, wooden drums and other carvings, plus model canoes, taro pounders, reef shoes, earrings and coconut bracelets. John Tangirere (☎ 34-054) makes wooden drums, wooden fruit bowls, model canoes, wooden necklaces and bamboo furniture.

On the women's side, Teremoana Tutu (☎ 34-036) and Tako Ruatoe (☎ 34-010) make household baskets, pandanus mats and long fishing baskets. Teremoana Ruatoe (☎ 34-010) makes tivaevaes, cushions and pillow cases. Plenty of other women also make tivaevaes but they are usually made only for home use.

Almost everyone makes *pupu eis* (long necklaces of tiny white or yellow shells). The tiny pupu shells from which the eis are made can only be found after rainfall. They're black and are found on the makatea, not by the water. Boiling them in caustic soda produces the typical yellow colour although they can also be grilled to make them white, or dyed a variety of colours. They're then individually pierced with a needle and threaded to make the finished ei. It's a time consuming business. On Rarotonga, pupu eis from Mangaia fetch as much as NZ$40 a dozen.

Getting There & Away

Air Air Rarotonga flies to Mangaia five times a week; the 203-km flight takes 40 minutes. Cost is NZ$127 one way (double for return), cheaper (NZ$180 return) on a Super Saver fare. If you visit any other southern group islands, you can get a 'Paradise Islands Pass', bringing the cost of each flight sector down to NZ$99. See the Getting Around chapter for details.

Sea See the Getting Around chapter for details on services and fares on passenger freighter ships operating from Raro to the other Cook Islands, including Mangaia. Mangaia is often included in trips around the southern islands.

Getting Around

Peiaa & Tutere Teinangaro (☎ 34-168) in Temakatea, Oneroa, have a couple of motorcycles which they will hire at NZ$20 per day including petrol, and a pick-up truck which can also be hired. They also have a boat for trips around the island. There are no other organised vehicle hires on the island but you could probably arrange something as there are plenty of motorcycles around.

Otherwise walking is fine, especially the route across the island via Rangimotia, but the distances around the coast are quite long and you can't count on getting a ride from a passing vehicle as there is so little traffic. Tony tried his luck one day while researching the first edition of this book and walked all the way from Ivirua via Tamarua to Oneroa, several hours' walk, and only saw one truck passing by – the wrong way.

The Northern Islands

The northern islands of the Cooks are scattered coral atolls, specks of land in a vast expanse of sea. They are all low-lying and from a ship cannot even be seen from much more than 10 km away. On many of the islands severe hurricanes will send waves right across the islands.

Although atolls such as these are the romantic image of a Pacific island – complete with sandy beaches, clear and shallow lagoons, swaying palm trees – in actual fact, life is hard on an atoll. Fish may be abundant in the lagoon but atoll soil is only marginally fertile and the range of foodstuffs which can be grown is very limited. Fresh water is always a problem. Shallow wells are often the only source of drinking water and the supply is generally limited and often not very pleasant to drink.

In the modern world atoll life has another drawback apart from these natural ones and that is sheer isolation. Today, people want economic opportunity, education for their children and contact with the outside world. On a tiny island where the only physical contact is a trading ship coming through a few times a year these things are clearly not available. Returning islanders and the radio whet the appetite for the outside world and consequently many of the northern islands are suffering from a declining population.

Literature

Several of the northern islands have figured prominently in the literature of the Cook Islands, both past and present. See the Books section in the Facts for the Visitor chapter, where many are mentioned.

For an account of a short visit to various northern group islands via the old Silk & Boyd freighter ships get yourself a copy of *How To Get Lost & Found in the Cook Islands* (Pukapuka, Nassau and Palmerston) or *Across the South Pacific* (Manihiki and Rakahanga).

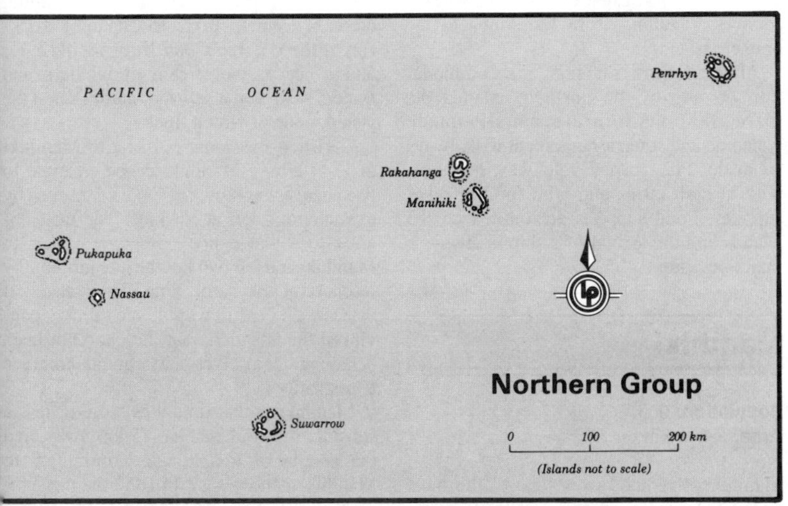

Getting There & Away

If you want to visit islands of the northern group you can fly to Pukapuka, Manihiki or Penrhyn, though the flights take a long time from Rarotonga (about 3½ to four hours) and are quite expensive. In fact it's only recently that the northern group islands have had regular air service at all – up until the early '90s the distance to these islands made the cost of flying there prohibitively high, so no flights went. The cost is still high – it costs just as much to fly to the northern group islands from Rarotonga as it does to fly to New Zealand, and can take even longer – but if you do get up there, you'll find these remote islands quite 'unspoiled'.

Otherwise the only regular way of getting there is on the inter-island shipping services which carry freight and passengers. The ships unload and load at the islands by day so if you're doing a circuit of the islands you can spend a day or two on a number of islands. If you want to stay longer you may be stuck with waiting until the next ship comes by – which could be quite a while, especially for the small islands that don't have airstrips. On the islands with airstrips you could always take the boat one way and fly one way. The Getting Around chapter has information on all the air and sea services travelling from Rarotonga to the northern islands.

Although there is no regular accommodation on any of the northern islands the infrequent visitors are usually made welcome and some arrangement will always be made. Plan to pay your way, however, both in cash terms and with food or other supplies. Food supplies are limited on the islands and the arrival of a ship is always a major occasion.

Manihiki

Population: 663
Area: 5.4 sq km

Manihiki is reputed to be one of the most beautiful atolls in the South Pacific. Although Aitutaki is sometimes called 'the Bora Bora of the Cook Islands' and is justly renowned for its beauty, those who have visited Manihiki often come back saying that Aitutaki is only second best.

Nearly 40 islands, some of them little more than tiny motus, encircle the four-km wide and totally enclosed lagoon of Manihiki. The main village is Tauhunu but there is a second village, Tukao. Manihiki has no safe anchorage for visiting ships which consequently stay offshore.

What it does have is pearls and pearl shells, especially the famous Manihiki black pearls which are the mainstay of the island and a significant export for the Cook Islands. The abilities of the island's pearl divers are legendary – they can dive effortlessly to great depths and stay submerged for minutes at a time.

Manihiki and Rakahanga were formerly lived on by the same group of people; they migrated between the two islands until the missionaries showed up and changed things.

History

Although some authorities consider that the Spanish explorer Pedro Fernandez de Quiros was the European discoverer of Manihiki, credit is normally given to Captain Patrickson of the US ship *Good Hope* in 1822. He and a successive stream of whalers and traders bestowed a series of names upon the island, none of which stuck.

Christian missionaries came to Manihiki in 1849 after a Manihiki canoe en route to Rakahanga was blown off course, rescued by a whaler and left at Manuae. The missionaries took the canoe passengers back to Manihiki and left two Polynesian missionary teachers at the same time. They also left disease. The ensuing epidemic quickly convinced the islanders that they had not been behaving themselves and should embrace Christianity.

Manihiki at that time was more-or-less a subsidiary of Rakahanga, 42 km away, and the people of Rakahanga 'commuted' to Manihiki as necessary. In 1852 the missionaries convinced the people to divide

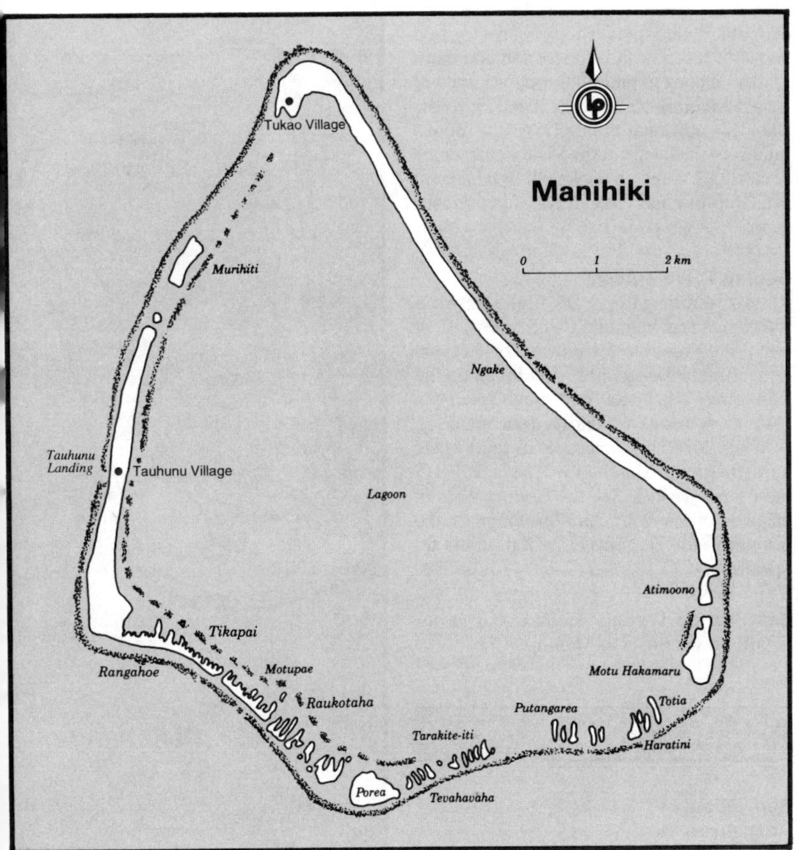

themselves between the two islands and settle permanently. See the Rakahanga section of this chapter for more about the relation between the two islands.

The women of Manihiki were famous for their beauty, a reputation which continues to this day. In the late 19th century, however, that belief led to raids by Peruvian slavers and a variety of other Pacific n'er-do-wells. In 1869 'Bully Hates' spirited off a number of islanders, supposedly for a visit to Rakahanga; in reality they ended up as plantation labourers in Fiji.

In 1889, when relations between the British and French in the Pacific were tense, the islanders fell out with their missionaries and invited the French from Tahiti to take over the island. A French warship duly turned up but the missionaries speedily hoisted the Union Jack and the French opted for discretion rather than valour. Later that year the island was officially taken under the British wing.

Literature

Manihikian literary giants are few and far between but one Manihikian author, Kauraka Kauraka, has published a number of books, including two books of poetry, two books of legends and stories, and one more academic book exploring the significance of an old Manihikian myth as it relates to the island's traditional culture. See the Books section of the Facts for the Visitor chapter for details on Kauraka's books, all of which are available in paperback in Rarotonga bookshops.

Getting There & Away

Air Air Rarotonga operates flights between Rarotonga and Manihiki twice weekly. Cost is NZ$500 (double for return) for the 3½-hour flight. Depending on demand, the flights may also be routed through Pukapuka (1½ hours away) or Penrhyn (one hour).

When Air Rarotonga starts its tours to the northern group, Manihiki will be included in the islands visited. See the Getting Around chapter; check with Air Rarotonga or the Rarotonga travel agents to see if the tours are operating.

Sea See the Getting Around chapter for details on sea travel to Manihiki.

Rakahanga

Population: 262
Area: 4.1 sq km

Only 42 km north of Manihiki, this rectangular atoll consists of two major islands and a host of smaller motus almost completely enclosing a central lagoon about four km long and two km wide at its widest points.

Without the pearl wealth of Manihiki, the island of Rakahanga is conspicuously quieter and less energetic. Copra is the only export product although the islanders grow breadfruit and a taro-like vegetable. The rito hats woven on Manihiki are particularly fine. The population is concentrated in the village of Nivano on the south-west corner of the atoll.

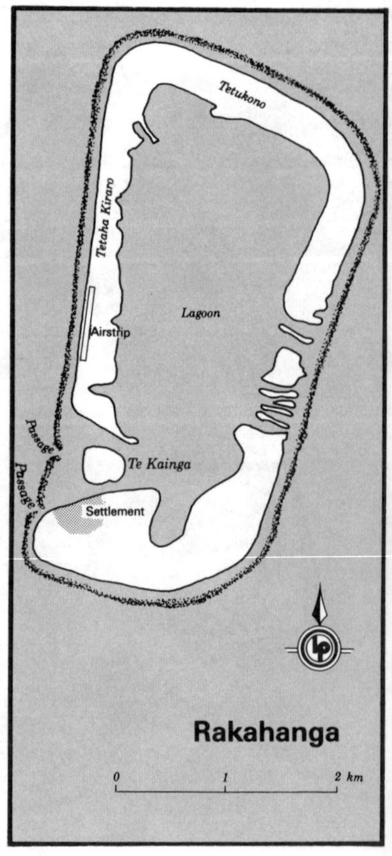

History

Legends tell of Rakahanga being hauled up from under the sea by three brothers and the island of Manihiki breaking off from the island and drifting away. There are a variety of similar legends including one which tells of the island subsequently being populated entirely by the offspring of one man and his wife, the man taking his four daughters as additional wives.

On 2 March 1606 the commander of the ships *Capitana* and *Almiranta*, Pedro Fernandez de Quiros, who as navigator to

Mendana had already discovered Pukapuka 10 years earlier, sighted the island. He reported that the islanders were:

> ...the most beautiful white and elegant people that were met during the voyage.

Furthermore, he continued, the women were exceptionally beautiful and:

> ...if properly dressed, would have advantages over our Spanish women.

Such reports were no doubt the genesis for many romantic notions of the South Seas! De Quiros was not the only member of the expedition to be impressed. A Franciscan friar accompanying the expedition named the discovery the island of Gente Hermosa, 'beautiful people'. At this time Rakahanga and Manihiki islands were both owned by the people of Rakahanga who used to commute between the two islands.

Over 200 years were to pass before the island was again visited by Western ships, first a Russian expedition in 1820 then a series of whalers and trading ships. As usual a number of easily forgotten names were bestowed on the island. In 1849 Polynesian missionaries arrived on Manihiki, although at that time it was still only settled by temporary groups from Rakahanga. The often-hazardous journey between the two islands resulted in numerous deaths at sea and in 1852 the missionaries convinced the islanders to divide themselves between the two atolls. Travelling between Manihiki and Rakahanga can still be dangerous.

Getting There & Away

Rakahanga has an airstrip but, so far, no regular flights are operating to the island. The only way to get to Rakahanga is by boat.

Penrhyn

Population: 503
Area: 9.8 sq km

Penrhyn, often still called by its traditional Maori name, Tongareva, is the northernmost of the Cook Islands and its lagoon is unlike most of the other Cook atolls in that it is very wide and easily accessible. From Omoka, one main village, Te Tautua, the other main village, isn't visible except for its church roof. Not only is the lagoon accessible to ships, it also has plenty of sharks, although most are harmless.

Penrhyn was famous throughout the Pacific at one time for its natural mother-of-pearl which is still found to this day. Some interesting shell jewellery is also produced and Penrhyn is noted for its fine rito hats.

Lost En Route

Although missionaries tried as early as 1852 to put an end to voyaging back and forth across the 40-odd km between Rakahanga and Manihiki, people continue to shuttle back and forth, sometimes with harrowing results. In June 1953, for example, nine islanders set out at night to sail from Manihiki to Rakahanga. Come dawn they were lost: a squall had blown them off course and where they were, relative to the two islands, was a mystery. Where they were relative to Pukapuka, 500 km downwind, didn't seem to be such a mystery because they set out to sail there. Five days later, in an extraordinary navigational feat, they arrived in Pukapuka.

In 1965 another small boat from Manihiki suffered engine failure midway between the islands and was swept away to the west by the steady three to four-knot current that runs between the islands. Sixty-five days and almost 3500 km later the crew landed at Erromanga in Vanuatu. The book *The Man who Refused to Die: Techu Makimare's 2000 Mile Drift in an Open Boat Across the South Seas* by Barry Wynne (Souvenir Press, London, 1966) recounts the tale of this extraordinary voyage and the persistence of Techu Makimare, the hero of the crew. ■

History

Polynesian legends relate that the island was fished up from the depths of the ocean by Vatea, the eldest son of the great mother in Avaiki. He used a fish-hook baited with a star but when that did not work he tore a piece of flesh from his thigh, baited the hook with that and promptly pulled up the island from the deep. He then hung the hook in the sky.

Although the local name Tongareva is still widely used the atoll takes its most un-Polynesian name from the British ship *Lady Penrhyn* which dropped by in 1788 on the way back to England from Australia. The ship was one of the 11 which carried the original convict settlers out to Sydney in Australia. The Maori name Tongareva could translate as something like 'to the south of the great emptiness' – there's a lot of nothing to the north of Penrhyn – or 'Tonga floating in space'. Another Maori name, Mangarongaro, is also sometimes used although some people say it was originally only the name of one of the islands in the atoll. There is no direct translation but a *mangaro* is a kind of coconut.

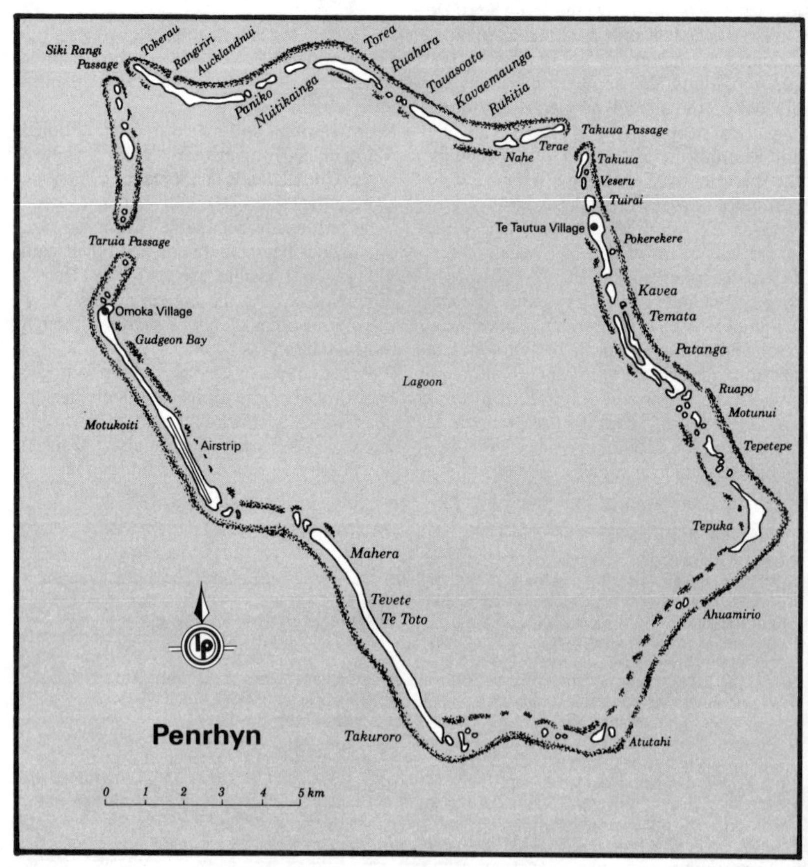

After the *Lady Penrhyn* it was 28 years before a visit by the Russian ship *Rurick* in 1816. The earliest Western accounts of Penrhyn all comment on the unusual fierceness and erratic behaviour of the island's inhabitants. The following extract is a typical description from a visit by the US ship *Porpoise* in 1841:

> ...each and all of them were talking in a language altogether unintelligible and in voices peculiarly harsh and discordant accompanying their words with every unimaginable contortion of the body and with the most diabolical expressions of countenance every muscle being brought into play and made to quiver apparently with rage & excitement, and their eyes fairly starting from their heads. It is utterly impossible for the mind to conceive and altogether out of my power to find words to express or convey any adequate idea of a scene so savage...

None of these early visitors dared to go ashore and they all tried to keep the inhabitants distinctly at arm's length. Despite this impression, when the American ship *Chatham* ran onto the reef in 1853 they were treated well, to the surprise and relief of the crew and passengers. Some of them were to remain on the island for almost a year before being rescued. E H Lamont, the trader who had chartered the unfortunate vessel, wrote *Wild Life among the Pacific Islanders* about his time on the island. He obviously entered into atoll life wholeheartedly because he married three women while he was there! Dr R in his account was the Dr Longghost of Herman Melville's *Omoo*.

The first missionaries arrived in 1854 and those warlike and terrifying islanders quickly became obedient churchgoers. So obedient that the four Polynesian teachers landed by the missionaries 'sold' their flock to Peruvian slavers in 1862 to 1863. They netted $5 a head and went along to South America as overseers for a salary of $100 a month. The island's population was decimated by the activities of the slavers who dubbed the island 'the island of the four evangelists'. That disastrous slaving foray left Penrhyn with a population of only 88 – down from an estimated 700 before the trade began, with around 470 persons taken to Peru, and another 130 to Tahiti. The population had rebounded to 445 by 1902 but the entire chiefly line disappeared during this period, so today Penrhyn is the only island in the Cooks with no ariki.

Literature

For an interesting account of the island's history during the last century look at *Impressions of Tongareva (Penrhyn Island), 1816-1901*, edited by Andrew Teariki Campbell (University of the South Pacific, 1984, paperback), available at the USP Centre on Rarotonga.

Getting There & Away

Air Penrhyn has an airstrip near Omoka village as a result of its use as an American airbase during WW II. The remains of the *Go-Gettin' Gal*, a four-engined bomber, still remain there although it's gradually being used up as a source of scrap metal.

The airstrip was disused for many years, but Air Rarotonga now operates weekly flights between Rarotonga and Penrhyn; cost is NZ$550 for the four-hour trip (double for return). The flights may be direct, or routed through Aitutaki or Manihiki.

Penrhyn will be included in the monthly northern group tours organised by Air Rarotonga. See the Getting Around chapter and check with Air Rarotonga for details.

Sea Penrhyn is also served by the inter-island shipping services. See the Getting Around chapter for details.

Pukapuka

Population: 670
Area: 5.1 sq km

Shaped like a three-bladed fan, Pukapuka's atoll has an island at each 'blade end' and another in the middle. The northernmost island gives its name to the whole atoll although it is also known, usually in paren-

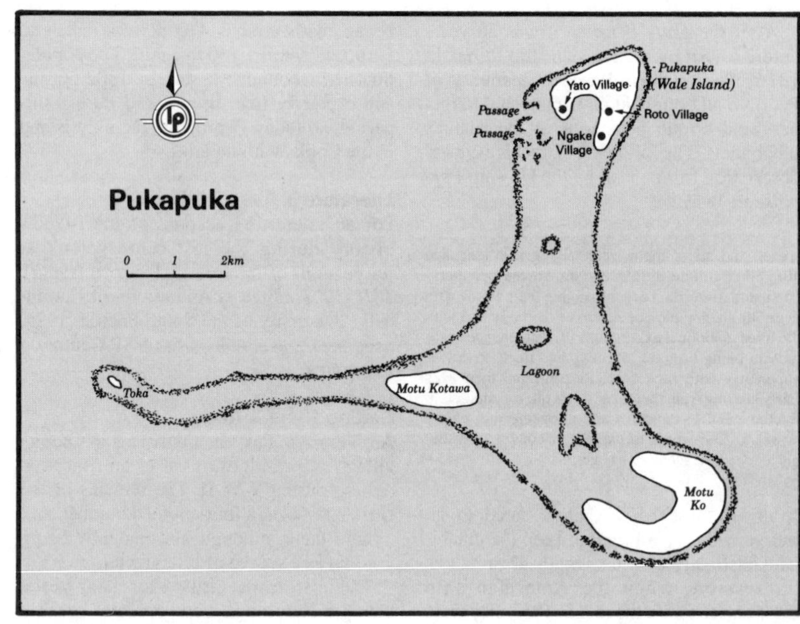

theses, as 'Wale'. The only landing place is reached by narrow and difficult passages through the reef on the western side of Wale Island.

There are three villages – Ngake, Roto and Yato – all on Wale Island. Copra and smaller quantities of bananas and papayas are grown. The relative proximity to Samoa has resulted in the islanders' customs and language relating more closely to Samoa than to the rest of the Cooks. There is a notably decorated Catholic church on the island and excellent swimming and snorkelling, particularly off the central island of Kotawa. Pukapuka is noted for its finely woven mats.

History

Early legends relate tales of the island rising from the deep with men inside it and of great voyages. Another tale tells of a great tidal wave about 400 years ago which left only two women and 15 men alive on the island; with considerable effort (on the women's part!) they managed to repopulate it. There may have been some truth in this tale as the islanders recall that it was during the rule of the fourth chief after the great disaster that the first Western visitors arrived.

That first Western visitor was the Spanish explorer Alvaro de Mendana who, with his navigator Pedro Fernandez de Quiros, sailed from Peru in 1595 and later that year discovered an island which he named San Bernardo. Although they did not attempt to land nor did they see signs of life, it is generally accepted that the island they sighted was Pukapuka. Over 150 years later in 1765 the British ships *Dolphin* and *Tamar* again sighted the island and again decided against attempting a landing due to the high surf. They named the atoll the Islands of Danger and Pukapuka is still sometimes referred to as Danger Island.

Further sightings and namings continued and finally in 1857 Polynesian missionaries were landed, followed in 1862 by a visit by

Robert Dean Frisbie

Robert Dean Frisbie never achieved his dream of writing a great book, a modern *Moby Dick*, but his accounts of life in the Pacific are still classics and if his life was hard it was also colourful. Born in 1896 in Cleveland, Ohio, his parents were strict and Frisbie was a frail, weak child. He joined the US Army during WW I but was discharged as medically unfit in 1918 with a warning that he was unlikely to survive another North American winter.

Two years later Frisbie, living in Tahiti with a Tahitian mistress named Terii, had become known as Ropati to his Polynesian neighbours and was running a small plantation and dreaming of that great book. In 1923 he set off on a sailing trip, with two partners, which would take them to Manihiki, Penrhyn and Suwarrow in the Cook Islands, to the Samoas and finally to Fiji where the now penniless adventurers had to sell their boat. Back in Tahiti, Frisbie learned that his first magazine article had been sold.

In 1924 he sailed to Rarotonga where he got a job running a trading store on Pukapuka and wrote of his experiences in a series of magazine articles which established that idyllic vision of warm seas, swaying palm trees and romantic and beautiful women. Many were published by the *Atlantic Monthly* and came out in book form as *The Book of Puka-Puka* in 1928. Frisbie spent four years on Pukapuka and married Ngatokorua, with whom he had five children.

In 1928 Frisbie and his wife travelled to Rarotonga and in 1930 his first child, a son named Charles, was born. Frisbie made a brief trip back to the USA but quickly returned to his beloved Pacific islands where he lived with Nga on Tahiti and continued to write magazine articles. In 1932 his daughter Florence was born in Papeete and was soon nicknamed 'Johnny', a name which stuck. Moving to Moorea he went into poultry farming and had a second son, William, who was always known as 'Jakey'.

In 1934 the Frisbie family, all except Charles who had remained on Rarotonga since his birth with a grand aunt, returned to Pukapuka and lived on the southern motu, Ko, where two more daughters, Elaine and Nga, were born. For a spell he had difficulty selling his articles but now his writing was again in demand. Then in 1938 his wife became so ill with tuberculosis that she had to be evacuated to Western Samoa for treatment. The Frisbies soon returned to Pukapuka where she died in early 1939.

That same year Frisbie's first novel, *Mr Moonlight's Island*, was published and in December 1941, unaware that the Japanese raid on Pearl Harbor had taken place earlier in the month, Frisbie and his four children set off on a Pacific cruise that was soon interrupted by a lengthy pause on the atoll of Suwarrow. The five Frisbies were soon joined by three New Zealand surveyors accompanied by three islanders from Manihiki and then by two yachtsmen. On 19 February 1942 the island was struck by an exceptionally severe hurricane. Waves as high as five metres swept right across the low-lying island, parts of the atoll which the New Zealanders had recently surveyed were totally reshaped and the yacht disappeared completely. Remarkably the nine adults and four children all survived and Frisbie was to write of this experience in *The Island of Desire* which was published in 1944. Desire was his late wife, Nga, and her island was Pukapuka but Suwarrow also features in this South Seas classic.

The later years of Frisbie's energetic life are told not only in his own writings but also in those of his daughter Johnny who, with help from her father, wrote *Miss Ulysses from Puka-Puka* when she was only 15 years old. It was published in 1948 with support from no less a Pacific luminary than James Michener. She also wrote *The Frisbies of the South Seas* which was published in 1959. His long time friend James Norman Hall also wrote of Frisbie in 'Frisbie of Danger Island' in his book *The Forgotten One* (1952) and he features in James Michener's book *Return to Paradise*.

From Suwarrow the Frisbies sailed to Manihiki where Frisbie remarried then moved on to Rarotonga where his new wife soon left him. On Rarotonga his decidedly able children had their first experience of school but soon the Frisbies were on the move again, first to Manihiki and then to Penrhyn from where he was rescued by a US Navy aircraft and taken to Pago Pago in American Samoa, dying from tuberculosis. On board the aircraft was James Michener. The well-travelled Frisbie children soon joined their remarkable father who proceeded to make an equally remarkable recovery and added schoolteacher to his list of occupations. From American Samoa the Frisbies moved to the quieter surroundings of Western Samoa, then on to Tahiti and back to Rarotonga where he completed his last work before he died of tetanus in 1948. It was not the great South Pacific novel he dreamed of but no matter, he'd led a full life and left works he will be remembered by. Robert Dean Frisbie's grave can be found by the CICC church in Avarua, Rarotonga. ■

the pioneer missionary William Wyatt Gill. A year later the population of the island was decimated by slave raids from Peru. In 1865 the London Missionary Society ship *John Williams* which had spent so much time in this region was wrecked on Pukapuka's reef.

During this century, South Seas character Robert Dean Frisbie lived for some time on the island and wrote *The Book of Puka-Puka* and *The Island of Desire*. His daughter Johnny Frisbie also wrote of the island in *Miss Ulysses from Puka-Puka*. Modern maps of Pukapuka are still based on Robert Dean Frisbie's 1925 survey.

Getting There & Away

Air Air travel to Pukapuka has been initiated only very recently. The island's airstrip was officially opened in early 1994 and Air Rarotonga began operating flights to the island via Manihiki. With the stop at Manihiki on the way, the flight from Rarotonga to Pukapuka takes about five hours. It's usually shorter on the way back to Rarotonga, being a direct flight. Cost between Rarotonga and Pukapuka is NZ$550 (double for return); between Pukapuka and Manihiki it's NZ$165 for the 1½-hour flight.

Pukapuka will be included on Air Rarotonga's northern group tours when they begin. See the Getting Around chapter and check with Air Rarotonga or the Rarotonga travel agents for details.

Sea Pukapuka is served by the passenger freighter ships coming from Rarotonga; see the Getting Around chapter for details. Since the island is closer to Samoa than to Rarotonga, some boat traffic also goes back and forth between Pukapuka and Samoa.

Nassau

Population: 102
Area: 1.2 sq km

The tiny island of Nassau was named after an American whaling ship. There's no atoll, just a fringing reef around a tiny, half-km long sand cay. There is a coconut plantation and taro is grown in the centre of the island.

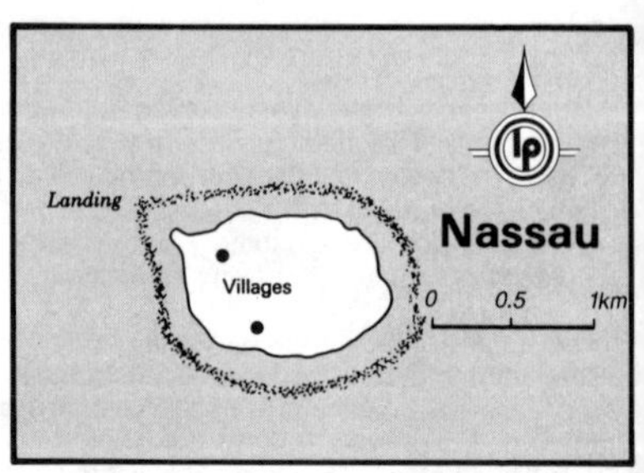

History

Lying 88 km south-east of Pukapuka, the island was effectively the property of the Pukapukans. It was probably first discovered by Europeans in 1803 and each successive visitor gave it a new name, usually that of the discovering ship. For some reason, however, it was the American whaler *Nassau's* visit, comparatively late in the day in 1835, which gave the island its present name.

The island did not have a permanent population although occasional groups from other islands stopped for longer or shorter periods. An American attempted to grow coconuts and other plants from 1876 and in later years a number of European-owned copra plantations were established. In 1945 these were sold to the colonial government for £2000. Six years later they were sold to the chiefs of Pukapuka for the same figure. Their temporary work groups have become a virtually permanent population.

Wreck of the Manuvai

The Scandinavian-built 50 metre (164 foot), 400-ton *Manuvai* carried freight and passengers throughout the Cook Islands for the Silk & Boyd shipping company, based on Rarotonga. There was space for 20 passengers in five four-berth cabins and 70 passengers on deck. On 27 December 1988, at around midnight, the *Manuvai* ran onto the reef on

Nassau as it was returning to Rarotonga from a northern group loop. No storm, no wind, it simply ran onto the reef!

It was windy for the next four days and the seas pushed the ship farther and farther up the reef. The old ship was damaged beyond repair; a Silk & Boyd team came up to salvage whatever was useful off the vessel, but its remains will probably be sitting on the reef for the next 100 years. It was quite an adventure for all, including the 100-odd population of the remote island who suddenly found themselves hosting the stranded 30-to-40 passengers and crew for the next two weeks, until an emergency ship could be brought up from Rarotonga to retrieve them.

Getting There & Away

The only way to get to Nassau is by the infrequent shipping services.

Suwarrow

Population: 6
Area: 0.4 sq km

The atoll of Suwarrow is one of the best known in the whole Cook Islands group due to a prolonged visit by one man. Between 1952 and his death in 1977, New Zealander Tom Neale lived on the island for extended periods as a virtual hermit and his book *An Island to Oneself* became a South Seas classic. If you want to know all about how to live on an atoll then this book is a must.

Although Tom Neale is long gone – he is buried in the cemetery opposite Rarotonga's airport – his memory lives on and yachties often call in to the atoll. It's one of the few in the northern Cooks with an accessible lagoon. Tom's room is still furnished just as it was when he lived there. Visiting yachts fill in a logbook left in the room. Pearl divers from Manihiki also visit occasionally.

Tom Neale wasn't the only writer to live on, and write about, Suwarrow. American-born Robert Dean Frisbie survived a terrible hurricane in 1942 and wrote of it in *Island of Desire*. His daughter Johnny Frisbie also wrote about the same hurricane in *The Frisbies of the South Seas*. Although the lagoon is large the scattered islands of Suwarrow are all very small and low-lying. Hurricanes have brought waves which wash right across even the highest of the islands and in 1942 the Frisbie group only survived by tying themselves to a tree.

Today the island is populated only by a caretaker and his family.

History

Suwarrow's curious name is neither English nor Polynesian. It was named by the Russian explorer Mikhail Lazarev in 1814 after his ship *Suvarov*. Nor has it always been uninhabited. There was an unsuccessful attempt to produce pearl shell here in the early part of this century while in the '20s and '30s copra was produced until a devastating termite infestation halted production. 'Coastwatchers' from New Zealand kept an eye on Japanese activity from Suwarrow during WW II and the remains of their buildings can still be seen on Anchorage Island.

There may well have been earlier visitors. In the mid-19th century the American whaler *Gem* was wrecked on the reef. A ship came from Tahiti to salvage the whaler's oil cargo and one of the visiting ship's officers dug up a box containing $15,000. Where this cache came from has never been satisfactorily explained, although the coins were thought to date from the mid-1700s and may have been connected with the first British Pacific expedition under Commodore George Anson in 1742. In 1876 another visitor found Spanish coins dating from the 1600s.

In 1860 the atoll was the scene of a dramatic and tragic dispute. First, a group of eight people, one of them an Englishman, drifted to Suwarrow after an abortive Manihiki-Rakahanga voyage. Later, a group of Penrhyn pearl divers with a European boss turned up and later still another European visitor was left on the atoll. Shortly after the arrival of the third European an argument broke out between the pearl divers and their

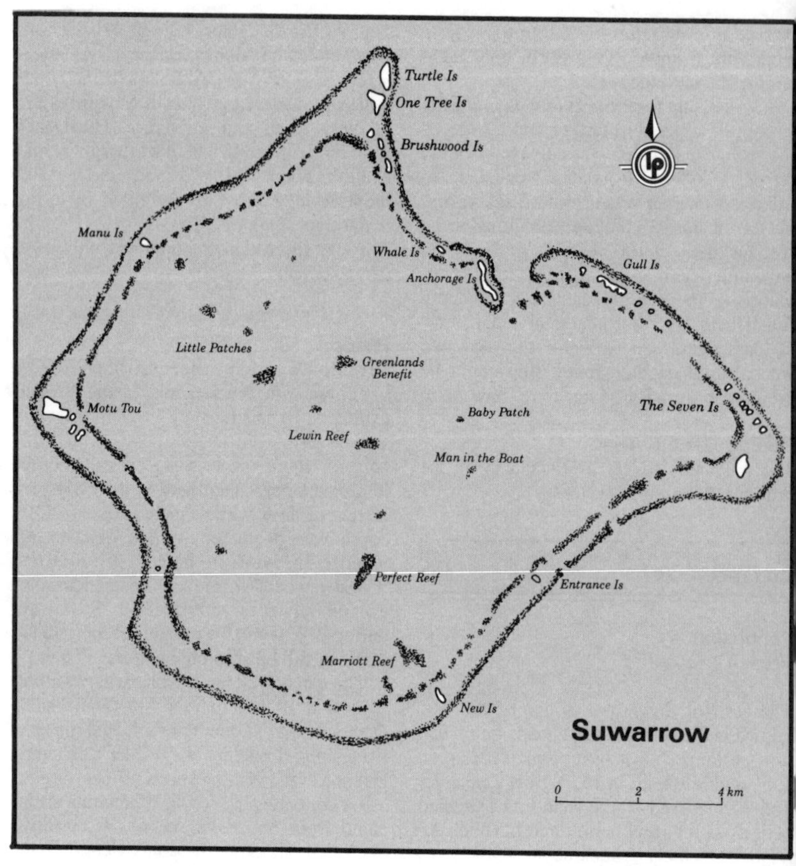

leader and all three Europeans were murdered.

In the mid-1870s more evidence of an early European visit was discovered when signs of habitation, various artefacts and skeletons were unearthed. Were they left by shipwrecked Spaniards? Or were they the remains of the English crew lost on a cutter from the ship *Pandora*, sent to the Pacific in 1791 to search for the mutineers of the *Bounty*?

Getting There & Away

Sea The only way to get to Suwarrow is on the extremely infrequent shipping services, or by private yacht.

Glossary

adze – axe-like hand tool with ceremonial importance in the Cook Islands
Ara Metua – ancient Polynesian road around the circumference of Rarotonga, inland from the newer coast road
Ara Tapu – coast road around Rarotonga
ariki – paramount chief; traditional head of a tribe, the same as a king or queen
Atua – God; the Christian God
Avaiki – legendary Polynesian ancestral homeland. No-one today knows precisely where Avaiki was, but many Polynesian islands, and the New Zealand Maori, say their ancestors originated from Avaiki (spelled various ways throughout Polynesia). The spirits of the dead are believed to return home to Avaiki after death

bush beer – locally produced moonshine beer brewed from oranges, bananas, pawpaws or hops; also called 'home brew'
bush beer school – communal drinking session where bush beer is consumed; also called a *tumunu*

CICC – Cook Island Christian Church, the Protestant church which continues from the original London Missionary Society churches
copra – coconut 'meat' from which coconut oil is produced, an important product throughout the Pacific. The problem with copra is the price is very volatile – it has reached as high as US$450 a ton but currently is much, much lower

ei – necklace
ei kaki – flower ei draped around the neck like a necklace; traditionally given to anyone arriving or departing on a journey
ei katu – flower tiara
ekalesia – church
eke – octopus
enua – land

ika – fish

kai – food
kikau – palm leaves, woven or thatched; a *kikau* hut is a traditional thatch-roofed hut
koutu – ancient Polynesian open-air royal courtyard, used for gatherings and political functions

LDS – Church of Jesus Christ of the Latter-Day Saints (Mormons)
LMS – London Missionary Society, the original missionary force in the Cook Islands and in many other regions of the Pacific

mataiapo – head of a sub-tribe, a rank down from an *ariki*
makatea – raised coral reef which forms a coastal plain around several islands of the southern group including Mangaia, Atiu, Mauke and Mitiaro
mana – power or influence
Maori – the Polynesian people of the Cook Islands and also of New Zealand, also the language of these people; literally means 'indigenous' or 'local'
marae – ancient open-air family or tribal religious meeting ground, marked by stones
maroro – flying fish
maunga – mountain
moana – sea; ocean
motu – lagoon islet

pandanus – type of palm leaf used for thatching the roofs of traditional houses and for mats, baskets, bags and *rito* hats
papa'a – Europeans and other foreigners; also, the English language
pareu – wrap-around sarong-type garment
pupu – tiny shells used to make necklaces

rangatira – landed gentry; lowest rank of Cook Islands royalty hierarchy, below *mataiapo* which is below *ariki*
rito – bleached pandanus or bleached, young palm leaves, used to make a variety of woven handicrafts including hats, fans, handbags etc

SDA – Seventh Day Adventist church, another popular Protestant church in the Cooks

Tangaroa – in traditional Polynesian religion, Tangaroa was the god of the sea and of fertility. His corpulent, phallic figure appears on the Cook Islands' one dollar coin and is a symbol of the Cook Islands
tapu – holy; sacred
taunga – expert
tiare – flower
tiare Maori – gardenia
tiki – symbolic human figure
tivaevae – tivaevaes are colourful and intricately sewn appliqué works which are traditionally made as burial shrouds but are also used as bedspreads, with smaller versions used as furniture covers, cushion covers and pillowcases
tivaivai – alternate spelling for *tivaevae*, used on the island of Atiu
tumunu – hollowed-out stump of a coconut tree used to brew bush beer; also refers to bush beer drinking sessions

umu – traditional Polynesian underground oven
umukai – traditional Polynesian food *(kai)* cooked in an underground oven *(umu)*

vaka – canoe

Index

ABBREVIATIONS

Ait – Aitutaki
At – Atiu
Mg – Mangaia
Man – Manihiki
Mau – Mauke
Mit – Mitiaro
Nas – Nassau
Pa – Palmerston
Pen – Penrhyn
Puk – Pukapuka
Rak – Rakahanga
Rar – Rarotonga

MAPS

TEXT

Map references are in **bold** type.

Lonely Planet Guidebooks

Lonely Planet guidebooks cover every accessible part of Asia as well as Australia, the Pacific, South America, Africa, the Middle East, Europe and parts of North America. There are five series: *travel survival kits*, covering a country for a range of budgets; *shoestring guides* with compact information for low-budget travel in a major region; *walking guides*; *city guides* and *phrasebooks*.

Australia & the Pacific

Australia
Bushwalking in Australia
Islands of Australia's Great Barrier Reef
Fiji
Melbourne city guide
Micronesia
New Caledonia
New Zealand
Tramping in New Zealand
Papua New Guinea
Bushwalking in Papua New Guinea
Papua New Guinea phrasebook
Rarotonga & the Cook Islands
Samoa
Solomon Islands
Sydney city guide
Tahiti & French Polynesia
Tonga
Vanuatu
Victoria

South-East Asia

Bali & Lombok
Bangkok city guide
Cambodia
Indonesia
Indonesia phrasebook
Laos
Malaysia, Singapore & Brunei
Myanmar (Burma)
Burmese phrasebook
Philippines
Pilipino phrasebook
Singapore city guide
South-East Asia on a shoestring
Thailand
Thai phrasebook
Vietnam
Vietnamese phrasebook

North-East Asia

China
Beijing city guide
Cantonese phrasebook
Mandarin Chinese phrasebook
Hong Kong, Macau & Canton
Japan
Japanese phrasebook
Korea
Korean phrasebook
Mongolia
North-East Asia on a shoestring
Seoul city guide
Taiwan
Tibet
Tibet phrasebook
Tokyo city guide

Middle East

Arab Gulf States
Egypt & the Sudan
Arabic (Egyptian) phrasebook
Iran
Israel
Jordan & Syria
Middle East
Turkish phrasebook
Trekking in Turkey
Yemen

Indian Ocean

Madagascar & Comoros
Maldives & Islands of the East Indian Ocean
Mauritius, Réunion & Seychelles

Mail Order

Lonely Planet guidebooks are distributed worldwide. They are also available by mail order from Lonely Planet, so if you have difficulty finding a title please write to us. US and Canadian residents should write to Embarcadero West, 155 Filbert St, Suite 251, Oakland CA 94607, USA; European residents should write to 10 Barley Mow Passage, Chiswick, London W4 4PH; and residents of other countries to PO Box 617, Hawthorn, Victoria 3122, Australia.

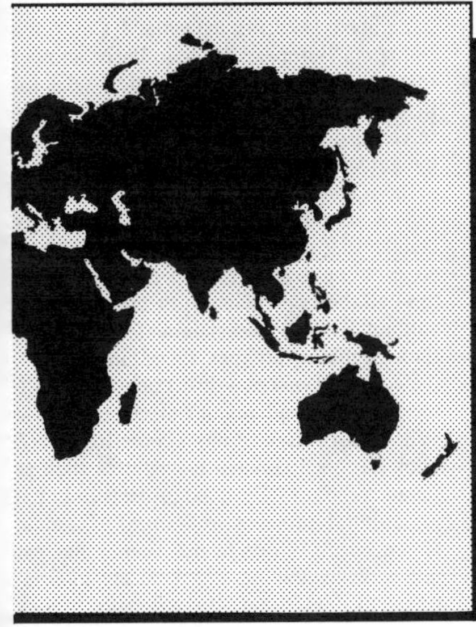

Europe

Baltic States & Kaliningrad
Dublin city guide
Eastern Europe on a shoestring
Eastern Europe phrasebook
Finland
France
Greece
Hungary
Iceland, Greenland & the Faroe Islands
Ireland
Italy
Mediterranean Europe on a shoestring
Mediterranean Europe phrasebook
Poland
Scandinavian & Baltic Europe on a shoestring
Scandinavian Europe phrasebook
Switzerland
Trekking in Spain
Trekking in Greece
USSR
Russian phrasebook
Western Europe on a shoestring
Western Europe phrasebook

Indian Subcontinent

Bangladesh
India
Hindi/Urdu phrasebook
Trekking in the Indian Himalaya
Karakoram Highway
Kashmir, Ladakh & Zanskar
Nepal
Trekking in the Nepal Himalaya
Nepali phrasebook
Pakistan
Sri Lanka
Sri Lanka phrasebook

Africa

Africa on a shoestring
Central Africa
East Africa
Trekking in East Africa
Kenya
Swahili phrasebook
Morocco, Algeria & Tunisia
Arabic (Moroccan) phrasebook
South Africa, Lesotho & Swaziland
Zimbabwe, Botswana & Namibia
West Africa

Central America

Baja California
Central America on a shoestring
Costa Rica
La Ruta Maya
Mexico

North America

Alaska
Canada
Hawaii

South America

Argentina, Uruguay & Paraguay
Bolivia
Brazil
Brazilian phrasebook
Chile & Easter Island
Colombia
Ecuador & the Galápagos Islands
Latin American Spanish phrasebook
Peru
Quechua phrasebook
South America on a shoestring
Trekking in the Patagonian Andes

The Lonely Planet Story

Lonely Planet published its first book in 1973 in response to the numerous 'How did you do it?' questions Maureen and Tony Wheeler were asked after driving, bussing, hitching, sailing and railing their way from England to Australia.

Written at a kitchen table and hand collated, trimmed and stapled, *Across Asia on the Cheap* became an instant local bestseller, inspiring thoughts of another book.

Eighteen months in South-East Asia resulted in their second guide, *South-East Asia on a shoestring*, which they put together in a backstreet Chinese hotel in Singapore in 1975. The 'yellow bible' as it quickly became known to backpackers around the world, soon became *the* guide to the region. It has sold well over half a million copies and is now in its 7th edition, still retaining its familiar yellow cover.

Today there are over 130 Lonely Planet titles in print – books that have that same adventurous approach to travel as those early guides; books that 'assume you know how to get your luggage off the carousel' as one reviewer put it.

Although Lonely Planet initially specialised in guides to Asia, they now cover most regions of the world, including the Pacific, South America, Africa, the Middle East and Europe. The list of *walking guides* and *phrasebooks* (for 'unusual' languages such as Quechua, Swahili, Nepali and Egyptian Arabic) is also growing rapidly.

The emphasis continues to be on travel for independent travellers. Tony and Maureen still travel for several months of each year and play an active part in the writing, updating and quality control of Lonely Planet's guides.

They have been joined by over 50 authors, 60 staff – mainly editors, cartographers & designers – at our office in Melbourne, Australia, at our US office in Oakland, California and at our European office in Paris; another five at our office in London handle sales for Britain, Europe and Africa. Travellers themselves also make a valuable contribution to the guides through the feedback we receive in thousands of letters each year.

The people at Lonely Planet strongly believe that travellers can make a positive contribution to the countries they visit, both through their appreciation of the countries' culture, wildlife and natural features, and through the money they spend. In addition, the company makes a direct contribution to the countries and regions it covers. Since 1986 a percentage of the income from each book has been donated to ventures such as famine relief in Africa; aid projects in India; agricultural projects in Central America; Greenpeace's efforts to halt French nuclear testing in the Pacific and Amnesty International. In 1994 $100,000 was donated to such causes.

Lonely Planet's basic travel philosophy is summed up in Tony Wheeler's comment, 'Don't worry about whether your trip will work out. Just go!'.